HOW TO
TUNEUP & REPAIR
YOUR OWN CAR

Other TAB books by the author:

HOW TO TUNEUP & REPAIR YOUR OWN CAR

BY JOHN E. TRAISTER

TAB BOOKS

BLUE RIDGE SUMMIT, PA. 17214

FIRST EDITION

FIRST PRINTING—SEPTEMBER 1979

Copyright © 1979 by TAB BOOKS

Printed in the United States of America

Library of Congress Cataloging in Publication Data

Traister, John E.
  How to tuneup & repair your own car.

  Includes index.
  1. Automobiles—Maintenance and repair. I. Title.
TL152.T7   629.28'8'22   79-17427
ISBN 0-8306-9767-5
ISBN 0-8306-1131-2 pbk.

Preface

This book is aimed at those individuals who need a basic understanding of automotive troubleshooting and maintenance procedures, whether they be students, professional mechanics or home do-it-yourselfers.

If you fit into any of the categories above, or if you plan to undertake automotive repairs, you will find this guidebook helpful. It gives much of the information you will need to know on how to detect and then repair almost any automotive problem that is likely to occur.

You'll learn how to keep vehicles in first-class running condition as well as maintaining that "new car" look.

I wish to thank the many manufacturers of autos and auto supplies for their help in supplying much of the reference data used in this book. I am especially indebted to Ford Motor Company, Chrysler Motor Corporation, and General Motors.

John E. Traister

Contents

Chapter 1

Introduction To
Troubleshooting Procedures

A great deal of the work performed by automotive mechanics involves the repair and maintenance of automobiles of all kinds. To properly maintain automotive systems, the mechanic must have a good knowledge of what is commonly known as *troubleshooting*, the ability to determine the cause of any problem in an automotive system and correct the problems in the shortest possible time and with the least amount of expense.

TROUBLESHOOTING

Troubleshooting covers a wide range of problems from such small jobs as finding a short circuit in the electrical system to the diagnosis of internal engine problems or emission control systems. In any case, troubleshooting usually requires a thorough knowledge of basic automotive systems and testing equipment. Also, a systematic and methodical approach to the problem is needed; test one part of the system at a time until the trouble is located.

Those involved in the maintenance and repair of automotive systems should keep in mind that every automotive problem can be solved—regardless of its nature. The chapters to follow are designed to aid those involved in such work to better solve the more common automotive problems in a safe and logical manner.

SAFETY PRECAUTIONS

Experience in the automotive industry has shown that all mechanics, at times, expose themselves to danger; newer mechanics do so because of inexperience and older ones have the problem because of over-confidence and habits of work which they form.

When working on any automotive system, always consider your personal safety first. Be extremely careful with gasoline fumes which can easily explode and also around refrigerants which can freeze the eyes and cause blindness.

To prevent damage to test instruments, always select a range (on meters with different ranges) that insures less than full-scale deflection of the needle or pointer. Also, a mid-scale deflection of the needle usually provides the most accurate reading.

The mechanic also has an obligation to the driver. Defective parts in a vehicle can cause accidents, and this fact has been noted by most state legislatures. Therefore, periodic inspections are required for vehicles that use public roads.

Listed below are safety checks that should be made at regular intervals during operation. The intervals should be no greater than six months or 6,000 miles, whichever occurs first (more often when the need is indicated). Any deficiencies should be repaired as soon as possible.

Starter Safety Switch. On automatic transmission, check the starter safety switch by placing the transmission in each of the driving gears while attempting to start the engine. The starter should operate only in *PARK* or neutral positions.

For manual transmissions, place the shift lever in neutral, depress the clutch halfway, and attempt to start the vehicle. On cars of recent manufacture, the starter should operate only when the clutch is fully depressed.

Steering Column Lock (when applicable). Check for proper operation by attempting to turn key to *LOCK* position in the various transmission gears with the vehicle stationary. The key should turn the lock only when the transmission control is in *PARK* on automatic transmission models and in reverse on manual transmission models. Of course, the key should be removable in the *LOCK* position.

Parking Brake and Transmission "PARK" Mechanism. Check parking brake holding ability by parking on a fairly steep slope and restraining the vehicle with the parking brake only. On vehicles with automatic transmissions, check the holding ability of the *PARK* mechanism by releasing all brakes after the transmission selector lever has been placed in *PARK* or *P* position.

Transmission Shift Indicator. Check to be sure automatic transmission shift indicator accurately indicates the shift position selected.

Steering. Be alert to any changes in steering action. The need for inspection or servicing may be indicated by "hard" steering, excessive free play or unusual sounds when turning or parking.

Wheel Alignment and Balance. In addition to abnormal tire wear as described in Chapter 14, the need for wheel alignment service may be indicated by a pull to the right or left when driving on a straight and level road. The need for wheel balancing is usually indicated by a vibration of the steering wheel or seat while driving at normal highway speeds.

Brakes. Be alert to illumination of the brake warning light or changes in braking action, such as repeated pulling to one side, unusual sounds when braking or increased brake pedal travel. Any of these could indicate the need for brake system inspection and/or service.

Exhaust System. Be alert to any change in the sound of the exhaust system or a smell of fumes which may indicate a leak; this could cause carbon monoxide poisoning.

Windshield Wipers and Washers. Check operation of wipers, as well as condition and alignment of wiper blades. Check amount and direction of fluid sprayed by washers during use.

Defrosters. Check performance by moving controls to *DEF* or *DEFROST* and noting amount of air directed against the windshield.

Rearview Mirrors and Sun Visors. Friction joints should be properly adjusted so that the mirrors and sun visors remain in the selected position.

Horn. The horn should be tested frequently (usually by the driver) to be sure that it works all the time.

Seat Belts. Check belts, buckles, retractors, and anchors for cuts, fraying or weakened portions, loose connections, damage and for proper operation. Check to make certain that anchor mounting bolts are tight.

Head Restraints. Check that head restraints, if present, adjust properly in the up detent positions, and that no components are missing, damaged or loose.

Seat Back Latches. If the vehicle is equipped with seat back latches, check to see that they are holding by pulling forward on the top of each folding seat back.

Lights and Buzzers. Check all instrument panel illuminating and warning lights, interior lights, license plate lights, side marker lights, headlamps, parking lamps, tail lamps, brake lights, turn signals, backup lamps and hazard warning flashers. Have someone observe operation of each exterior light while you activate the controls.

Glass. Check for broken, scratched, dirty or damaged glass on vehicle that could obscure vision or become an injury hazard.

Door Latches. Check for positive closing, latching and locking.

Hood Latches. Check to make sure the hood closes firmly by lifting on the hood after each closing. Check also for broken, damaged or missing parts which might prevent secure latching.

Fluid Leaks. Check for fuel, water, oil or other fluid leaks by observing the ground beneath the vehicle after it has been parked for a while. If gasoline fumes or fluid are noticed at any time, the cause should be determined and corrected without delay because of the possibility of fire.

Tires and Wheels. Check tires for excessive wear, nails, glass, cuts or other damage. Make certain wheels are not bent or cracked and wheel nuts are tight. Uneven or abnormal tire wear may indicate the need for alignment service. Tire inflation pressure should be checked by the owner at least monthly, or more often if daily visual inspection indicates the need. Refer to Chapter 14 on tire wear information.

ENGINE SYSTEMS CHECKS

Exhaust System. Check complete exhaust system and nearby body areas for broken, damaged, missing or mispositioned parts, open seams, holes, loose connections or other deterioration which could permit exhaust fumes to seep into the passenger compartment. Dust or water in the passenger compartment may be an indication of a problem in one of these areas. Any defects should be corrected immediately to help insure continued integrity. Exhaust system pipes and resonators rearward of the muffler should be replaced whenever a new muffler is installed.

Engine Drive Belts. Check the driving fan, compressor, alternator, and power steering pump for cracks, fraying, wear and tension. Adjust and replace as necessary.

Suspension and Steering. Check for damaged, loose or missing parts, or parts showing visible signs of excessive wear or lack of lubrication in front and rear suspension and steering system. Questionable parts found should be replaced immediately.

Brakes and Power Steering. Check lines and hoses for proper attachment, leaks, cracks, chafing, deterioration, etc., and replace any questionable parts without delay. When abrasion or wear is evident on lines or hoses, the cause must be corrected.

Be alert for disc brake wear indicator sound and check pads and condition of rotors while wheels are removed during tire rotation.

Drum brakes should be checked for the condition of the linings and other internal brake components at each wheel. The parking brake adjustment also should be checked for drag and lubricated at every chassis lube period.

Throttle Linkage. Check for damaged or missing parts, interference or binding. Any deficiences should be corrected without delay.

Headlights. Check for proper aim, and correct as necessary. More frequent checks should be made if oncoming motorists signal when lights are already on low beam, or if illumination of the area ahead seems inadequate.

Underbody. In geographic areas using a heavy concentration of road salt or other corrosive materials for snow removal or road dust control, flush and inspect the complete underside of the car at least once each year, preferably after a winter's exposure. Particular attention should be given to cleaning out underbody members where dirt and other foreign materials may have collected.

EMISSION CONTROL MAINTENANCE

Thermostatically Controlled Air Cleaner. Inspect installation to make certain that all hoses and ducts are connected and correctly installed. Also check valves for proper operation.

Carburetor Choke. Check choke mechanism for free operation. Any binding condition which may have developed due to petroleum gum formation on the choke shaft or from damage should be corrected.

TUNEUP

Adjust dwell (on cars equipped with conventional ignition) and then adjust timing and carburetor idle speed accurately at the first 3 months or 3,000 miles of operation. Then do so at 12-month or 12,000-mile intervals thereafter. Adjustments must be made with test equipment known to be accurate.

In general, the tuneup should consist of replacing distributor points (on vehicles so equipped) every 12 months or 12,000 miles. The cam lubricator should be replaced every 24 months or 24,000 miles. In addition, carefully inspect the interior and exterior of the distributor cap, distributor rotor and coil for cracks, carbon tracking and terminal corrosion. Clean or replace as necessary, at least once each year, to prevent misfiring and/or deterioration.

Those vehicles equipped with electronic ignitions differ greatly from those equipped with conventional mechanical points. However, there are few differences in the servicing of the unit. In electronic-ignition systems, the distributor cam is replaced by an *armature* or *timing core* along with a pickup coil that replaces the ignition points and a transistorized control box. As the distributor shaft turns, the teeth of the armature pass the pickup coil—which is an *electromagnet*—and upsets the magnetic field, creating an interruption of current to the coil and a pulse of power to the spark plugs.

Proper functioning of the carburetor is particularly essential to emission control. Correct mixtures for emission compliance and idle quality have been preset by manufacturers in most cases. Plastic idle mixture limiters are installed on the idle mixture screws to preclude unauthorized adjustment. These idle limiters are not to be removed unless some major carburetor repair or replacement which affects the idle screw adjustment has been necessary.

Manifold Heat Valve. Some engines are equipped with a manifold heat valve which should be inspected and repaired as necessary to insure free operation.

Carburetor Mounting. Torque carburetor attaching bolts and/or nuts to compensate for compression of the gasket at the first four months or 6,000 miles of vehicle operation, then at every 12,000 miles thereafter.

Spark Plugs. Replace spark plugs at 6,000-mile intervals when operating with leaded fuels or at 12,000-mile intervals when using unleaded fuels. Use of leaded fuels results in lead deposits on spark plugs and can cause misfiring at mileages less than 12,000. Where misfiring occurs prior to 6,000 miles, spark plugs in good condition can often be cleaned, tested and reinstalled in an engine with acceptable results.

Exhaust Gas Recirculation (EGR) System. At 12-month or 12,000-mile intervals when operating with leaded fuels, or at 24-month or 24,000-mile intervals when operating with unleaded fuels, remove and inspect the *EGR* system. If deposits exist, clean the *EGR* valve. Inspect the *EGR* passages in the inlet manifold and clean as required. If the valve is damaged, it should be replaced.

Carburetor Fuel Inlet Filter. Replace the filter at least once each year or 12,000 miles, whichever occurs first. Do this more frequently if the filter is clogged.

Thermal Vacuum Switch and Hoses. Check for proper operation. A malfunctioning switch must be replaced. Also check hoses for proper connection, cracking, abrasion or deterioration and replace as necessary.

Vacuum Advance Solenoid and Hoses. Check both the vacuum and electrical functions of this valve. An inoperative or leaking valve should be replaced. Check the condition of wires and connections as well as hoses for proper connection, cracking, abrasion or deterioration and replace as necessary.

Transmission Control Switch. Check the electrical function of this switch. An inoperative switch should be replaced. Also check condition of wires and connections.

Idle Stop Solenoid. Check for proper operation and replace if found defective.

Positive Crankcase Ventilation System (PCV). Check the PCV system for satisfactory operation at 12-month intervals using an approved tester. Replace the PCV valve at 24-month intervals; blow out the PCV valve hose with compressed air and replace the filter. Under unusual driving conditions, the valve should be replaced at 12-month intervals.

Engine Compression. Test engine cranking compression. If a problem exists, have correction made. The minimum compression recorded in any one cylinder should not be less than 70 percent of the highest cylinder. To illustrate, if the highest pressure in any one cylinder is 160 pounds the lowest allowable pressure for any other cylinder would be 160×70 percent $= 112$ pounds.

Evaporation Control System. Check all fuel lines and hoses for proper connections and correct routing as well as condition. Remove the canister and check for cracks or damage. Replace damaged or deteriorated parts as necessary. Replace the filter in the lower section of the canister.

Fuel Cap, Fuel Lines and Fuel Tank. Inspect the fuel tank, cap and lines for damage which could cause leakage. Inspect fuel cap for correct sealing ability and indications of physical damage. Replace any damaged or malfunctioning parts.

Air Injector Reactor System Hoses and Connections. Check these items for loose connections and deterioration. Test diverter valve for proper operation. Malfunctioning diverter valves and deteriorated hoses must be replaced.

Air Cleaner Element. Replace the engine air cleaner element under normal operating conditions every 12,000 miles. However, operation of vehicle in dusty areas will necessitate more frequent element replacement.

Spark Plug and Ignition Coil Wires. Inspect spark plug and ignition coil wires for evidence of checking, burning, or cracking of exterior insulation and tight fit at distributor cap, coil and spark plugs. The wires' exterior should be cleaned and any evidence of corrosion on the end of terminals should be removed. Wires should be replaced as necessary to prevent misfiring and/or deterioration.

The chapters to follow give details as to how most of these service problems are handled

Chapter 2

Tools Of The Trade
—and How to Use Them

High quality work in any trade or profession can be accomplished only with high quality tools and a proper knowledge of their use. This chapter, therefore, will deal with tools commonly needed by the automotive mechanic to perform good work on the usual kinds of engine tuneup and repair projects. The tools should be of the best quality that the mechanic can afford as the better tools will last a lifetime.

GENERAL AUTOMOTIVE TOOLS

The type of work normally encountered in automotive repair, maintenance and tuneup will probably require the use of pliers, wrenches, and screwdrivers more than any of the other hand tools. Almost everyone is familiar with these tools, but a review is in order to make sure that the proper tools will be used to their best advantage on the various projects.

Pliers

The variety of cutting and gripping pliers shown in Fig. 2-1 come in a number of sizes and each has a specific purpose. Pliers can be ruined if they are used for the wrong job.

Adjustable combination pliers have a definite place in every automotive mechanic's toolbox. In general, a slip joint holds the two parts of the pliers together so that the jaws can be opened or closed to hold large or small objects. Most adjustable combination pliers have two cutting edges at the back of the jaws for wire cutting, but

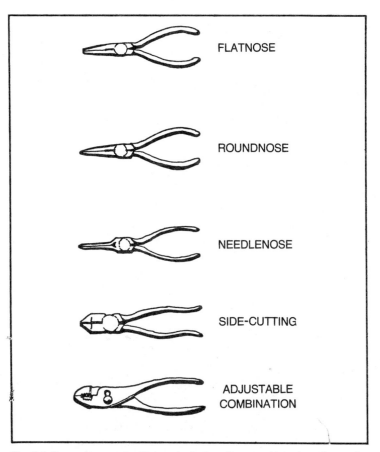

Fig. 2-1. Several types of cutting and gripping pliers used in automotive work.

their main purpose is for gripping, like holding a small part against a grinding wheel. Such pliers are not normally intended to loosen or tighten screws or nuts as this will often damage the screw or nut. A wrench should be used instead.

Longnose pliers—often called "needlenose" pliers—are used with small objects in hard-to-get-at locations, such as starting a nut on the end of a bolt that can't be reached with the fingers. The tips of these pliers are easily bent if they are misused, like trying to tighten or loosen a nut. Other types of pliers similar to long-nose pliers include roundnose pliers and flatnose pliers; both types are used for situations similar to what the long-nose pliers face.

Side-cutting pliers are used in automotive work for cutting wire or other small wire-type items such as the legs from cotter pins. Their use on heavy material will quickly nick or dull the cutting edge.

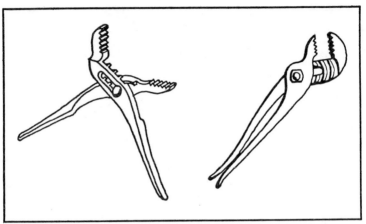

Fig. 2-2. Pump pliers have a quick adjustment for widening or narrowing the jaws to hold various sizes of materials.

Pump pliers (Fig. 2-2) have a quick adjustment for widening or narrowing the jaws to hold various materials, especially round objects. The interlocking tongues and grooves on the two parts of the pliers enable the jaws to be moved closer together or farther apart.

Self-adjustable locking pliers (vise grips) (Fig. 2-3) act as a small portable vise. These pliers have a toggle and floating wedge arrangement that automatically adjusts the jaws of the pliers to the size of the object. Pressure on the handle then enables the jaws to lock around the object very tightly and remain in this position until reverse pressure is applied to release the vise grips.

Screwdrivers

Screwdrivers are available in a wide assortment of sizes, shapes and lengths. Quality is determined by the type of metal in the blade, the method used in grinding the blade, and how the blade is attached to the handle. The material used for the handle construction is also an important feature in determining quality.

If the metal used in a screwdriver is of poor quality, it will easily chip and crumble under pressure. If the tip is improperly ground and flares too much, it will rise out of the screw slot during use. Blades improperly attached to the screwdriver handle (or if the handle is made of poor material) will eventually work loose—probably splitting or breaking the handle—and again render the screwdriver useless.

The most common type of screwdriver is the one for slotted screw heads as shown in Fig. 2-4. The Phillips-head screwdriver

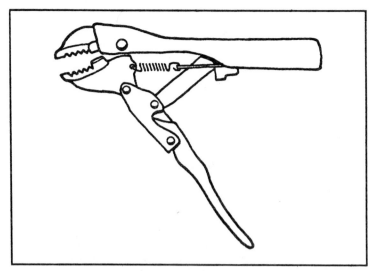

Fig. 2-3. Self-adjustable locking pliers acts as a small portable vise for gripping.

(Fig. 2-5) has slots that cross at the center to fit into Phillips-head screws. This type of screw is widely used for trim and molding on autos to cut down on the chance that the screwdriver will slip out of the slots and damage the finish.

Other types of screwdrivers include the offset screwdriver, for use in places where it is impossible to reach with ordinary drivers; spiral screwholder blades used to start screws in hard to reach spots; and offset screwdrivers with ratchets. All of these types can be seen and demonstrated at your local hardware or automotive tool supply stores. A visit to either of these stores—when they are not busy—is a good education for anyone wanting to learn about the various tools available to the automotive mechanic.

Wrenches

Types of wrenches found in every automotive shop include open-end, box, combination open-end and box, socket, nut driver, torque, Allen and adjustable. As an automotive mechanic—either hobby or professional—you'll find that hardly any project can be

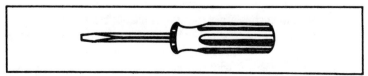

Fig. 2-4. Common screwdriver used to drive slotted screws.

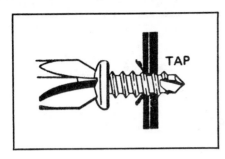

Fig. 2-5. Typical Phillips-head screwdriver.

completed without the use of one or more types of wrenches just mentioned.

Open-end wrenches are designed to tighten or loosen nuts and bolts. The opening at the end of the wrench as shown in Fig. 2-6 is usually at an angle to its body to permit turning a nut or bolt in a restricted space. This permits the wrench to be turned over for further turning after it has been turned as far as it will go on one side.

When using an open-end wrench, always pull on the wrench rather than push if at all possible. Pushing on a wrench with the fingers wrapped around the wrench handle is a good way to skin your knuckles should the nut or bolt suddenly give.

Select a wrench that fits the nut or bolthead snugly. A loose fit can damage both the nut or bolthead as well as the wrench. In such instances, the wrench will be put under excessive strain which can spring or break either the jaws or the handle. Never use a hammer to strike on a wrench to loosen, say, a tight-fitting nut, unless the wrench is specifically designed for such usage. Since most wrench handles are designed to withstand the maximum leverage that can be applied to their ends, don't use a pipe or another wrench on the end for additional leverage. This additional leverage may cause the wrench to break.

Box wrenches serve the same purpose as open-end wrenches, except that the opening on the box wrench completely surrounds (boxes in) the nut or bolthead. Combination open-end wrenches have a box wrench on one end and an open-end wrench on the other as shown in Fig. 2-7. The box wrench is normally used for breaking loose and final tightening of a nut while the open-end wrench is best suited for running a nut or bolt off. Usually both ends of such a wrench fit the same size nut or bolt.

Socket wrenches are somewhat similar to box wrenches in that the opening into which the nut or bolthead fits completely surrounds the nut or bolthead. However, socket wrenches have detachable sockets which are used with special handles. The socket can then be selected for a specific job, using only one handle.

Fig. 2-6. Open-end wrenches are designed to tighten or loosen nuts and bolts.

Most handles for use with sockets are of the ratchet type. Therefore, the socket doesn't have to be lifted from the nut or the bolt at the end of the swing like a conventional box wrench. Rather, the handle of the ratchet can be returned to the original position to start a new pull, and the socket stays stationary. The lock position of the ratchet—for either tightening or loosening—can be changed by a lever. Some ratchet handles even have a third lock position that stops the ratchet action altogether, allowing the socket to be used like a regular box-end wrench.

For very cramped spaces, a sliding offset handle is available. This type of handle employs a universal joint (see Fig. 2-8) permitting the use of any of the handles at an angle to the axis of the socket.

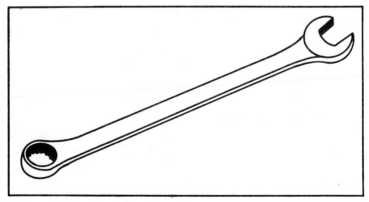

Fig. 2-7. Combination open-end wrench.

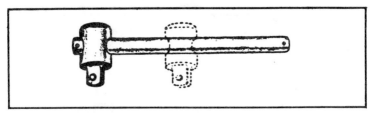

Fig. 2-8. A sliding offset handle for socket wrench.

A hinged offset handle is also used on socket wrenches to turn the socket quickly, as shown in Fig. 2-9. With such a handle, a bolt can be run and then the handle can be swung to 90 degrees for final tightening.

Fig. 2-9. A hinged offset handle for use with socket wrench.

Torque wrenches (Fig. 2-10) are necessary for working on several automotive parts where nuts and bolts must be tightened to special specifications. Air conditioner compressors, engine heads, etc., must be tightened to the manufacturers specifications. Excessive tightening might cause distortion of the parts and the possibility of stripped threads or broken bolts. Insufficient tightening will allow the nut or bolt to loosen with possible damage to the part. With a torque wrench, the dial on the wrench can be read to see the amount of torque being applied to the nut or bolt as it is being tightened. Thus, you can tighten within the specified limits.

Fig. 2-10. Typical torque wrench.

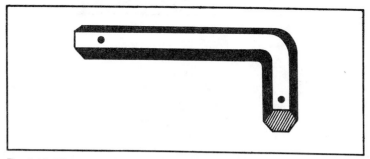

Fig. 2-11. Allen wrenches are used for tightening or loosening setscrews and Allen screws.

Allen wrenches (Fig. 2-11) are used for setscrews and for Allen screws, such as the ones shown in Fig. 2-12. The Allen setscrew is widely used on automotive parts to hold collars, pulleys and fans in place on shafts.

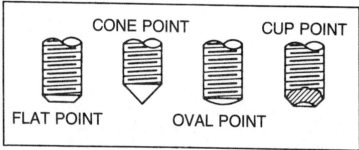

Fig. 2-12. Examples of setscrews and Allen screws.

An adjustable wrench like the one shown in Fig. 2-13 has an adjustable jaw to fit nuts and bolts of various sizes. Figure 2-14 shows the correct way to use an adjustable wrench (pressure is against the stationary jaw) while Fig. 2-15 shows the incorrect way (pressure is against the movable jaw).

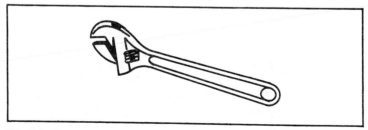

Fig. 2-13. Typical adjustable wrench.

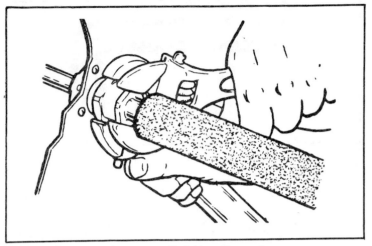
Fig. 2-14. Correct way to use an adjustable-end wrench.

Hammers

Ball pein hammers are the type commonly used on automotive projects and metal work of all kinds. A typical ball pein hammer is shown in Fig. 2-16. When using this type of hammer, always check the hammerhead for tightness before use. If you find it loose, a wedge or screw in the head end of the handle spreads it and keeps the head from coming off. Obviously, if the head should fly off during use, it could easily injure someone who may happen to be standing nearby.

One use of the ball pein hammer is for setting rivets, such as the ones in Fig. 2-17. Note that one end of the rivet has a head while the remaining shank is straight. When two pieces of metal are to be fastened together, a hole is drilled to accept the rivet. Then a ball pein hammer and a rivet set are used to form a head on the other end of the rivet as shown in Fig. 2-18.

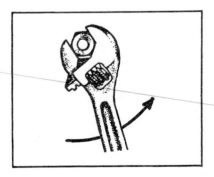

Fig. 2-15. Incorrect way of using adjustable-end wrench.

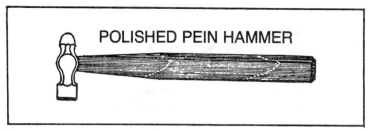

Fig. 2-16. Typical ball pein hammer.

Hammers are often used in conjunction with chisels to cut metal by driving the chisel into the metal with the hammer. There are several different shapes and sizes of chisels, some of which are shown in Fig. 2-19. When using any of them, hold the chisel in the opposite hand from the one you hold the hammer with. The ball pein

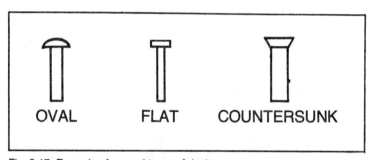

Fig. 2-17. Example of several types of rivets.

hammer should strike the head of the chisel with quick, sharp blows. Be sure to hold the chisel rather loosely in your hand. If the hammer misses and strikes your hand, less injury will occur since your loosely held chisel hand will give somewhat from the blow.

It is also a good idea to wear goggles when using a chisel to avert the possibility of chips flying into your eye.

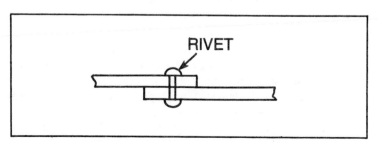

Fig. 2-18. Rivet having been set with a ball pein hammer.

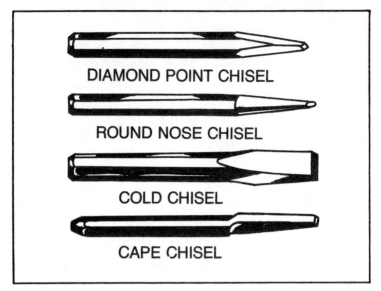

Fig. 2-19. Several types of chisels.

Punches

Punches, at first glance, might resemble chisels, except that chisels are designed for cutting and punches are used to knock out rivets and pins. Also, they align parts for assembly and mark locations of holes to be drilled in metal. A starting punch (Fig. 2-20) is used to break a rivet or pin loose and the pin punch is then used to drive the rivet or pin out. In the case of a rivet, the rivet head must first be ground off with a grinder or else cut with a cold chisel.

A center punch is worth its weight in gold when drilling into hard metal with a metal drill. Without a punched guide, the drill bit will slide and make it almost impossible to drill the hole where it is wanted. With a center punch mark at the location of the hole, the drill will not wander. Center punch marks are also useful for marking parts before they are disassembled so that they can be reassembled in the same relative locations.

Saws

Most people are familiar with the common hacksaw (Fig. 2-21) which is used mostly to cut metal of all types. Blades are available in a variety of sizes (teeth per inch) for all types of cutting. For example, the very fine-toothed blades of 32 teeth per inch are used to cut extra thin materials, light angle irons, wire cable, etc. The medium blade with 18 teeth per inch is a good all-purpose blade suitable for cutting

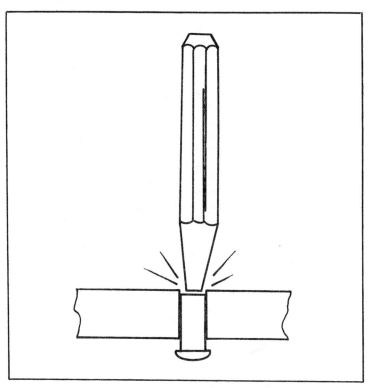

Fig. 2-20. Typical starting punch used to break a rivet or pin loose.

light angle iron, tool steel, iron pipe and similar items. High speed blades are made for cutting hard, extra tough steel.

Hacksaw frames vary in style and price, but all of them can be adjusted to accept different blade lengths. Some frames are designed for holding the blade in both a vertical and horizontal position. Some of the tubular frames provide room for extra blade storage.

When deciding which blade to use for a particular application, a good rule of thumb is to always have at least three teeth in contact

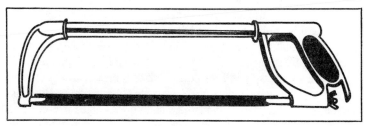

Fig. 2-21. Common hacksaw.

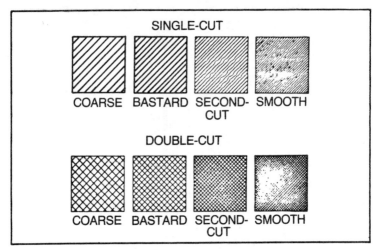

Fig. 2-22. Various types of cutting teeth used on files.

with the material in which you are cutting. This is especially true for coarse teeth as they have a tendency to snap and break off when used on thin material, in which less than three teeth are in contact with the material.

Files

Files are metal cutting tools with a large number of cutting teeth as shown in Fig. 2-22. Files have many uses. Consequently, there are hundreds of types of files available. The mechanic should learn to select the type that will give the best results. For rough and fine filing, a fast accurate file, having the proper cut is required. With a full assortment of files, a good mechanic is able to do all the filing necessary in making parts and repairing of autos. The parts of a typical file are shown in Fig. 2-23.

The cuts made across the face of a file to form the file teeth are either fine, coarse or the degree in between. The coarser the file, the more metal it removes with each file stroke, and the rougher it leaves the filed surface. A coarse file is usually used for rough cutting a part and is then finished with a fine-cut file.

When only one series of parallel cuts has been taken across the face of the file, the file is known as a single-cut file. When the file has two series of cuts (see Fig. 2-22) across the face in two different directions, it is known as a double-cut file. In addition to single-and double-cut classification, and their coarseness, files are classified according to their shape. For example, they may be flat, triangular, square, half-round, etc.

Most of the tools mentioned above are available in tool kits complete with a tool box. A small set, suitable for the home mechanic, may be purchased for under $50 while complete sets of hand tools for the professional may cost as much as $1000.

A set of tools which will fill the needs of most home mechanics, and is also a good starter set for the professional, follows:

- One ¼-inch ratchet driver with eight 6-point SAE sockets (3/16 to 7/16 inch)
- Three 8-point SAE sockets (¼, 15/16, and ⅜ inch).
- One spinner handle.
- One ⅜-inch ratchet driver with two 6-point SAE sockets (⅜ and 7/16 inch), five 12-point SAE sockets (½ to ¾ inch), four 6-point SAE sockets (½ to ¾ inch), two 6 point SAE sparkplug sockets (⅝ and 13/16 inch), ⅜-inch F x ¼-inch M adapter, two extensions (5 and 12 inch), ratchet and speeder handle.
- One ½-inch ratchet drive with six 12-point SAE sockets (¾ to 1-1/16 inch), 5-inch extension, ratchet and spin disc.
- Six open end wrenches (⅜ to l inch)
- One pair of 6 inch combination pliers.
- Two square-bar screwdrivers (4 and 6 inch)
- One 3-inch No. 1 Phillips screwdriver.
- Twenty-piece hex key set.
- One hacksaw with an assortment of blades.
- One tool box.

All of these tools can be purchased for around $100 at the time of this writing.

POWER TOOLS

Since all power tools are potentially dangerous, certain precautions should always be taken when they are in use. Here are a few of these precautions include.

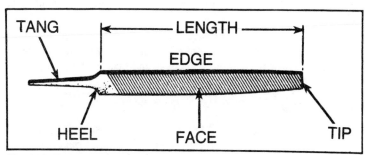

Fig. 2-23. Parts of a typical file.

1. Make certain the switch is in the OFF position before connecting the power supply.
2. Think "safety."
3. Plan ahead.
4. Keep children away.
5. Dress properly. Never wear loose clothing that might become entangled in the moving parts of the saw.
6. Disconnect the power cord before making any kind of adjustment or changing the blade of a power saw, bits in a drill, etc.
7. Never run a power tool in an enclosed area where there is any chance of explosion of fire through the presence of gasoline or any other explosive or inflammable substance.
8. Make sure electric power tools are properly grounded and, as an extra precaution, keep hands and feet dry when operating power tools.
9. When using extension cords over long distances, make sure that the wire size is sufficient to keep the voltage drop to a minimum and routed properly to prevent tripping or coming into contact with liquids.
10. Never remove any guard or other safety device provided for the power tool. One common fault is removing the grounding prong from power cords; this eliminates grounding protection.
11. Wear glasses or goggles when operating power tools.

IMPACT WRENCHES

Both air operated and electric impact wrenches are available in sizes from 2200 impacts per minute at 75 feet-pounds of torque to over 250 feet-pounds of torque. These wrenches are great time-saving devices for mechanics and the cost is not exorbitant for the home mechanic. Nearly all of them are equipped with ball bearings, reverse operation and a built-in regulator for positive speed control. The two most common sizes are ½-and ⅜-inch.

Other power tools related to the impact wrench include a right-angle attachment for converting impact wrenches to right-angle tools, power ratchet wrenches, and power chisels that produce up to 35 impacts per minute.

DRILLING TOOLS

The auto mechanic will find numerous occasions to drill holes through various types of materials around the shop. For light drilling, hand drills will suffice. However, for most drilling applications, the portable electric drill is the most convenient. These useful tools are very reasonably priced and will find many uses around the shop, as well as in the home. The smallest normally found around an automotive shop is the ¼-inch size. Such drills offer sufficient power for drilling in all types of metal and other materials when the proper bit is used. Many accessories—such as a disc sander, drill press, etc.—make them excellent power tools to have around any shop.

Single speed models operate at one speed only, while variable speed models offer speed or torque control from zero to maximum revolutions per minute. Another model incorporates a two-speed switch which runs the drill on high and low speeds. The method of changing speed varies with the different brands, but the most common method is a special trigger control that changes the speed by varying the finger pressure on the switch. Another model used a dial control to vary the speed.

The next size hand drill is the ⅜-inch model. Most of these drills—in addition to having a slightly larger chuck capacity—are normally built with double-reduction gears to provide more torque and to operate at lower speeds. Some of these models are even equipped with reversible motors for backing out of tight holes if the bit becomes locked.

Bits are available in a wide variety of sizes and types, for drilling in almost any material. The auto mechanic will be more concerned with metal-cutting bits that enable holes to be drilled in all types of metal. The selection of the correct bit for the job is of great importance, and an entire book could be filled on the selection of the correct bit alone. Therefore, it is suggested that the reader obtain several catalogs from the manufacturers of drill bits. The information in these catalogs will help greatly in selecting the correct bit for any given project.

Other than a drill motor and an assortment of drill bits, the home or even the professional mechanic should go slowly when purchasing any other power tools. The expense can run into the thousands in a very short time. Therefore, purchase power tools only when you are sure that you need them. Some relatively expensive power tools might be handy at times, but if they are used infrequently, it may be best to rent them until the tool is needed more often.

TESTING EQUIPMENT

Experts disagree, but if most professionals were limited to one testing tool, they would choose a volt-ohmmeter (VOM) for most of their troubleshooting problems. The volt-ohmmeter shown in Fig. 2-24 is capable of testing and locating the cause of trouble in an

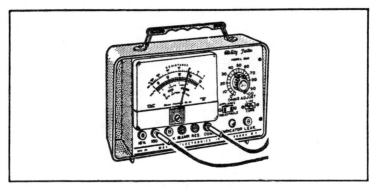

Fig. 2-24. Volt-ohmmeter (VOM) used for testing and locating troubles in automotive electrical systems.

automotive electrical system and the initial cash outlay is relatively small. It would be impractical within the scope of this book to fully cover the many ways in which a VOM may be used to test and locate the cause of trouble in all automotive electrical components, but some of the more common problems follow.

Testing Storage Batteries

Although storage batteries are frequently tested by simply connecting a tester to the battery, the proper way to test a battery is under load. This can best be accomplished by turning on all lights, radio, heater blower and all other accessories. Then connect the "-" test lead of the VOM to the negative (-) post of the battery as shown in Fig. 2-25. The positive lead is then connected to the positive (+) terminal of the battery, after the meter has been calibrated to 15V DC scale. The exact voltage reading can then be read on the meter and should not have a variation of more than one volt.

Testing the Cigarette Lighter

Use the resistance range of the VOM to check the lighter element for continuity. Be sure to depress the lighter before reading the meter. If the element checks good, use voltage range to check for voltage at the socket. With the lighter out of the socket, connect or touch one lead to the frame and the other lead to the center of the socket. The meter should read the battery voltage.

Testing the Circuit Breaker

Disconnect the circuit breaker for testing. Since the circuit breaker contacts are normally closed when that part is in use, the resistance range is used to check for continuity (See Fig. 2-26). If

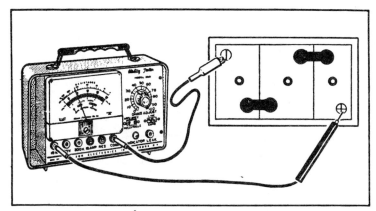

Fig. 2-25. Connection of VOM for testing storage batteries.

the meter does not indicate continuity, the unit is defective. You can then attempt to repair, re-test or replace the unit.

If the circuit breaker is of the magnetic type (includes a coil), the coil and its lead should also be tested for a possible break.

Testing Hydraulic Stop Light Switches

You need not disconnect this switch. Use the voltage range. The meter should read the battery voltage when the foot brake is *off* and zero volts when the foot brake is *on*. The ignition switch should be *on* when this test is being made.

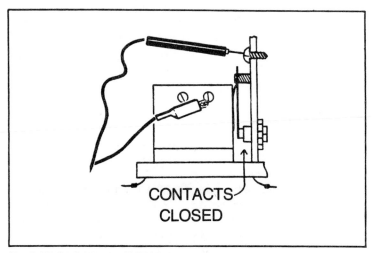

CONTACTS
CLOSED

Fig. 2-26. Connections of VOM for testing circuit breakers.

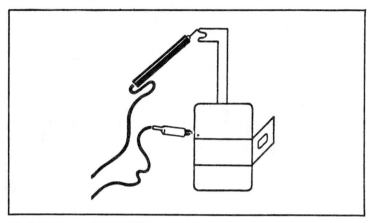

Fig. 2-27. Connections of VOM for testing condensers.

Testing Condensers

Use resistance range (Fig. 2-27). A good condenser should not cause the meter to read. If the meter does indicate resistance, the condenser is defective.

Checking Complete Operation of the Flasher Unit

To make this test, turn on the ignition switch. Use the 15-volt range to check the voltage at the flasher terminals. Meter should read battery voltage at both terminals. If the meter reads battery voltage on only one terminal, the flasher is open.

If battery voltage is measured at both terminals, disconnect the wire that connects the flasher unit to the directional lever switch. Connect the 15 amp range of the VOM from the disconnected flasher terminal to the chassis. If the flasher is good, the meter will indicate the current drawn by the flasher each time the flasher "clicks". No meter reading indicates a bad flasher unit.

Testing the Distributor

Turn the test meter for 15V DC range and connect the test leads across the breaker points of the distributor as shown in Fig. 2-28. The meter should read approximately six volts with the points open and about nine volts intermittently while cranking the engine. If the meter reads without interruption while cranking the engine, the points are not closing properly. If the meter does not read at all, the trouble can be caused by a short-circuit in the condenser, an open coil, an open ballast resistor, or points that are not opening properly.

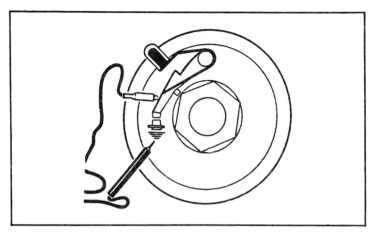

Fig. 2-28. Connections of VOM for testing distributor.

Testing the Alternator

Again use the voltage range (15VC DC) of the VOM and connect the leads as shown in Fig. 2-29. Now start the engine and let it idle while you observe the meter reading. At idle speed, the meter should read a low voltage at the armature terminal, but should increase as the gas pedal is pressed down to maximum. If no voltage or low voltage shows on the meter, the cause of the trouble is due to either a burned out field coil, defective brush, defective armature or shorted condenser.

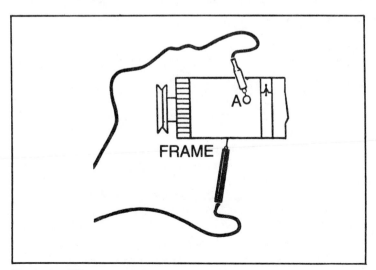

Fig. 2-29. VOM connections for testing generator.

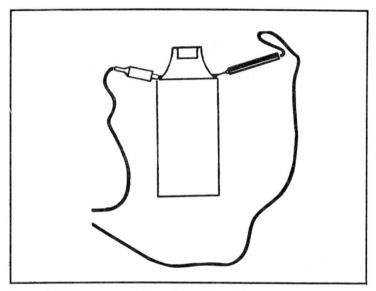

Fig. 2-30. VOM connections for testing ignition coils.

If the alternator under test does not have an external field coil terminal, the test previously described will show the condition of both the armature and field coil combined. If the alternator has an external field coil terminal, the voltage at the field coil terminal should increase with the motor speed in a manner similar to armature terminal voltage test outlined previously. No voltage or low voltage indicates a burned out or shorted field coil.

Testing Ignition Coils

The ohmmeter is used to test the primary coil for continuity. Connect the test leads as shown in Fig. 2-30. No reading indicates that the primary coil is open. If the ignition coil under test is of the single post type instead of the two-post type illustrated in Fig. 2-30, use the following test.

Remove the lead from the low voltage post. Connect one of the test leads (from the VOM set on 12V DC) to the grounded chassis. Then turn the ignition switch to *ON* and touch the other lead to the disconnected post on the coil. The meter should read 12 volts.

VACUUM GAUGE

A vacuum gauge can be purchased at any of the automotive supply houses for about $5. It can be used to check vacuum systems as well as for general tune-up tests and several other applications.

For tuneup tests, the vacuum gauge is connected directly to the engine's intake manifold. The vacuum here is controlled by the engine's valves, piston rings, head gasket, timing, speed and the throttle position. The reading on the gauge and the movement of the needle will detect many problems in the engine and may be used to select the proper idle mixture. Begin by selecting a vacuum hose on

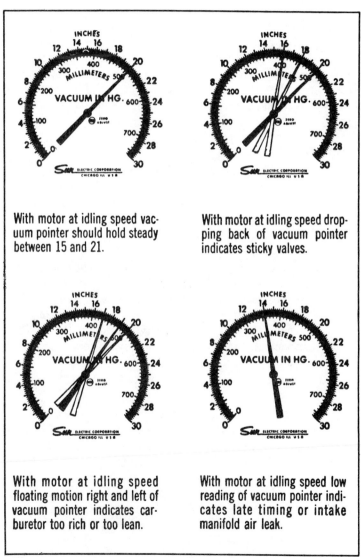

With motor at idling speed vacuum pointer should hold steady between 15 and 21.

With motor at idling speed dropping back of vacuum pointer indicates sticky valves.

With motor at idling speed floating motion right and left of vacuum pointer indicates carburetor too rich or too lean.

With motor at idling speed low reading of vacuum pointer indicates late timing or intake manifold air leak.

Fig. 2-31. Typical vacuum gauge reactions and some of their causes (courtesy Sun Electric Corporation).

the car that is connected directly to the intake manifold. Remove this hose and install the vacuum-gauge test hose to this point.

Some vacuum circuits have a built-in bleed to limit the maximum vacuum in that circuit. To check if the point you have connected the hose to has such a bleed, temporarily connect the gauge to the manifold and start the engine. You are looking for a circuit where the vacuum at idle is between 15 and 22 inches as the engine is accelerated and decelerated (Fig. 2-31).

When using the vacuum gauge, remember that readings have been calibrated for use at sea level. For all altitudes higher than sea level, readings will drop by one division on the dial for every 1000 feet over sea level. Thus, a reading of 20 inches of mercury at sea level would be only 19 inches at 1000 feet, 18 inches at 2000 feet, etc.

Tuneup Tests

This test is a quick way to determine if the engine has any mechanical problems—burnt valves, a blown head gasket, broken rings, or a cracked block or head—which will affect the engine's compression.

1. Ground out the coil's high tension lead so the engine will not start.
2. Crank the engine and watch the vacuum gauge. If the vacuum indicated is very low (less than 1 inch), you may have to back out the idle-speed screw or disconnect the idle stop solenoid to increase the reading. Cranking vacuum readings are normally between 2 and 10 inches. The amount of vacuum is controlled by the cranking speed, throttle position, and condition of the engine.
3. Be sure to reset the idle speed or reconnect the solenoid before starting the engine.

If the vacuum reading has a slight pulsation or is steady, this is acceptable. You will normally see between 1 and 2 inches of swing to the needle as the engine cranks. If, however, the reading drops toward zero occasionally, it needs service. If the vacuum gauge has indicated a loss in compression in one or more cylinders due to mechanical problems, a compression test should be made to pinpoint the cylinder that has the problem and determine the cause.

Positive Crankcase Ventilation (PCV) Test

This test checks the PCV (positive crankcase ventilation) system.

While cranking the engine, remove the PCV valve and close off the end or alternately pinch the PCV hose closed. Watch the vacuum gauge. It is acceptable if the vacuum increases slightly when the PCV hose or valve is closed off. If there is no change in vacuum, cleaning or replacing the PCV valve is necessary. Be sure to check PCV hoses for build-up of oil or dirt.

Idle Vacuum

This checks the engine condition and carburetor mixture at idle. Reconnect the coil lead, start the engine, and allow it to warm up. Read the vacuum gauge while the engine is at specified idle rpm. The vacuum should be steady and should read: late model cars 15 to 22 inches, older models 18 to 22 inches. Long-duration, high-performance cams may cause lower, and less steady, vacuum readings. If the reading is low or unsteady, one of the following is wrong and corrective action may be taken.

1. Lower than normal readings are caused by incorrect ignition timing, valve timing or adjustment, misadjusted idle mixture, worn piston rings or a leak in the intake manifold.
2. Readings that slowly change (3 to 5 inches(indicate incorrect idle-mixture adjustment.
3. Readings that oscillate rapidly are due to sticking valves, a leak in the head gasket, or worn valve guides. Increase the engine speed to 2000 rpm. If the gauge becomes steady, the problem is probably worn valve guides.

High Speed Vacuum

This test will detect a restriction in the exhaust system which may be the cause of a loss of high-speed performance or weak valve springs.

1. Note vacuum at idle.
2. Increase the engine speed to about 2000 rpm. Read vacuum. The vacuum should be steady and higher at 2000 rpm than at idle.

If the vacuum falls below the reading at idle or the vacuum oscillates, the engine needs service. The fall in vacuum is due to a restriction in the exhaust system. Check for a crushed tailpipe, a muffler that is choked up with rust and has loose baffles, or a collapsed header pipe. To isolate the problem, remove each section, starting with the rearmost one, and repeat the test. On some large displacement engines you may have to conduct this test while the car is on the road. To do this, connect the vacuum gauge (use a "tee" fitting so the accessory is also connected and will operate) and run the hose back through the window into the car. Drive the car through the speed range where performance starts to fall off while watching the gauge.

The oscillations at high speeds mentioned earlier are due to weak valve springs.

Carburetor Adjustment

The vacuum gauge may be used to set the idle mixture. Be sure the compression is good and the ignition system is in proper working order before attempting to set the carburetor. The engine must be at correct operation temperature.

1. Set idle speed to manufacturer's specifications.
2. Turn the idle mixture screw out (counterclockwise) until the vacuum starts to drop.
3. Turn the screw in (clockwise) slowly until maximum vacuum is seen without a loss in engine rpm.

On multiple-barrel carburetors, adjust each mixture screw separately. On some emission-controlled engines, the manufacturer specifies that you must turn the idle mixture screw in after reaching the best idle speed until the engine slows down a specified amount. Use a tachometer for this final adjustment. During mixture adjustments maintain idle rpm within 50 rpm of the specified idle speed by adjusting the idle speed screw.

Measuring Vacuum and Detecting Vacuum Leaks

The vacuum gauge may be used to test the amount of vacuum used to operate accessories, headlight covers or emission controls. It also will detect any vacuum leaks which reduce the effectiveness of the system. Some tests may require the use of a "tee" fitting so the circuit may be monitored while under normal operation.

1. Connect the vacuum gauge to the vacuum line; use a "tee" fitting if the system is to operate while you are making the test.
2. Operate the engine. Read the vacuum.

The vacuum should be within the manufacturer's specification. If not, headlight covers, air-conditioner controls and most vacuum-powered accessories have a modulated vacuum and normally will read about 4 to 8 inches. Power brakes and accessories with vacuum boosters and reservoirs will read close to full manifold vacuum.

If the vacuum is below the amount specified, inspect the hoses, especially at connection points, for cracks and splits and replace as necessary. A small amount of soap-and-water solution may be brushed on the hose in question to find the leak. When the solution is pulled into the hose the indicated vacuum will increase. You can also move the "tee" fitting to the other end of the hose and compare readings. If there is a leak, the vacuum will be considerably lower on the side of the leak away from the intake manifold. Be sure you reconnect all vacuum lines correctly. Incorrect connections may affect the performance, reliability, and safety of your vehicle.

Fuel Pump Tests

This is a simple way to determine the overall condition of the fuel pump and fuel lines. Use extreme care when making fuel pump tests. Keep fire and sparks away from the gasoline.

1. Disconnect the fuel line between the fuel pump and carburetor.
2. Connect the gauge's hose to the fuel pump.
3. Operate the engine at idle rpm. Read the 0-10 psi pressure scale.
4. Stop the engine and note the pressure gauge for 15 seconds.

The pressure should be within manufacturer's specifications or between 2 - 5 psi if specifications are not known and pressure holds after the engine is stopped.

If the pressure is too low, visually inspect for a crimped fuel line or leaks between the tank and fuel pump. If the line is not restricted or leaking, then the fuel pump's spring is weak. Repair or replace the pump. The vehicle may have an electric fuel pump and regulator; be sure pressure is not too high. Should this occur, check the fuel pressure regulator. You need to replace the pump as its check valves are leaking if the pressure drops to ½ of maximum reading or less within 15 seconds after stopping the engine.

Volume Test

This test does not require the use of the gauge; however, it's included as it is part of a complete fuel pump test.

1. Direct the flow of fuel from the pump into a graduated container. Place the hose at the bottom of the container.
2. Run the engine for 30 seconds and measure the amount of gas pumped.

At least one pint should be pumped in 30 seconds unless more is specified by the manufacturer. If less fuel than specified is pumped or a large amount of bubbles is seen coming out of the hose, check for a crimped, restricted or leaking fuel line. If volume is low but pressure was okay, inspect the pump's operating cam or rod and cam lobe for wear. If bubbles are seen, check for a leak between the fuel tank and the fuel pump.

Fuel Pump Vacuum Test

This test determines how much vacuum the fuel pump can develop to pull the fuel from the tank. It is made to pinpoint the cause of failure noted in the above fuel pump test.

1. Disconnect the fuel line from the pump inlet.
2. Connect the vacuum hose to the inlet of the fuel pump.
3. Start the engine and run it at idle. Watch the vacuum gauge.

The pump will not produce any vacuum until the fuel level in the carburetor drops and the pump attempts to fill the carburetor bowl. On some engines this may require two to three minutes. There should be from 2 to 10 inches of vacuum. If little or no vacuum is produced, the pump has a leak, a ruptured diaphragm or a leaking check valve. Repair or replace it. If this test is run at the end of the fuel line near the fuel tank, it will also check for fuel leaks in that line.

TESTING INSTRUMENTS

There are several testing instruments which are found in every automotive repair shop. A dwell/tachometer, timing light, and a compression tester are necessary for engine tune-ups. An electronic components analyzer saves time and eliminates guesswork when troubleshooting electronic ignition systems, etc. There are also a large array of sophisticated engine analyzers, charging-starting-battery analyzers and automotive oscilloscopes.

One type of professional engine analyzer, for example, provides complete diagnostic testing on most cars and trucks, including solid-state electronic and HEI ignition systems. It measures cam angle dwell from 0-60 degrees in 1 degree increments for precision dwell adjustment. The analyzer can determine engine speed from 0-1200 rpm for all carburetor adjustments and 0-6000 rpm for high speed tests. The color-coded meter scale gives "good/bad" indication of complete primary circuit resistance. Prefocused light allows precise engine timing at all speeds and in all lighting conditions. The analyzer measures mechanical, vacuum and total degrees of distribution advances from 0-60 degrees, gives "go" or "no go" reading for battery bolts, measures starter draw from 0-800 amps and alternators output from 0-200 amps, determines resistance for 0-500,000 ohms, and detects defective points, condenser, coil, distributor cap, rotor, and spark plug wires.

A typical charging-starting-battery analyzer will perform tests on all types of 6, 12, 24 and 32-volt batteries. Most are designed to electronically isolate problems with the battery, starter, regulator, alternator or generator.

Solid-state oscilloscopes are frequently used for testing conventional, breakerless, electronic and ignition systems. Tests can be made on secondary and primary circuits in parade with superimposed, individual cylinder displays. Peak voltage tests can be made and automatic rate adjusts circuits for stable patterns at all rpm's.

Dwell-Tach-Points Tester

This instrument is used to test and adjust dwell, along with setting idle speed and mixture adjustments. In addition, it may be used to test the PVC system, cylinder power balance, air cleaner efficiency and air-fuel ratio. Used with a compression tester, vacuum and fuel pump gauge and a timing light, it gives full testing and tune-up capabilities. Most Tach-Dwell testers feature all solid state circuitry and requires no internal battery or connections to the engine other than the two test leads.

Most instruments are equipped with a zero adjuster on the meter face to reset the mechanical zero position of the pointer. Before using the instrument, always check that the pointer is on zero before connecting the test leads. If it is not, turn the adjuster to left or right or rezero the meter. For best reading accuracy always zero the meter in the position that it will be read, that is, laying flat, upright or at an angle.

Most testers may be used on four, six or eight cylinder engines, and on 12 volt negative or positive ground with conventional point controlled and breakerless electronic or capacitor discharge ignition systems. In addition, many may be used on rotary (Wankel) type engines.

One hook-up allows the Dwell-Tach-Points Tester to perform or function as described. For negative ground vehicles, connect *RED* lead to the distributor terminal of the ignition coil and the *BLACK* lead to any good engine ground. For positive ground vehicles, connect the *BLACK* lead to the distributor terminal of the ignition coil and the *RED* lead to any good engine ground. If the ignition system has a *Tachometer* terminal or connection point, connect the *RED* lead to this point and the *BLACK* to ground. On *Breakerless* electronic systems and General Motors V8 engines attach *RED* lead to *Tach* terminal on distributor, *BLACK* to ground. Most others connect *RED* lead to coils distributor or *DEC* (Ford systems) terminal and *BLACK* to ground.

Points Test

This test function is used to test the ignition points for excessive resistance or poor contact. Problems here will reduce ignition efficiency and cause misfiring, hard starting and poor gas economy.

1. Slide the "dwell-tach" switch to dwell. The switch is in position when the function name is uncovered.
2. Turn the vehicle's ignition key on.
3. Slide the points ("pts") switch toward the meter.
4. If the meter reads in the open band the ignition points are open, bump the engine over slightly with the starter to close the points.
5. If the meter now reads in the green "OK" band the ignition points are good. Proceed to the dwell tests.
6. If the meter reads in the red "points resist" band, the points have excessive resistance. Replace the ignition points.

Point resistance may also be due to a broken strand in the coil to distributor wire or poor connections at the coil or distributor. To test the coil to distributor lead and its connections, move it back and forth. If the meter moves from the "OK" to the "bad" band replace this wire or repair any loose connections.

Dwell Test:

Dwell is defined as the period of time the ignition points remain closed during the ignition cycle. Proper dwell angle allows full energy build up in the coil (saturation) for good spark at all engine speeds. Excessive dwell results in point burning and rapid deterioration while too little dwell reduces the available spark voltage resulting in poor acceleration and engine misfiring at high rpm's.

Vehicles with breakerless ignitions do not have a conventional dwell period. The electronic circuitry controls the "on time" of the ignition coil and, when measured with a dwellmeter, the indicated dwell varies with engine rpm. For this reason the car manufacturers do not specify a dwell setting. You do not have to make the following dwell tests if your car has a breakerless ignition system. Refer to the manufacturer's specification for the correct dwell angle specification.

1. Slide the "dwell-tach" switch to the "dwell" position.
2. To test dwell, read the proper dwell scale while the engine is at idle rpm. (Double the eight cylinder reading for four cylinder engines.)

3. To set or adjust dwell with Delco window type distributors:
   - Operate the engine at idle rpm.
   - Lift the window and use a tool to turn the adjustor until the proper dwell setting is obtained.

4. To set or adjust dwell with other types of distributors with single ignition points:
   - Remove distributor's cap and rotor.
   - Loosen the ignition points' hold-down screws.
   - Crank engine and turn the adjuster until the   proper dwell setting is obtained.
   - Tighten hold-down screws and recheck dwell.

Dual Point Distributors

Two types of dual point installations are in use. One has two individual points, each independently controlling the coil. The other type uses two sets of ignition points in parallel to extend the total dwell period. The first type will have a distributor cam with only half the distributor cam lobes as there are cylinders. The second type will have the same number of distributor cam lobes as cylinders. To adjust either type, always block open one set of points with a clean piece of smooth card stock while adjusting the other set. After setting one set, remove the card stock and move it to the other set and adjust remaining point set. Some emission controlled engines have a separate control circuit to cut-in or out the second set of points. Refer to the manufacturer's manual for proper method of setting these points. On vehicles with the points in parallel, after setting the individual point dwell for each set, check that the total dwell is also within manufacturer's specifications, by removing the card stock and measuring the total dwell.

Testing For Dwell Variations:

Dwell variation (a change in the dwell reading as engine speed is increased) is caused by wear in the distributor shaft's breaker plate bearings, or a bent distributor shaft.

1. Increase engine speed to about 1,500 rpm.
2. Watch the dwell meter. The dwell should not change more than 3 degrees unless the vehicle's manufacturer specifies a larger amount is acceptable. (Some manufacturers specify 5-7 degrees as acceptable.

Tachometer

The tachometer is used to measure engine rpm. It is used while making idle speed and mixture settings. The tachometer also may be used to make tests of the carburetor's air fuel ratio setting, the PCV system, air cleaner efficiency and the distributor's mechanical advance system. The following is how to make idle speed and mixture setting.

1. Slide the "dwell-tach" switch to the "tach" position.
2. Adjust the idle speed screw on a fully warmed up engine until the engine is at the manufacturer's specified idle rpm. While following steps three and four of this procedure, readjust the idle speed as necessary to hold engine speed within 50 rpm of the specified idle rpm.
3. Turn the idle mixture screw in until the engine rpm slows. Then back out until the engine reaches highest rpm. This is the proper idle mixture for setting pre-emission controlled vehicles.
4. On engines with emission controls, do not remove idle mixture plastic caps if fitted. On all vehicles manufactured since 1968 (1966 in California), turn the idle mixture screw in (clockwise) until engine speed drops 50 rpm or the amount specified by the manufacturer. (On two or four barrel carburetors adjust each mixture individually following steps three and four).
5. Follow the manufacturer's procedures for setting final hot idle speed, i.e. transmission in drive, air conditioner on, head lights on, etc. Set idle speed adjustment to manufacturer's specified idle rpm.

For a simple quick check of the idle mixture, use the following method.

1. Remove the air cleaner.
2. Be sure the engine is fully warmed up, the choke is fully open and engine is at correct idle rpm.
3. Slide a flat plate slowly over the carburetor's air horn to block off air flow. If the engine speed increases, the idle mixture is too lean. If the engine speed decreases, idle mixture is too rich. Little or no change in speed as the air horn is almost closed off indicates the mixture is acceptable.

The following test determines if each cylinder of the engine is producing equal power. Unequal power indicates problems in the ignition, compression or fuel system.

1. Set the engine speed to any steady speed between idle and 1,000 rpm. Be sure the engine is at its normal operating temperatures.
2. One by one remove, and reconnect each spark plug wire. As each wire is removed the rpm will decrease. Record the rpm for each cylinder while the spark plug wire is removed.
3. Compare these rpm readings:

• If all are within 50 rpm of each other, the engine has equal power output from each cylinder. This indicates no unusual problems exist in any one cylinder's ignition, compression or fuel system.

• If any cylinder is more than 50 rpm different than the others, check those with the highest rpm. They have ignition, compression or fuel system problems that are causing those cylinders to produce less power than the others. (On some late model (1971 and later cars) with exhaust gas recirculating type emission controls, this test will give erroneous results. Some "good condition" cylinders will show no decrease or an increase in speed).

Another test using the tachometer is to check the operation of the PCV system.

1. Set the engine at idle rpm.
2. Remove the PCV hose from the valve cover. Leave the other end connected to the intake manifold.
3. Close off the end of the PCV hose with your finger. Note rpm. (If the PCV valve cannot be easily removed, this test may also be run by pinching closed the PCV hose at any point.).
4. If the PCV system is functioning properly, the engine should slow down a minimum of 50 rpm. If the engine does not slow down at least 50 rpm, replace a PCV valve and clean out the PCV hose.

This test checks the condition of the air filter to determine if it is causing a reduction of air flow to dirt or damage.

1. Remove the air cleaner cover and filter.
2. Note rpm.
3. Replace air filter and tighten cover securely. If engine speed decreases, inspect the air filter for excessive dirt or damage which may restrict air flow.

This test determines if the distributor's mechanical advance mechanism is working.

1. Set the engine to the lowest idling speed possible.
2. Loosen the distributor and rotate it slightly until the engine runs at the highest rpm. Hold distributor in this position.
3. Increase the engine speed to approximately 1,000 rpm and hold this throttle setting.
4. Rotate the distributor again and note the maximum increase in rpm. If the engine speed increases more than 100 rpm the mechanical advance mechanism is not working properly and the distributor should be removed and checked for binding, wear or damage.
5. Return the engine speed to the correct idle rpm and reset the initial timing to factory specifications. (Do not attempt to set timing by "peaking" rpm while turning distributor. On late model, emission controlled vehicles this may lead to overheating and possible engine damage).

Most Dwell-Tach-Points testers may also be used on rotary (Wankel) engines equipped with point controlled ignition systems. The design of this type of engine provides for one spark plug firing per crankshaft revolution.

Ignition Timing Light

An ignition timing light in essence is a stroboscopic beam (intermittent flashes of light that are synchronized with each revolution of the timing mark). Thus, every time the timing mark makes a complete cycle the light flashes on. This has the illusion of arresting all motion and enables the user to observe the action of the ignition even while it is operating at high speeds. Since the timing mark appears to be standing still, it is a simple matter to make ignition timing adjustment.

All auto manufacturers do not employ a universal set of specifications for setting ignition timing. Normally timing specifications are given for the Number one cylinder (the one next to the radiator). When this cylinder fires the timing mark must align with the reference pointer. If they are not aligned this means that the distributor breaker contacts opened either too early or too late. Ignition timing adjustments must then be made.

Initial Check Out Points

1. Make sure that distributor points and spark plugs are properly cleaned and set.
2. Rev the engine until it reaches a normal operating temperature.

3. Check the manufacturer's specifications for idling speed. Normally this is between 300 and 600 rpm.

4. When testing a V-type engine remember that *right hand* or *left hand* refers to that side as viewed from the driver's seat.

5. When testing an engine that has the timing marks located on the front of the engine near the fan blades, loosen the fan belt to keep it from revolving. This precaution will avoid injury to your hands or to the timing light.

To operate the timing light, first locate the reference pointer and timing mark. This can be determined from the manufacturer's specifications, and may be in any one of several places—on the harmonic balancer, damper fly wheel, crankshaft impulse neutralizer located on the front of the engine, or a line or steel ball embedded in the flywheel at the back of the engine. Turn the engine over slowly until this timing mark appears.

Mark the location with a piece of chalk or quick drying enamel. Make a white line about ⅛ inch wide and directly over the mark. This easily pinpoints the mark when it is in motion.

Start the engine. After it has warmed up to normal operating temperature, shut it off and disconnect the ignition wire from the Number one cylinder spark plug. Now push the spring male terminal of the timing light into the terminal of the ignition wire and the other terminal of the timing light on the terminal of the Number one cylinder spark plug. The timing light is now connected in series with the plug, and every time the plug fires the light will flash.

Start the engine again and rev to idling speed. Now point the light at the timing mark. If the timing mark and reference point do not align, loosen the locking screw on the distributor and rotate either clockwise or counterclockwise until alignment is obtained. This is done while the engine is still running. After proper alignment has been achieved, re-tighten the distributor locking screw.

Testing Automatic Spark Advance

After timing adjustments have been made, and with the timing light still connected up in series, gradually increase the engine speed while noting the timing mark. Timing mark should remain stationary until automatic advance cuts in (between 500 and 1000 rpm). From this point on, as engine speed is increased, the timing mark should gradually move. If it does not move, or if it moves suddenly, the advance mechanism is either frozen or sticking and should be repaired or replaced.

Checking Synchronization of Double Points

First make timing mark adjustments. Timing light is then connected in series to the spark plug of the cylinder indicated at the second timing mark. This mark is generally indicated as "Syn 2-7" or "Ign 2-7". This indicates the Number two or Number seven plug which should fire when the timing mark and reference pointer are aligned. If they fail to align, shut off the engine and adjust the removable breaker points until they are in synchronization with the stationary points.

Many ignition timing lights are equipped with a remote starter switch which can be attached to any engine having a solenoid starter switch. This permits the mechanic to make motor tests and adjustments without the aid of a second person inside the car. In using this device, always connect the remote starter leads to the solenoid and never to the starter motor. Operating instructions are as follows:

1. On engines where ignition must be on before starter will operate, leave ignition in *off* position. Connect one lead wire of the flat twin cord to the ungrounded terminal of the battery. Connect the other lead wire to the ungrounded terminal of the starter relay or solenoid. Press the starter button to turn over the engine.

2. On engines where it is not necessary to turn on the ignition to operate the starter, connect one lead wire of the flat twin cord to the switch side of relay or solenoid and the other lead wire to ground. Press the starter button to turn over the engine.

Compression Tester

The three types of compression testers in normal operation are the offset stem model, seal quick-flex drive model, and the screw-in flex drive models. The general instructions for testing engine compression with any of these are as follows.

1. Run the engine until it is at normal operating temperature.

2. Loosen all spark plugs one or two turns and crank the engine (do not attempt to start engine) five to 10 seconds. This will blow out any dirt around the base of the spark plug so it doesn't fall into the cylinder.

3. Carefully remove all spark plugs. A visual inspection of the plugs will detect many problems. Look for oily plugs that indicate bad rings or worn valve guides and burnt plugs indicating a vacuum leak.

4. Open the carburetor throttle fully for accurate results.

5. Insert your compression tester—refer to specific instructions for your model.
6. Crank the engine until you go through four compression strokes. At each compression stroke the gauge will pulse slightly. Note the readings of the first and last stroke. Be sure the battery is fully charged and the starter is in good condition and cranks the engine at normal speed. Low cranking speeds may give erroneous results.

After testing as indicated above, the engine is in good condition if the first stroke was 50-70 pounds and the last stroke was within the manufacturer's specifications. It's also okay if the compression difference between cylinders is less than the amount specified by the manufacturer.

Results that indicate problems in the engine are as follows:

1. Low compression on the first stroke and the pressure building up only 10-20 psi per stroke indicates sticking valves or burnt seats.
2. Low compression one or all cylinders is undersirable. To determine if the piston rings or cylinder walls are bad, squirt a small quantity of oil into the cylinder. Crank the engine a couple of times and then repeat the compression test. If the results are now okay then the rings or cylinder walls are worn. The oil seals off any small leaks around the rings. If the results are still low, then the problem is in the valves or head gasket. If there is only a slight improvement then rings, valves and/or head gasket are bad.
3. Higher than normal compression is caused by carbon build-up in the cylinder.
4. Low reading on recently overhauled engines where new rings were installed may be caused by low compression. Eventually the rings will seat properly.

Chapter 3

Lubrication

The time or mileage intervals for lubrications and maintenance services outlined in this chapter are intended as a general guide for establishing regular maintenance and lubrication periods. Sustained heavy duty and high speed operation or operation under adverse conditions may require more frequent servicing (Fig. 3-1).

For normal operation, engine oil should be changed each three months or 3,000 miles, whichever comes first. However, engine oil should be changed every two months or 3,000 miles, whichever occurs first, under any of the following conditions.

1. Driving in dusty conditions.
2. Driving in snowy or muddy conditions where slipping of traction is frequent.
3. Pulling camping trailer or mobile home.
4. Frequent long runs at high speeds and high ambient temperatures.
5. Excessive idling.
6. Stop and go driving or short trips in freezing temperatures (engine not thoroughly warmed up).

Replace the oil filter at the first oil change, and every second oil change thereafter. The proper oil viscosity should be given consideration for operating at various temperatures. For example, for operation in temperatures from -30 degrees Fahrenheit to 20 degrees Fahrneheit, 5W-20 or 5W-30 is recommended. For temperatures from 0 degrees to 90 degrees Fahrenheit, 10W-30 or 10W-40

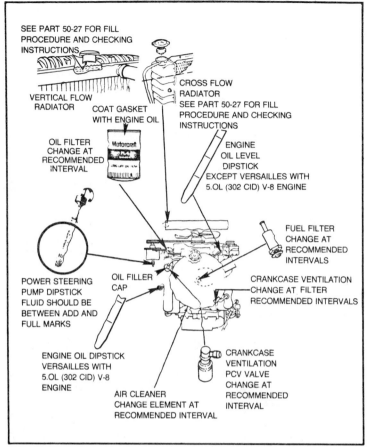

SEE PART 50-27 FOR FILL
PROCEDURE AND CHECKING
INSTRUCTIONS

VERTICAL FLOW
RADIATOR

COAT GASKET
WITH ENGINE OIL

CROSS FLOW
RADIATOR

SEE PART 50-27 FOR FILL
PROCEDURE AND CHECKING
INSTRUCTIONS

OIL FILTER
CHANGE AT
RECOMMENDED
INTERVAL

ENGINE
OIL LEVEL
DIPSTICK
EXCEPT VERSAILLES WITH
5.0L (302 CID) V-8 ENGINE

FUEL FILTER
CHANGE AT
RECOMMENDED
INTERVALS

POWER STEERING
PUMP DIPSTICK
FLUID SHOULD BE
BETWEEN ADD AND
FULL MARKS

OIL FILLER
CAP

CRANKCASE VENTILATION
CHANGE AT FILTER
RECOMMENDED INTERVALS

ENGINE OIL DIPSTICK
VERSAILLES WITH
5.0L (302 CID) V-8
ENGINE

AIR CLEANER
CHANGE ELEMENT AT
RECOMMENDED INTERVAL

CRANKCASE
VENTILATION
PCV VALVE
CHANGE AT
RECOMMENDED
INTERVAL

Fig. 3-1. Engine lubrication rack service points.

is recommended. The 10W-30 is probably the best all-around oil viscosity to use in most American-made vehicles.

LUBE AND GENERAL MAINTENANCE

Lubricate all grease fittings in front suspension, steering linkage, and constant velocity universal joint. Remove the lubrication plugs. Use a hand-operated, low-pressure grease gun fitted with a rubber tip and loaded with multi-purpose long-life lubricant. Force the lubricant into the joint only until the ball joint seals can be felt or seen to swell, indicating that the seal is full of lubricant. Do not, however, lubricate until the lubricant escapes from the seal as this will destroy the weather-tight seal. Re-install the lubrication plug.

Also lubricate the transmission shift linkage, hood latch, hood hinges, parking brake cable guides and linkage, clutch linkage, propeller shaft slip joint, universal joints and brake and clutch pedal springs. Lubricate suspension and steering linkage every two months or 3,000 miles when operating under dusty or muddy conditions and in extensive off-road use.

Four wheel drive vehicles should also have the centering ball at the transfer case end of the front propeller shaft lubricated every 6,000 miles with water resistant chassis lubricant. The front axle should be checked every 6,000 miles or four months and refilled with gear lubricant when necessary. If the differential is at operating temperature, fill to the level of the filler plug hole; if below operating temperatures, fill to ½ inch below the filler plug hole.

Check the transfer case on four wheel drive vehicles every 6,000 miles and, if necessary, lubricate as follows.

1. Add gear lubricant to bring to the level of the filler plug hole.
2. Brush or spray engine oil on the control   lever pivot point and on all exposed control linkage every   6,000 miles or four months, whichever occurs first.

BODY LUBRICATION

Normal use of a vehicle causes metal-to-metal movement at certain points in the body and must be provided with a protective film of lubricant to prevent noise, wear and improper operation at these points. For exposed surfaces, such as door checks, door lock bolts, etc., apply a thin film of light engine oil. Where holes are provided in body parts, a dripless oil can be safely used, but any lubricant should be used sparingly. After application, all excess should be carefully wiped off.

There are other points on auto bodies which may occasionally require lubrication and which are difficult to service. The seat adjusters and seat track, for example, are often overlooked. These should be lubricated with water resistant chassis lubricant. Window regulators and controls are confined in the space between the upholstery and the outside door panel. Easy access to the working parts may be made by removing the trim. Door weatherstrips and rubber hood bumpers should be lightly coated with a rubber lubricant.

The effects of salt and other corrosive materials used for ice and snow removal on the highways can result in accelerated rusting and deterioration of underbody components such as brake and fuel lines, frame, underbody floor pan, exhaust system, etc. These corrosive effects, however, can be reduced by periodic flushing of the underbody with plain water. This should be done at least once each year. Dirt and other foreign matter should also be cleaned out at least once each year.

REAR AXLES

The lubricant level should be checked in the rear axle every four months or 6,000 miles, whichever occurs first. If the lubricant is low, add the fill to the filler plug hole. It is usually a good idea to drain the rear axle lubricant every 24,000 miles and refill with new. If the vehicle is operated in exceptionally heavy work or at continuous high speeds, the lubricant should be changed every 12,000 miles. It may even be necessary to change the rear axle even more often—such as every 12,000 miles—if the vehicle is used off road in dusty areas.

Propeller shaft slip joints should be lubricated every 6,000 miles or four months with water resistance chassis lubricant which meets the manufacturer s specifications. Also, lubricate the universal joint equipped with lube fittings every 6,000 miles or four months with the same water resistant lubricant. More frequent lubes may be required for "off the road" operations like in the case of four wheel drive vehicles.

WHEEL BEARINGS

Due to the weight of the tire and wheel assembly on many vehicles, it is recommended that they be removed from the hub before lubricating wheel bearings to prevent damage to the oil seal. Then remove the front wheel hub to lubricate the bearings (Fig. 3-2). The bearings should be thoroughly cleaned before repacking with lubricant. This should be performed every 24,000 miles.

Since the rear wheel bearings receive their lubrication from the rear axle on most autos, new or cleaned wheel bearings should be greased with wheel bearing grease before replacing them.

STEERING

Manual steering gears are factory-filled with steering lubricant and usually no lubrication is required for the life of the steering gear. However, every 36,000 miles the gear should be inspected for seal leakage and if a seal is replaced or the gear is overhauled, the gear housing should be refilled with steering gear lubricant.

On power steering systems, the fluid level in the pump reservoir should be checked at each oil change. Add power steering fluid or automatic transmission fluid as necessary to bring the fluid level into proper range on the filler cap indicator, depending upon the fluid temperature.

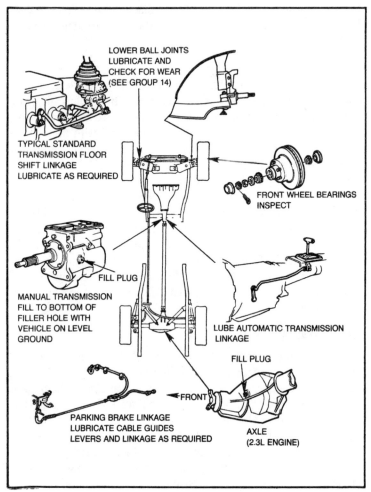

LOWER BALL JOINTS
LUBRICATE AND
CHECK FOR WEAR
(SEE GROUP 14)

TYPICAL STANDARD
TRANSMISSION FLOOR
SHIFT LINKAGE
LUBRICATE AS REQUIRED

FRONT WHEEL BEARINGS
INSPECT

FILL PLUG

MANUAL TRANSMISSION
FILL TO BOTTOM OF
FILLER HOLE WITH
VEHICLE ON LEVEL
GROUND

LUBE AUTOMATIC TRANSMISSION
LINKAGE

FILL PLUG

FRONT

PARKING BRAKE LINKAGE
LUBRICATE CABLE GUIDES
LEVERS AND LINKAGE AS REQUIRED

AXLE
(2.3L ENGINE)

Fig. 3-2. Typical chassis lubrication points.

If the operating temperature of approximately 150 degrees
Fahrenheit is reached (hot to the touch), the fluid should be between
hot and *cold* on the indicator stick. If at lower temperatures—such as
70 degrees Fahrenheit—the fluid level should show between *add*
and *cold*. In any case, the fluid does not require periodic changing.

To maintain correct front end alignment and to provide easy
steering, longer tire life, and driving stability, the steering linkage
and suspension should be checked and lubricated at regular
intervals—about every 6,000 miles. Lubricate tie rods, upper and
lower control arms, and ball joints at fittings with water resistant
chassis lubricant.

HOOD LATCH AND HOOD HINGE

As with body lubrication, discussed earlier, the hood latch assembly and hood hinge assembly should be lubricated every 6,000 miles or four months, whichever occurs first. Proceed as follows:

1. Wipe off any accumulation of dirt or contamination on latch parts.
2. Apply lubricant (of an approved type) to the latch pilot bolt and latch locking plate.
3. Apply light engine oil to all pivot points in the release mechanism, as well as primary and secondary latch mechanisms.
4. Lubricate hood hinges.
5. Make a hood hinge and latch mechanism functional check to assure the assembly is working correctly.

MISCELLANEOUS APPLICATIONS

Under normal driving conditions, the automatic transmission fluid should be changed and the sump filter replaced every 24,000 miles. Under unusual conditions, such as constant driving in heavy city traffic during hot weather, trailer pulling, etc., these services should be performed at 12,000-mile intervals.

Replace the fuel filter element located in the carburetor inlet every 24,000 miles for normal driving conditions and more often for abnormal conditions. The cam lubricator in the distributor where applicable should also be replaced at 24,000-mile intervals.

Lubricate accelerator linkage every 24,000 miles. On most V8 engines the ball stud at the carburetor should be lubricated. On six cylinder engines, there are usually two ball studs at the carburetor lever to lubricate and also a lever mounting stud. Do not, however, lubricate the accelerator cable.

To check automatic transmission fluid, drive the engine several miles if the engine is cold, making frequent starts and stops, to bring the transmission up to normal operating temperature (between 150-190 degrees Fahrenheit). Then park vehicle on a level surface and with the selector lever in *park*, leave the engine running. Remove the dipstick and wipe clean. Reinsert dipstick until the cap seats and then remove again and note reading. If the oil level is at or below the *add* mark on the dipstick, oil should be added as necessary, but do not overfill.

Figures 3-1 and 3-2 detail engine rack service points, chassis lubrication points and lubrication specifications for Ford products. Keep these illustrations in mind for future reference.

Chapter 4

Engine And Engine Tuneup

Engine tuneup is very important to the modern automotive engine as it has a decided effect on power, performance and fuel consumption. A properly tuned engine will run smoother, making the vehicle ride more comfortably. It will also obtain the best possible gas mileage and accelerate and perform at its best. On the other hand, a poorly tuned engine will often miss while idling as well as at various road speeds. The engine will frequently stall. Original power is reduced and gas mileage is poor.

In general, an engine tuneup should be performed by following a definite and thorough procedure of analysis and correction of all items affecting power, performance and economy. This is best performed in two parts: mechanical checks and adjustments will be performed first, then an instrument checkout follows.

Before attempting an engine tuneup, a basic knowledge of how an engine operates is required. Then with this basic knowledge, the reader should have little trouble in following and understanding the more detailed procedures presented in this chapter.

THEORY OF ENGINE OPERATION

All conventional automotive engines have one thing in common—they operate on the four-stroke cycle principle. During this cycle the piston travels the length of its stroke four times up, down, up, down (or vice versa). As the piston travels the length of its stroke—up or down—the crankshaft is rotated halfway or 180 degrees. Therefore, since the piston travels the length of its stroke four times, the crankshaft rotates two complete turns during one cycle. The camshaft, which controls the opening and closing of the valves, is driven by the crankshaft at half the crankshaft speed. Valve action—intake and exhaust (requiring two strokes)—occurs once in each four-stroke cycle and the piston acts as a compressor during the two remaining strokes by pumping air. All of the components just mentioned are shown in Fig. 4-1.

Stroke One

During normal operation, the intake valve opens as the piston moves in the cylinder as shown in Fig. 4-2. The piston traveling

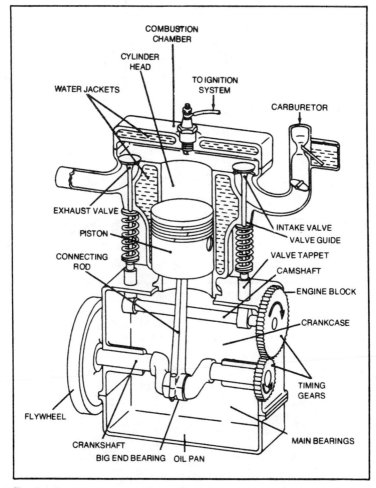

Fig. 4-1. Basic components of a four-stroke internal combustion engine.

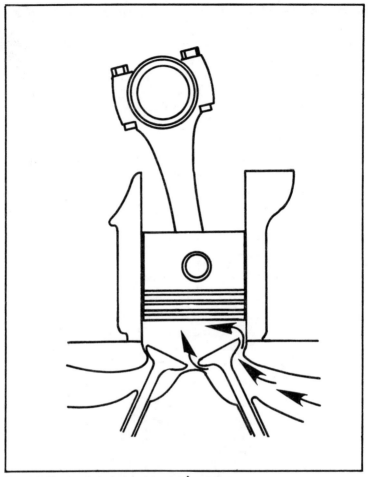

Fig. 4-2. Sectional view of a piston intake stroke.

downward in the cylinder creates an area of pressure lower than that of the atmosphere surrounding the engine. Atmospheric pressure will cause air to flow into this low pressure area, and by directing the air flow through the carburetor, a measured amount of fuel is added. When the piston reaches the bottom of the intake stroke, the cylinder is filled with air and vaporized fuel. The exhaust valve is closed during the intake stroke.

Stroke Two

The compression stroke begins as the piston begins to move upward (Fig. 4-3). Since the intake valve closes on this stroke, the air-fuel mixture is trapped in the cylinder. As the piston continues on this upward movement, it compresses the air-fuel mixture to a fraction of its original volume. The exact pressure of this compression will vary—depending on the amount of carburetor throttle opening and also on the compression ratio of the engine.

Stroke Three

The power stroke is produced by igniting the compressed air-fuel mixture. The igniting takes place when the spark plug arcs—not as an explosion—but as a very rapid igniting and burning action. The extremely high temperature caused by the igniting of the air-fuel mixture expands the gases, creating a very high pressure on the top of the piston which drives the piston down. This downward

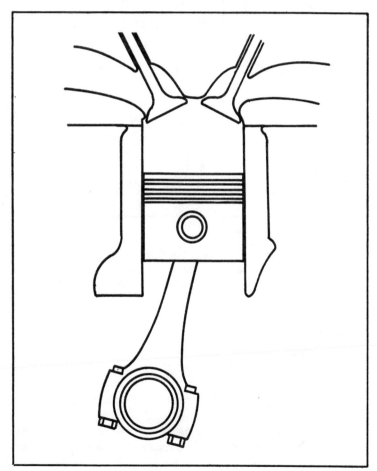

Fig. 4-3. Piston compression stroke.

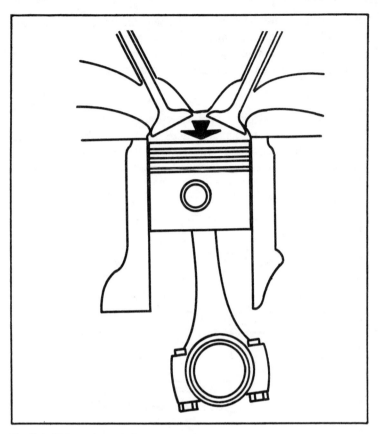

Fig. 4-4. Piston power stroke.

motion of the piston is transmitted through the connecting rod and is converted to rotary motion by the crankshaft. Both the intake and exhaust valves are still closed during this stroke as shown in Fig. 4-4.

Stroke Four

The final stroke in a four-stroke cycle is the exhaust stroke (Fig. 4-5). Pressure in the cylinder at this time causes the exhaust gas to rush into the exhaust manifold. The upward motion of the piston on its exhaust stroke expels most of the remaining exhaust gas.

During the end of the exhaust stroke, the piston pauses momentarily and the inertia of the exhaust gas tends to remove any remaining gas in the combustion chamber. However, a small amount of exhaust gas always remains to be mixed with the incoming mixture; this unexpelled gas is captured in the clearance area between the piston and the cylinder head. Thus one four-stroke cycle is completed.

COMBUSTION

The power delivered from the piston to the crankshaft is the result of a pressure increase in the gas mixture above the piston. This pressure increase occurs as the air-fuel (gas) mixture is heated, first by compression, and then on the down stroke by burning. The burning fuel supplies heat that raises temperature and at the same time also raises pressure. Actually, about 4/5 of the mixture in the

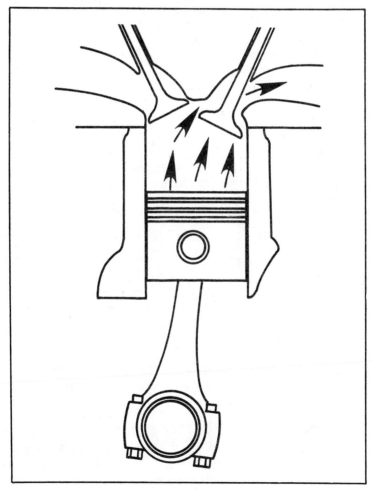

Fig. 4-5. Piston exhaust stroke.

cylinder is composed of nitrogen gas that does not burn but expands when heated by the burning of the combustible elements. This expanding nitrogen supplies most of the pressure on the piston.

Burning of the fuel and oxygen mixture must burn evenly as the flame moves across the combustion chamber; otherwise maximum power would not be delivered. Instead, the entire force would be spent in one sharp blow, occurring too fast for the piston to follow.

The burning of the fuel-air mixture must also be completed by the time the piston is about half-way down, so that maximum pressure will be developed in the cylinder when the piston sends its greatest force to the crankshaft.

At the beginning of the power stroke, as the piston is driven downward by this pressure, the volume above the piston increases. If it were not for the continuance of the combustion process at this point, the pressure in the cylinder would drop. The continuance of the combustion process therefore raises the temperature of the gases, expanding them and causing them to maintain a constant pressure on the piston as it travels downward. This provides a smooth application of power throughout the effective part of the power stroke to make the most efficient use of the energy released by the burning fuel.

From the previous paragraphs, we can see that the fuel is not used to cause an explosion in an internal combustion engine; rather, the burning causes a high pressure within the cylinder to push the piston down smoothly during the power stroke.

COMPRESSION RATIO

The compression ratio is a comparison of the volume of the cylinder and combustion chamber when the piston is all the way down, to the volume remaining when the piston is all the way up.

The main advantage of a high compression ratio is that it enables the engine to develop more power from a given charge of fuel. The combustion pressure exerted downward on a piston is always three or four times as great as the compression pressure. Consequently, an increase in compression pressure (input) means at least three times as great an increase in combustion pressure (output).

VALVE TIMING

In most four-stroke engines, the intake valve begins to open before the piston reaches the top, and the exhaust valve remains open until after the piston reaches the very top of its length. Therefore, both the intake and exhaust valves are open for a short period of time. The valve timing is arranged this way to use the inertia of the gas in evacuating and in filling the cylinders.

During this filling of the cylinder with the air-fuel mixture and evacuating the exhaust gases, the weight of these gases provides momentum in the established direction. When a valve opens, the initial air flow is slow, requiring valve timing to allow for this lag in starting and stopping in the flow. Each valve opens earlier and closes later than would be necessary if the air-fuel mixture and the exhaust gases were weightless. This action insures that the maximum air-fuel mixture will enter the cylinder.

On the intake stroke, the exhaust valve remains open a little after the piston has started down (after top center) to take advantage of the momentum of the exhaust gases rushing out through the valve. Therefore, the cylinder continues to empty itself because of this momentum.

The intake valve stays open on the compression stroke a little past bottom center because incoming gases will continue to pack their way in for a short time after the piston reverses direction, due to the momentum of the air-fuel mixture.

On the power stroke, the exhaust valve opens before bottom center to start the exhaust gases out of the cylinder. On the exhaust stroke, the intake valve opens early to start the fuel mixture moving into the cylinder.

Unlike ignition timing, valve timing is not variable with the speed and load of the engine. Except for very small variations due to the stack of tolerances in the valve train, valves always open and close at the same time in the cycle. There is, however, one particular speed for a given engine at which the air-fuel mixture will pack itself into the cylinders most effectively. This is the speed at which the engine puts out its peak torque.

Peak torque is not reached at other speeds because at low speeds, for example, compression is somewhat suppressed. This is due to the slight reverse flow through the valves just as they open or close, when the mixture is not moving fast enough to take advantage of the time lag. At very high speeds, the valve timing does not allow quite enough time during the opening and closing periods for effective packing of the air-fuel mixture into the cylinders.

MECHANICAL CHECKS AND ADJUSTMENTS

As mentioned previously, an engine tuneup will consist of two parts. The first part should consist of mechanical checks and adjustments; the second part should consist of an instrument checkout. The first part will be discussed briefly in this section.

Spark Plug Removal. Before removing any of the plugs, eliminate any foreign matter from around the spark plugs by blowing out with compressed air. Then the wires can be disconnected and the plugs removed. When disconnecting the plug wires, do not pull on the plug wires; rather, grasp the boot portion of the wire and apply only enough force to remove the boot.

Test Compression. Once the plugs are removed, a compression check should be made because an engine with a low or uneven compression cannot be tuned successfully. If any problems are discovered during this check, they should be corrected before proceeding with the engine tuneup. If a weak cylinder cannot be located with the compression check, a cylinder balance test should be performed. A description of this test follows.

CYLINDER BALANCE TEST

The compression test, discussed previously, will not always locate a weak cylinder. For example, a leaky intake manifold cannot be detected by the compression test, nor can a valve not opening properly due to a worn camshaft, or a defective spark plug. A cylinder balance test can be performed by checking the power output of one cylinder against another, using a set of grounding leads in conjunction with a tachometer and vacuum gauge.

Service and Spark Plug Test. Each plug should be examined carefully for badly worn electrodes, glazed, broken, or blistered porcelains, etc. Then test each plug with a spark plug tester. Serviceable spark plugs should then be cleaned and the center electrode filed flat. Adjust spark plug gaps to specifications using a round feeler gauge. Re-install the plugs and torque to specifications.

Service Ignition System. The ignition system, consisting of the distributor, points, condenser, etc., should be carefully checked as described in following chapters. Also, check and service the battery and battery cables as well as the alternator, voltage regulator and related pulley belts.

Manifold Servicing. Check the manifold heat control valve for freedom of operation and, if sticking, free it with manifold heat control solvent. The manifold bolts should be tightened to specifications in the proper sequence as outlined in the manufacturer's shop manual. Only a slight leak at the intake manifold lowers engine performance and economy.

Servicing Fuel System. Inspect all fuel lines for kinks, bends and leaks and correct any defects found. Continue by inspecting the fuel filter. If poor high speed performance exists on the vehicle, the fuel pump should be checked.

Servicing Cooling System. The entire cooling system should be checked for leaks, weak hoses, loose hose clamps and correct coolant level during the tuneup. Any faults should be corrected.

Crankcase Ventilation. All internal combustion engines have a ventilation system that utilizes manifold vacuum to draw fumes and contaminating vapors into the combustion chamber where they are burned. Since it affects every part of the engine, crankcase ventilation is an important function and should be understood and serviced properly.

Miscellaneous Checks. On engines so equipped, check out the air injecion reactor system, exhaust gas recirculation valve, and finally inspect the choke valve, choke rod, shock coil and housing for proper alignment. Make necessary corrections to assure proper choke operation and then adjust the choke as described in the chapters to follow.

INSTRUMENT CHECK OUT

For a proper engine tuneup, the mechanic should have a vacuum gauge, dwell meter, tachometer and a timing light besides the conventional tools described in Chapter 2. With these instruments connected as recommended by the manufacturer of the equipment being used, commence the following checks.

Check and Adjust Dwell. Start engine and check ignition dwell. If it is not within specifications, adjust dwell according to the manufacturer's shop manual.

Check Dwell Variation. With the dwell meter still connected, slowly accelerate engine to approximately 1750 rpm (depending upon the make) and note the dwell reading. If dwell exceeds specifications, check for a worn distributor shaft and bushing or loose breaker plate.

Check and Adjust Ignition Timing. Disconnect the distributor spark advance hose and plug the vacuum source opening before running the engine at idle speed. Aim the timing light at the timing tab (location varies on different makes of engines). Adjust the timing by loosening the distributor clamp and rotating the distributor body as required, then tighten the clamp and recheck the timing. Stop engine and remove timing light and reconnect the spark advance hose.

Adjust Idle Speed. The idle speed should be set during every tuneup operation. Procedures vary with the different makes of engines but a general description follows.

The engine should be running at operating temperature with the air cleaner installed, the air conditioning in the *off* position, and the choke valve in the fully open position. Adjust idle stop solenoid to obtain 600 rpm; then place transmission in *park* or neutral and adjust the carburetor fast idle speed to obtain approximately 1800 rpm or as recommended by the manufacturer. Finish this phase of the tuneup by adjusting the idle mixture according to the manufacturer's recommendations.

Data presented thus far are meant to give the reader an overview of the automotive internal combustion engine, its operation and how tuneup procedures should progress. The data to follow will cover, in detail, the necessary procedures and other details to enable the reader to obtain a better understanding of internal combustion engines, their maintenance, and how to tune them to obtain the highest performance and economy.

WHEN IS A TUNEUP NEEDED?

The owner's manual that accompanies all new cars suggests when routine maintenance should be performed. Occasionally, however, it becomes necessary to perform the maintenance without benefit of a schedule, due to unexpected engine problems. Some of these problems include poor gas mileage, hard starting, power loss, missing engine, stalling and rough idling. Any of these problems point to the possibility that a tuneup is needed.

INITIAL INSPECTION

A visual inspection of the engine and its related systems is usually the first step towards tuning an automotive engine. Vacuum lines, fuel lines and all electrical wiring and components should be checked for cracks, breaks, loose connections and dirt or corrosion. Then the emission control system should be checked to determine the condition of its components. Finally, the fuel system should be checked for cleanliness. The carburetor especially must be cleaned prior to the actual tuning of the engine.

An inspection of the wiring and vacuum lines are necessary to insure that these two systems will not interfere with the performance of the engine—either during or after the tuneup. Cracked or frayed ignition wires, for example, can cause shorts that will interfere with the operation of the ignition system. The ignition wiring should also be checked for loose connections as they can decrease the efficiency of the ignition system tremendously.

Anytime the vacuum system leaks, the vacuum advance on the distributor malfunctions. When the vacuum advance is not operating properly, the ignition does not advance as engine increases. This situation interferes with the timing of the engine and makes it virtually impossible to perform a tuneup.

If any kinks or breaks are present in the fuel lines, the engine will obviously be deprived of fuel which prevents accurately adjusting the fuel system. Broken fuel lines do not directly affect tuneup procedures, but while tuning up a vehicle, any defects that are discovered should be repaired. When looking for fuel line breaks, pay special attention to any rubber fuel line connections as they are often the source of leaks.

Tuneup time is also a good time to check for oil leaks. Since oil and dirt act as an abrasive solvent on wiring and rubber hoses, repairing oil leaks is a good preventive maintenance procedure. By stopping the source of a potential problem—like corroded wires caused by oil spills—the need for tuneup and other repairs is lessened.

Tuning an engine is a good time to inspect any part of the engine that is not normally checked during the usual maintenance of the engine. Deciding exactly what should be checked, however, is governed by the age of the engine and the amount of time available for performing the tuneup operation.

A series of tests are performed to determine the condition of existing engine components. A compression test, for example, will give a good indication of the conditions of the cylinders, pistons and valve train. While the spark plugs are removed for the compression test, they should be inspected for spark, gap, etc., and be replaced if necessary.

Continue the inspection by checking the distributor along with the contact points (if characteristic of the engine in question). If points are changed, the timing and the dwell angle should be reset. The centrifugal advance and the vacuum advance systems are next in line, and then the carburetor should be adjusted to the manufacturer's specifications. When all of these steps are completed correctly, the engine should be ready for the major tuneup procedures.

CARBURETOR PREPARATION

Start the engine. When it reaches operating temperature, apply a cleaning solvent to the carburetor. The solvent will remove any deposits in the carburetor and, at the same time, loosen carbon deposits in the cylinders. Carburetor solvents are distributed in both liquid and spray form. The easiest one to apply is the spray type.

To apply the spray solvent, remove the air cleaner and while controlling the throttle by hand, spray the solvent into the carburetor throat. The engine speed will start to decrease so this decrease in speed must be compensated for by increasing the throttle opening. Continue spraying the solvent into the carburetor until the throttle is roughly half open. Spray the remainder of the can into the carburetor while maintaining the half open throttle. When the can is almost empty, allow the engine to die while continuing to spray. After the engine quits running, let it sit for approximately one hour to allow the solvent time to do its job.

After the one-hour waiting period, restart the engine and again allow it to reach normal operating temperature. The throttle should also be operated at its wide open position for a few seconds at a time until the exhaust quits smoking and the engine quits missing. The use of the solvent in the carburetor may cause spark plug fouling, but since the spark plugs must be removed and inspected during the tuneup, they can be cleaned at that time.

THE BATTERY

While the engine is cooling from the carburetor cleaning procedure, check the battery. The battery should be tested with a voltmeter (see Chapter 2) to make sure it is fully charged. Any corrosion around the battery terminals should be removed. To clean the battery terminals, remove the battery cables. Using a battery post brush or just a plain wire brush, remove all deposits on or around the post. Check the battery cable connections for corrosion and/or wear. Cleaning these connections can be done with a piece of sandpaper, but the battery post brush is simpler and more efficient. It is also a good idea to clean any dirt or salt deposits off the top of the battery. This will prevent the battery from self discharging by grounding through the electrical path that is set up by the dirt and battery acid salts. When cleaning the top of the battery, use a baking soda and water solution. This type of solution neutralizes any acid that is present—making it safe to rinse the battery with clean water.

When putting the battery back in service, coat the battery post and connectors with vaseline. This helps to slow down the build up of corrosion around the terminals. There are several spray lubricants (like WD-40) on the market that can be used in the place of vaseline. These sprays can be used for several other purposes in maintaining an engine. For that reason, they are a good investment for any home or professional mechanic.

THE COMPRESSION TEST

When the battery is finished, the engine should still be warm. If not, restart the engine long enough for the engine to get warm, not hot. When the engine is warm but not hot to the touch, the compression test should be run. The compression test gives some insight into the condition of the valves, pistons and cylinders. If the compression is low, there are problems that a tuneup will not be able to correct.

To begin the compression test, remove the spark plugs, being careful not to allow any dirt to enter the cylinders. Since all the spark plugs should be out when running a compression test, be sure to note the arrangement of the spark plug wires so that the wires can be put back at the right cylinder. On most engines the spark plug wires are kept in the order that they should be attached by harnesses. If there is no built-in way to keep track of the wires, you should tag the wires for identification. In any case, once the spark plugs are out of the engine, the compression tester should be attached.

There are several types of compression testers as pointed out in Chapter 2. No matter what type of compression tester is used, either a remote starting switch or a helper is needed to run the test. The compression tester is pushed into the spark plug hole for the cylinder that is being tested. Hold the tester in position while turning the engine over at least four compression strokes. Record the highest pressure reading that the gauge reads during the test. When the pressures for all of the cylinders have been recorded, compare them. If one or more of the cylinders has a significantly lower pressure reading than the other cylinders, there is a problem with the valves, piston or the cylinder wall. This problem cannot be repaired by a tuneup but will require major engine repairs. If the compression readings are all approximately the same, the engine is basically in good shape and the tuneup may improve engine performance.

SPARK PLUGS

While the spark plugs are out for the compression test, they should be inspected for damage and replaced if necessary. The normal life of a spark plug is approximately 12,000 miles, but plug life can be seriously reduced by several factors. The fact that spark plugs can be affected by the condition of the engine is used in determining the causes of several tuneup related problems. Using the spark plugs as a barometer for engine condition is called reading the plugs. Learning to read plugs comes with practice but the following information should help (Fig. 4-6).

Normal spark plugs will have a characteristic light tan or gray color if commercial grade gasolines have been used. The spark plugs' electrode should not show any evidence of burning, and the increase in the gap should exceed specifications by only .001 inch per 1000 miles. Those that exhibit only normal wear can usually be cleaned, regapped and then reused.

The best method for cleaning a spark plug is sandblasting, as this most effectively removes the deposits on the spark plug. If a sandblaster is not available and the spark plugs are going to be reused, they should be cleaned with a wire brush to remove as much of the deposits as possible, then regapped and reinstalled. Spark plugs that exhibit more than normal wear should be replaced.

Cold fouling occurs when carbon deposits build up on the spark plugs. The carbon deposits can be caused by improperly adjusted choke and idle fuel mixture or a dirty air cleaner or carburetor. If only one or two of the plugs exhibit this type of wear it is probably because that spark plug is not firing. If this is the case, the engine should be checked for a stuck valve or an ignition wire problem. Cold fouling can also result if the engine is continuously being operated at idle. When the engine is going to be operated continuously at idle speeds, the spark plugs should be replaced with spark plugs having a higher heat range. Heat range does not refer to the heat of the spark, but to the temperature at the tip of the spark plugs.

Spark plugs that have a wet coating of oil of them are referred to as wet fouled. The condition is caused by engine oil getting into the combustion chamber. This type of spark plug damage usually indicates the need for an engine overhaul because it means that oil is getting past either the valves or the piston rings. In a new engine that has not been broken in, some wet fouling can be expected. If the engine is old and an overhaul is trying to be put off, the heat range of the spark plugs can be increased as a temporary measure. But this is only a temporary solution and the cause of the problem should be identified and corrected as soon as possible.

Occasionally, deposits that have accumulated after a long period of engine misfiring dislodge from the cylinder and hit the hot insulator surface. This usually happens after new spark plugs are installed because the engine combustion temperature returns to normal. Since the spark plugs are usually new ones, it is a good idea to sandblast them rather than replace them. Like normally worn spark plugs, splash fouled spark plugs take readily to being cleaned.

Spark plugs that cause high speed misfiring at speeds greater than 50-60 mph usually are found to have a glaze on them. This type of spark plug problem is called high-speed glaze. High-speed glazing is caused by sudden increases in the engine temperature while accelerating. When the spark plug temperature increases in this

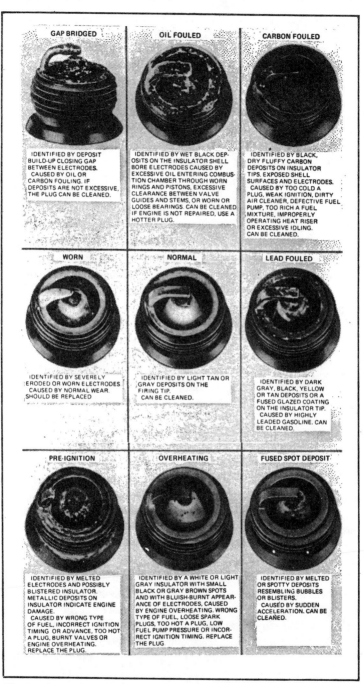

GAP BRIDGED

IDENTIFIED BY DEPOSIT BUILD-UP CLOSING GAP BETWEEN ELECTRODES. CAUSED BY OIL OR CARBON FOULING. IF DEPOSITS ARE NOT EXCESSIVE, THE PLUG CAN BE CLEANED.

OIL FOULED

IDENTIFIED BY WET BLACK DEPOSITS ON THE INSULATOR SHELL BORE ELECTRODES CAUSED BY EXCESSIVE OIL ENTERING COMBUSTION CHAMBER THROUGH WORN RINGS AND PISTONS, EXCESSIVE CLEARANCE BETWEEN VALVE GUIDES AND STEMS, OR WORN OR LOOSE BEARINGS. CAN BE CLEANED. IF ENGINE IS NOT REPAIRED, USE A HOTTER PLUG.

CARBON FOULED

IDENTIFIED BY BLACK, DRY FLUFFY CARBON DEPOSITS ON INSULATOR TIPS. EXPOSED SHELL SURFACES AND ELECTRODES. CAUSED BY TOO COLD A PLUG, WEAK IGNITION, DIRTY AIR CLEANER, DEFECTIVE FUEL PUMP, TOO RICH A FUEL MIXTURE, IMPROPERLY OPERATING HEAT RISER OR EXCESSIVE IDLING. CAN BE CLEANED.

WORN

IDENTIFIED BY SEVERELY ERODED OR WORN ELECTRODES CAUSED BY NORMAL WEAR. SHOULD BE REPLACED

NORMAL

IDENTIFIED BY LIGHT TAN OR GRAY DEPOSITS ON THE FIRING TIP. CAN BE CLEANED.

LEAD FOULED

IDENTIFIED BY DARK GRAY, BLACK, YELLOW OR TAN DEPOSITS OR A FUSED GLAZED COATING ON THE INSULATOR TIP. CAUSED BY HIGHLY LEADED GASOLINE. CAN BE CLEANED.

PRE-IGNITION

IDENTIFIED BY MELTED ELECTRODES AND POSSIBLY BLISTERED INSULATOR. METALLIC DEPOSITS ON INSULATOR INDICATE ENGINE DAMAGE. CAUSED BY WRONG TYPE OF FUEL, INCORRECT IGNITION TIMING OR ADVANCE, TOO HOT A PLUG, BURNT VALVES OR ENGINE OVERHEATING. REPLACE THE PLUG.

OVERHEATING

IDENTIFIED BY A WHITE OR LIGHT GRAY INSULATOR WITH SMALL BLACK OR GRAY BROWN SPOTS AND WITH BLUISH-BURNT APPEARANCE OF ELECTRODES, CAUSED BY ENGINE OVERHEATING. WRONG TYPE OF FUEL, LOOSE SPARK PLUGS, TOO HOT A PLUG, LOW FUEL PUMP PRESSURE OR INCORRECT IGNITION TIMING. REPLACE THE PLUG.

FUSED SPOT DEPOSIT

IDENTIFIED BY MELTED OR SPOTTY DEPOSITS RESEMBLING BUBBLES OR BLISTERS. CAUSED BY SUDDEN ACCELERATION. CAN BE CLEANED.

Fig. 4-6. Spark plug evaluation chart (courtesy Ford Motor Company).

manner, the normal deposits melt, causing the formation of a conductive glaze. If this type of spark plug wear is noticed during the tuneup, try running a colder range spark plug.

Scavenger deposits are commonly found on spark plugs. Although the deposits look abnormal, the opposite is true. This type of deposit is caused by certain gasoline additives and the action of certain chemicals on the normal deposits on the spark plugs. However, this type of deposit comes off easily—allowing the spark plug to be cleaned and reused.

Spark plugs that exhibit the wear are usually found in engines that are overheating. Electrode gap wear in an overheated spark plug usually exceeds .001 inch/1000 miles. The overheating problem should be corrected during the tuneup procedures so the new, or freshly cleaned, spark plugs are not ruined. This type of problem may also be caused by the spark plug heat range being too high.

Turbulence burning is caused by the turbulence in the combustion chamber. In certain engines this is normal as long as the full normal life of the spark plug is reached. On the other hand, if the spark plug is exhibiting this type of wear prematurely, the reason is usually due to an excessive spark plug heat range. Correct by replacing the spark plugs with colder range plugs.

Preignition damage is a warning that the engine has a potentially damaging problem that must be corrected as soon as possible. This type of damage is most frequently caused, in late model cars, by detonation. This condition occurs if the ignition timing is set too advanced or if the gasoline being used has too low an octane rating. The excessive temperatures that occur during detonation cause the spark plug electrode to melt. When the damage is severe, other engine parts may become damaged also.

If the ignition coil has been recently installed and the spark plugs indicate a dished ground electrode, the polarity on the coil is wrong. The spark plugs should be replaced and the primary coil leads should be reversed.

These examples of spark plug wear are not meant to be definitive since most spark plugs will exhibit more than one type of wear. However, if the examples are used in examining the spark plugs, some insight into the condition of the engine can be gained while doing a tuneup. This information can help in correcting problems that will affect the life of the engine. Once the spark plugs have been "read", they should be gapped and reinstalled.

When gapping and reinstalling spark plugs, a few precautions should be observed. First, when gapping the plugs be careful not to crack the porcelain insulator. Be sure the center electrode on the spark plug is flat; if it is not, file the electrode carefully. This should not be a problem with new spark plugs, only reused ones. Use a wire feeler gauge to check the gap against the manufacturer's specifications.

If new plugs are being installed and they are the pregapped type, check the gap anyway. The gap can change during shipment. Use new gaskets on reused plugs to insure a proper seal. The spark plugs should be installed with a torque wrench if possible, as the spark plugs can burn if the torque is not adequate. If the torque is too great, the spark gap may be incorrect. The most common size spark plugs should have a 30 foot-pound torque when installed in a case iron cylinder head. For aluminum heads, the torque should be 27 feet-pounds. Another reason for torquing the spark plugs, especially in aluminum, is to avoid the possibility of stripping the spark plug threads.

AIR CLEANER SYSTEM

The air cleaner, especially in late model engines, can affect the performance of an engine drastically. For this reason, it is very important to make sure that the air cleaner is clean and unplugged. The air cleaners can be made of foam or wire mesh, but the most common type has a paper element. Foam or mesh type air cleaners can be cleaned and then blown dry with compressed air, but paper type air cleaners should be replaced when they begin to show excessive dirt caught in the paper. When replacing the air cleaner, make sure that the rubber gaskets on the top and bottom of the air cleaner seat against the air cleaner can. If air can get around the filter, it is not cleaning correctly, so check for a good tight fit.

Between the air cleaner can and the carburetor, there is a round gasket which should fit snugly. This is important for the same reasons that the air cleaner gaskets must seat. If air can get into the carburetor without passing through the filter element first, the air cleaner is of no use.

While the air cleaner is out, check the filter for the crankcase vent. This is found where the hose from the rocker cover enters the air cleaner can. Crankcase vents are found on all engines equipped with a closed crankcase ventilation system. Once the vent filter is located, remove it for inspection. If it is a dirty gray color, replace it. In older engines, the vent filter was designed so it could be cleaned. Since the new emission standards have come out, it is a good idea to replace both the air cleaner and the vent filter at the same time.

The "smog" valve should be checked next. This valve is found at the end of the hose leading from the air cleaner can to the rocker cover. The valve is usually held in by friction against a rubber grommet in the rocker cover. Pull the valve out and check it by shaking it. If you can hear a clicking sound when the valve is shaken it is functioning. If the clicking sound is absent, replace the valve. Do not attempt to clean the valve as this will not return it to a satisfactory condition. Since the valve is inexpensive and can affect the performance of the engine, it is a good investment to purchase a new valve approximately every 25,000 miles or as recommended by the manufacturer.

THE DISTRIBUTOR CAP AND WIRES

When preparing to service the ignition system during a tuneup, start with the distributor. First, inspect the distributor cap and the spark plug and coil wires. The distributor cap should not be cracked and the spark plug wires should be resilient and devoid of any cracks. Check the contacts inside each of the towers on the distributor cap for any built up corrosion that might interfere with the electric current. Make sure that the nipples on the spark plug wires fit snugly on the spark plugs and the distributor cap towers.

Remove the distributor cap, usually held down by springs or by screws. The spring type clamps can be carefully pried open with a screw driver. The screw type clamps are part of the distributor cap and should be turned to release the cap. Look inside the cap to see if any carbon tracks are present.

Carbon tracks make an electrical bridge between the contacts inside the distributor causing the engine to misfire. These carbon tracks can be removed by cleaning the cap in a warm, mild soap solution. Be sure to rinse the cap well to make sure there is no soap residue left. Also be sure that the cap is dry before reinstalling it. Dry it with a clean lint free cloth, or spray it with one of the ignition system water displacing sprays like WD-40.

If the distributor cap has corrosion in the towers, clean them out by using a piece of emory cloth or a wire brush. The metal that makes up the contacts should be as clean and shiny as possible. If the contacts cannot be cleaned or if they are corroded to the point that the metal is breaking, replace the cap. The cap should also be replaced if there is any evidence of cracking.

The spark plug wires should be checked next. The rubber nipples at the ends of the wires should be soft and pliable. If not, they should be replaced. These nipples or boots prevent dirt and moisture from getting on the spark plug ends and into the distributor cap towers. If moisture can get into these areas, there is a possibility that the water will cause shorting and thereby cause the engine to misfire.

If the wires are of the resistance type, they have a specified resistance that should be checked. If not, they should be replaced. To check the resistance type spark plug wires, attach an ohmmeter to the opppsite ends of the wire and read the resistance. Compare this resistance with the specifications.

Check the cables for a tight fit on the spark plug ends and for a snug fit in the distributor cap towers. If any of the connections are loose, clamp the metal end that fits on the spark plug. If the ends that fit into the distributor cap towers are loose, take a screwdriver and gently pry the metal terminal apart so that the terminal fits snugly into the tower. Check these terminals for any evidence of corrosion. If the terminals are corroded, try to clean them with a wire brush. If the terminals are corroded to the point that they cannot be cleaned, they will have to be replaced. The metal terminal itself can be replaced without having to replace the wires if the wire is still in good condition. The metal ends can be purchased at an auto parts store, and it is a simple matter of removing the old clips and clamping on the new ones.

THE ROTOR

The rotor should be checked for any signs of burning or pitting on the blade surface. If the rotor is pitted or burned slightly, it can be cleaned by running a file across it a few times. Be careful not to over file the rotor or it will cause misfiring. If the points are more than slightly burned or pitted they should be replaced. Check the button on the top of the rotor to see if it has any deposits of carbon on it. Carbon on the rotor button can usually be wiped off with a clean rag. Any pitting in the rotor button should be removed with a fine emery paper.

THE DISTRIBUTOR

With the rotor off, the distributor should be checked for any signs of wear. Start by examining the distributor shaft cam for any signs of scouring on the cam lobes. If the lobes are scoured or worn in excess, the distributor shaft will have to be replaced. Wear on the cam lobes should be minimal unless the cam has never been lubricated.

Next, check the breaker plate assembly to see if it is distorted in any way. If the plate is distorted, it will interfere with the function of the breaker points. Also look for any wear or damage that might interfere with the movement of the breaker points. The assembly will have to be replaced if there is any indication of damage.

Look for any evidence of cracking at the base of the distributor. The distributor should be repaired if there is any evidence of cracking. Also check the rest of the distributor housing for cracks. If the distributor has to be removed to repair any cracks, be sure to mark the distributor so it can be replaced in the same position. Removing the distributor will be covered in greater detail in Chapter five.

IGNITION BREAKER POINT REPLACEMENT

Replacing the breaker points (in engines equipped with them) is a relatively simple procedure as long as a few rules are observed. First, when replacing breaker points, proceed slowly and make sure to note the position of all wire leads so they can be put back in the same place and in the same order. This is very important since some breaker point assemblies will not function if the wires are put back on in a different order. This type of point assembly usually has an insulator separating the wires. If the wires are allowed to touch one another, they cause the ignition system to short out. This can cause a great deal of extra work when it comes to finding out what the proper order was supposed to be. To avoid this type of problem, observe the positioning of the wires before going to disassemble the points. Then when the points are out, reinstall the new points as soon as possible so that the wire positions are still fresh in your mind.

Second, check the points for proper alignment before reinstalling them. Even a new set of ignition points can be misaligned which will cause the points to burn prematurely. The contact faces on the points should be parallel to each other without any overlap. Points manufactured by General Motors can have the contacts aligned while they are out of the distributor since they are made in one piece. To align the points, bend only the stationary point arm. On other contact points, the stationary arm and the movable contact arm are separately installed and the point alignment can only be adjusted after the points are installed. Again, bend only the stationary contact arm to adjust the alignment.

Depending on the design of the points, certain adjustments may need to be made. The points installed in Delco distributors, however, do not need the point gap adjusted before starting the engine. The point gap is set with an Allen wrench while setting the dwell angle. Distributors that have this type of ignition points have a sliding metal door that allows access to the Allen set screw on the points assembly.

Most other distributors need to have the point gap set with a feeler gauge according to a set of specifications. To set the gap on this type of points, make sure that the rubbing block of the points is sitting on the high point of the cam lobe. To get the rubbing block to this high point, it is necessary to turn the engine over until the cam lobe is immediately underneath the rubbing block. This can be accomplished by bumping the starter until the distributor shaft turns, stopping on the cam lobe. If the spark plugs are still out, turn the engine over by hand. The easiest method of adjusting the point gap, though, is to loosen the distributor hold down nut and then turn the distributor until the rubbing block sits on one of the cam lobes. This method works since the point gap can be adjusted on any of the cam lobes. If this method is to be used, be sure to turn the distributor back to approximately the same position. This will ensure easy starting.

THE CONDENSER

When replacing the ignition points, always replace the condenser. Even if the condenser tests out all right, it should be replaced as a preventive measure. The only precaution that should be taken is to make sure that the lead coming from the condenser is attached to the points in the same way that the original was. Check to make sure that the condenser cannot slip out of the metal band that is holding it. If the metal band that is provided to hold the condenser in place is spot welded to the condenser, there should not be any problem. Some of the hold-downs only rely on friction to hold the condenser in place. If the condenser should slip out of the hold-down while the engine is being operated, it may become damaged.

DWELL ANGLE

On most ignition points, the dwell angle can be set when the points are gapped. However, using a dwell meter is more accurate, and, in the case of points equipped with an Allen set screw, the only way to set the dwell angle is by using a dwell meter. The dwell meter is usually incorporated into a unit that also measures engine rpm, so it is usually called a dwell/tachometer. In any case, the meter should be connected between the distributor side of the coil and some grounding point on the engine.

Start the engine with the meter attached and check the meter reading against the manufacturer's specifications; if the dwell angle is off, open the sliding door on the side of the distributor cap. Using an Allen wrench, turn the set screw until the dwell reading is correct. When using the Allen wrench, be careful not to ground the points as this can cause a shock to the mechanic performing the operation. If the specifications give a range of degrees at which the dwell angle can be set, adjust the dwell to read at the high end of the scale. This is done because the dwell angle will decrease as the points wear and the gap increases.

To set the dwell on points not having a set-screw adjustment, the point gap must be set while watching the dwell angle indicated on the meter. Remove the distributor cap and rotor; then attach the leads from the dwell/tachometer—one to the distributor side of the coil and the other to some grounding point on the engine. With a remote start switch or a helper, crank the engine with the starter motor and watch the reading on the meter. Loosen the screw that holds the points in place and then open or close the points (as required) until the dwell/tachometer reading matches the specifications. If the dwell reading is high, increase the point gap; when the reading is low, decrease the point gap.

Most points have a place provided in them to wedge a screw driver to make the adjustments to the point gap. When setting the dwell in this manner, remember not to run the starter motor for extremely long periods of time or the battery may become discharged.

IGNITION TIMING

The ignition timing is an adjustment thet is made to insure that the proper opening and closing of the ignition points will occur. There are two main ways to set the timing, with a timing light or with a test lamp. The latter method is called "static timing" and is not the recommended method in most cases.

The most common method for adjusting the ignition timing is with the use of a stroboscopic light that is triggered by the current going to the spark plug on the number one cylinder. This method is the most accurate and should be used whenever possible. Never set the ignition timing by "ear"; this will only result in prematurely burned ignition points and possible damage to the emission control system.

To set the ignition timing using a strobe light, attach the timing light leads to the battery and the number one spark plug. If the specifications call for the vacuum advance unit to be disconnected, pull the vacuum hose off of the advance unit and plug the hose with a pencil or some similar object. Attach a tachometer so that the idle speed can be set at the specifications for timing. Then start the engine and allow it to warm up to the recommended temperature before setting the idle by turning the idle adjustment screws on the carburetor. On most engines, the idle speed for setting the timing is different from the regular idle speed.

Air the timing light at the timing marks. If these marks are hard to see, mark them with either a piece of chalk or some light colored paint. Loosen the distributor and turn it in the direction necessary for the marks to align. When the marks line up, tighten the distributor, without moving it, and recheck the marks to make sure they have not shifted. The engine ignition is now in "time."

VACUUM ADVANCE

The vacuum advance operation can be checked by simply watching the timing marks with a timing light while accelerating the engine. If the timing marks separate, with the pulley mark moving in the direction of engine revolution, the ignition is being advanced. Now disconnect the vacuum line to the advance unit and accelerate the engine; the engine should not advance as far as with the vacuum line attached. However, the engine should still advance due to the operation of the centrifugal advance mechanism. This is only a qualitative test; if the advance unit is suspected of not advancing the engine enough, the total amount of advance due to the vacuum unit by itself must be determined. To do this, the amount of advance must be measured by translating, to degrees, the number of inches around the pulley that the timing mark advances.

To find the number of degrees to an inch, divide the circumference of the timing pulley by 360 degrees. Then the amount of advance caused by the centrifugal advance must be subtracted from the total measured advance. Both of these measurements must be made at the same rpm. Compare the difference with the specifications set forth in the shop manual for the engine being worked on.

CENTRIFUGAL ADVANCE

Testing the centrifugal advance operation is simply a matter of disconnecting the vacuum advance unit and checking the amount of advance that occurs at the timing marks. Translate the number of inches that the pulley moves into degrees as previously explained and check the result against the manufacturer's specifications. Even if the amount of advance provided by the centrifugal advance is within specifications, the weights and springs should be checked to see what their condition is.

Checking the advance weights and springs on a Delco distributor is easy since they are located immediately below the rotor. Most other distributors require the removal of the breaker plate to gain access to the centrifugal advance unit. The weights and springs should be cleaned and oiled so they can move freely. If the springs are badly corroded, they should be replaced before they have a chance to fail.

ELECTRONIC IGNITIONS

In recent years each of the major automobile engine manufacturers have designed ignition systems that do not require the conventional ignition points, condenser or distributor cam. These systems use a magnetic sensing unit and a transistorized control module to interrupt the primary ignition circuit, thereby creating a spark at the spark plugs. Since this system eliminates the need for points and condenser, the only steps involved in tuning the ignition are checking the rotor and distributor cap and setting the timing. The system should also be checked for loose connections between the magnetic sensing unit and the control module. Electronic ignitions use a totally enclosed coil so special places are provided for the attachment of a tachometer for setting the engine idle.

The Chrysler electronic ignition does require one additional adjustment. The distance between the reluctor (the rotating part on the distributor shaft), and the tooth on the coil pickup, has to be adjusted to 0.008 inch. This adjustment should be made with a non-magnetic feeler gauge; the pickup coil tooth has a screw that when loosened will allow the tooth to be moved. Place the feeler gauge between the reluctor and the tooth. When the space between the reluctor and the pickup coil is filled completely by the feeler gauge, retighten the screw. This is the only adjustment necessary on the Chrysler.

Each of the electronic ignitions are different. Any work that is to be done on them should be checked against the recommended procedures in the shop manual for the particular system that is going to be serviced.

The procedures for checking out the rest of the system, such as the distributor cap and wires, are the same as for a conventional ignition system. The timing is set in the same manner. The only difference is that the timing will not change since there are no breaker points to wear. The dwell angle cannot be set either due to the lack of contact points.

HEAT RISER

Check the heat riser valve on the exhaust manifold to see if it is free to move. If the valve is stuck you will have to tap it with a hammer while applying penetrating oil. Some heat risers are controlled by the engine's vacuum. This type of heat riser can only be checked while the engine is running. With the engine idling, snap the throttle valve open and watch the heat riser. The counterweight on the heat riser should move. If it does not move, either the valve is stuck or the vacuum diaphragm has a hole in it.

A valve in the air cleaner, which closes to allow warm air from the exhaust manifold to enter, is part of the heat riser system. When the valve is operating correctly, the engine can warm up faster. The valve should be closed, allowing cool air in once the engine warms up. To check this valve, look in the air cleaner horn. When the engine has just been started and is still cold, the valve should be cold. Wait until the engine warms up and then recheck the valve. It should now be open.

FUEL FILTERS

Most fuel filters are located on or near the carburetor. The filters should be replaced periodically according to the manufacturer's recommendations. In-line fuel filters on some carburetors can have the filtering element replaced; other carburetors call for the entire unit to be replaced. In either case, when removing the filter, be sure to use a back-up wrench. This is done to avoid stripping any threads in the carburetor body. Use the back-up wrench when replacing the filter units also. While the filter unit is open, clean out any accumulated foreign matter in the housing that holds the filter.

CARBURETOR ADJUSTMENTS

During the tuneup process, the idle speed of the engine must be changed several times while adjusting the dwell or the timing. The idle speed that is used for these adjustments frequently differs from the manufacturers specified idle for the best operation of the engine. The idle mixture can also change due to wear on various parts of the carburetor, which means that the idle mixture will need some adjusting. Even if the idle mixture seems to be all right, it is a good idea to check it during the tuneup since it is so important to the performance of the engine. The choke on the carburetor should also be checked for proper functioning and adjustment. Adjusting the carburetor should be done in a systematic manner to make sure that everything necessary is done.

Since the idle mixture affects the engine idle speed, it should be adjusted first. Prior to the emission control age, the adjustments done to the idle mixture were simple and straightforward. Now, however, the need to minimize the amount of pollution contributed by the internal combustion engine has made it necessary to add quite a few emission controls which, in turn, affect the idle mixture adjustments. Although the procedures are more complex, the basic adjustment procedure still involves the turning of the idle mixture screws, either in, to lean the mixture, or out to richen the mixture. The main difference is in how to determine when the screws are adjusted correctly.

On most engines built prior to the new emission standards, the amount that a idle mixture screw was supposed to be turned was specified in terms of a certain number of turns. For pre-emission engines, 1½ to 2 turns open from the fully closed position would usually be enough to adjust the carburetor. Now, almost every engine has a different recommended method for adjusting the idle mixture. Some engines require the use of exhaust gas analyzers which detect the amount of carbon monoxide and unburnt hydrocarbons present in the exhaust gasses. These machines translate the amounts of these gasses to an air/fuel ratio. If the manufacturer gives specifications on the proper air/fuel ratio, the carburetor can be adjusted by reading the analyzer and turning the idle mixture screws until the mixture meets the specifications. This sounds simple, but, since the analyzers are so sensitive, any adjustments must be made very slowly to make sure that the machine works properly.

Most of the analyzers are ineffective with air/fuel mixtures in excess of 15:1, which means that as the amount of air used increases with respect to the amount of fuel used, the analyzers become unusable for idle mixture adjustments. In some states, like California, there are indications that they will require the use of infrared analyzers in the near future. Usually, the shop manual that is printed for each engine model year has all the information necessary for setting the carburetor idle mixture and, as was pointed out earlier, each manufacturer has a different set of specifications for this adjustment. Consult the manual before attempting to set the mixture.

Another place to look for specifications concerning adjustments for the idle mixture is the vehicle emission control decal. This decal is usually located somewhere under the hood of the automobile or it may be attached to the engine itself. The decal gives information on the spark plug gap, the idle speed, the timing, the point gap (if applicable) and the idle mixture setting. This decal should always be consulted when doing adjustments on the carburetor or when performing a tuneup. If the decal has deteriorated, as they often do, all of the specifications can be found in the shop manual written for the engine in question. The decal also gives information on the method to use when adjusting the idle mixture. The information concerning the idle mixture adjustments is usually minimal and then refers you to the shop manual. There is always going to be a need for a shop manual when going to adjust the new emission control carburetors.

Another concern when starting to adjust the idle mixture on the carburetor is the conditions which need to be set up for the adjustments to be correct. Usually the prior preparations that are spelled out by the manufacturer consist of engine temperature, idle speed, whether or not the engine should be in gear, and what vacuum hoses should be disconnected or plugged. All of the items should be checked before trying to set the idle mixture.

After the idle mixture has been set, the fast idle should be checked and adjusted to comply with specifications. The fast idle can be found on the emission control decal along with all of the previously mentioned information. The fast idle is necessary to keep the engine running when the choke is in operation. To adjust the fast idle, a screw on the fast idle cam must be turned so that the idle when the choke is operating is at the specified rpm. Connect a tachometer and start the engine.

Some engines require that the fast idle be set with the engine cold so all adjustments should be completed before the engine heats up. Once the tach is attached and the engine is running, the fast idle cam should be set on the specified step and the fast idle screw should be turned until the tach indicates the proper idle speed. Like with the idle mixture settings, there are many variations on this simple procedure, so the shop manual will have to be consulted for the specific procedures. The previously mentioned procedure will usually get the speed close to specified idle.

The last adjustment on the carburetor is the idle speed. The idle speed is the speed that the engine should run at when it is just sitting. Some engines are equipped with a solenoid. On this type of carburetor, the idle speed is set by using the adjustment on the solenoid. Before making any adjustments, determine whether or not the solenoid should be energized. Some manufacturers specify that the solenoid be energized so that it is operating when the adjustments are made; others specify that it be disconnected. In either case, the speed setting will require the use of a tachometer. Now set the idle speed according to the specifications by turning the adjustment on the solenoid. If the carburetor is not equipped with a solenoid, make the adjustment with the idle speed screw located on the throttle shaft.

EMISSIONS CONTROLS

There are many new devices being attached to engines these days to control the amount of pollutants given off in the process of burning gasoline. Since these devices can effect the operation of the engine, they should be checked at frequent intervals and the tuneup is an ideal opportunity to check them out. Most vehicles with internal combustion engines produced after 1975 are equipped with a catalytic converter. This convertor causes the exhaust gasses to be burned again before they leave the exhaust system. These catalytic convertors can be destroyed by fuels containing lead so engines equipped with them are required to use unleaded fuel. The convertors can also be ruined if the engine is running on too rich an air/fuel mixture. Since the rich mixture condition occurs whenever an engine is decelerated from a high speed, most systems have a catalyst protection system.

The shop manual will give the location and methods for checking the many different systems found on each type of engine. Each of the major manufacturers has its own system and so the catalyst protection system is different. These systems are usually run off of vacuum, but Chrysler has had a system that operates electronically.

In addition to the advent of the catalytic converter, the spark advance systems have been changed by each manfacturer. The new advance systems differ from vehicle to vehicle even within the same manufacturer. The heat risers have been changed in some cases to operate off of engine vacuum as well as engine temperature. To lower the amount of nitrogen oxides emitted by the engine, the exhaust gasses are being recirculated so they can be combined with the air/fuel mixture to lower the combustion temperatures. Lower combustion temperatures result in fewer nitrogen oxides being produced. With each passing year new developments in the emission standards will result in more pollution control equipment being added to the engine. Almost all of this new equipment will result in additional checks, tests and repairs being done during the tuneup. The days of the simple spark plug, points and condenser change in the backyard are probably gone forever.

Chapter 5

The Cooling System

The engine cooling system is to maintain the engine at its most efficient operating temperature. Two methods are employed to regulate the temperature—water-cooling systems and air-cooling systems. Of these two types, the water-cooling system is by far the most common and is used on practically all American-made automobiles. For this reason, the water-cooled engine will be discussed in this chapter.

In general, those autos cooled with a water-circulating pressure type engine cooling system employ a thermostatic control to regulate the flow of coolant. The system is then sealed by a pressure type radiator filler cap. This pressure cap is designed to operate the cooling system at higher than atmospheric pressure which increases the efficiency of the radiator.

The radiator filler cap (Fig. 5-1) contains a pressure relief valve and a vacuum relief valve. The pressure relief valve is held against its seat by a spring which, when compressed, allows excessive pressure to be relieved out the radiator overflow.

The vacuum valve is also held against its seat by a spring which, when compressed, opens the valve and relieves the vacuum created when the system cools.

Radiators are designed to hold a large volume of coolant so that the coolant is also exposed to a large volume of air. The object is to transfer heat produced during combustion to the coolant and then to transfer heat in the coolant to air flowing through the radiator.

Radiators used on vehicles equipped with automatic transmissions may, in some instances, have oil coolers within the output

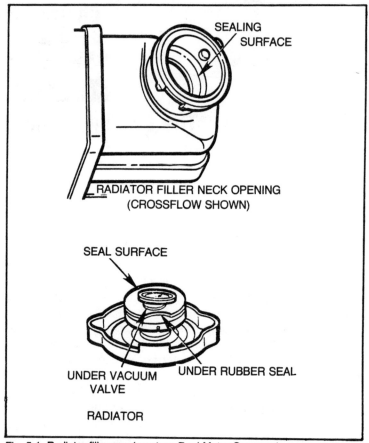

SEALING SURFACE

RADIATOR FILLER NECK OPENING
(CROSSFLOW SHOWN)

SEAL SURFACE

UNDER VACUUM VALVE

UNDER RUBBER SEAL

RADIATOR

Fig. 5-1. Radiator filler cap (courtesy Ford Motor Company).

tank. Inlet and outlet fittings for transmission fluid circulation are positioned vertically on the tank.

The cooling system water pump is usually of the centrifugal vane impeller type. The impeller turns on a steel shaft that rotates on a double row of permanently lubricated ball bearings, which are sealed during manufacture to prevent loss of lubricant and to prevent the entry of dirt and water.

A cooling fan is located on the end of the water pump shaft and is driven by the same belt that drives the pump. Basically, there are two types— fixed drive fan and the automatic fan clutch. The former operates at engine rpm and an explanation of the latter follows.

A typical automatic fan clutch is shown in Fig. 5-2. Basically, it is a hydraulic device used to vary the speed of the fan in relation to the engine temperature. Therefore, such a unit permits the use of a high delivery fan to insure adequate cooling at reduced engine speeds while eliminating overcooling, excessive noise and power loss at high speeds.

When the engine is cold or operated at high speeds, the fan clutch will be in the disengaged mode. As the temperature of the engine rises, so does the temperature of a bimetallic coil connected to the arm shaft. The rise in temperature causes the shaft to move the arm which exposes an opening in the pump plate. This opening allows the silicone fluid (contained in the reservoir area during the disengaged mode) to flow from the reservoir into the working chamber of the automatic fan clutch.

The silicone fluid is kept circulating through the fan clutch by wipers located on the pump plate. The speed differential between the clutch plate and the pump plate develops high pressure areas in front of the wipers and forces the fluid back into the reservoir. But as the temperature rises, the arm uncovers more and more of the large opening and allows more of the silicone fluid to re-enter the working chamber.

The automatic fan clutch becomes fully engaged when the silicone fluid, circulating between the working chamber and the reservoir, reaches a sufficient level in the working chamber to completely fill the grooves in the clutch body and clutch plate. The reverse situation occurs when the temperature drops; that is, the arm slowly closes off the return hole thus blocking the fluid flow from the reservoir into the working chamber.

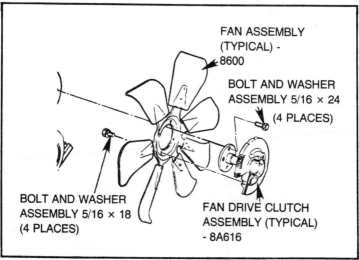

Fig. 5-2. Typical automatic fan clutch.

Temperatures at which the automatic fan clutch engages and disengages is controlled by the setting of the bimetallic coil. This setting is set to satisfy the cooling requirements of each model of engine.

THEORY OF OPERATION

The drawing in Fig. 5-3 shows a cross-section of an engine block and its related cooling system. During combustion of the air-fuel mixture, combustion gas temperatures may be as high as 4500 degrees. Some of this heat is absorbed by the engine components and they, in turn, must be provided with some means of cooling to prevent permanent damage. However, removing too much of the heat would lower the thermal efficiency of the engine. Therefore, most cooling systems are designed to remove approximately 35 percent of the heat produced during combustion.

In general, the water pump discharges coolant into the water jacket chamber and flows from the front of the bank around each cylinder and toward the rear of the block. Large passages connecting the block to the cylinder head directs coolant over and around the alternately spaced inlet and exhaust ports, as well as around the exposed exhaust valve guide inserts. Smaller circular holes permit metered amounts of coolant to pass from the cylinder block to cored passages surrounding the spark plugs.

During engine warm-up, when the thermostat is closed, coolant is redirected to the water pump through a coolant by-pass in the cylinder head and block. Coolant circulation, after normal operating temperatures are reached, flows through the coolant outlet and the pellet-type thermostat to the radiator.

The radiator is made of many thin tubes and metal fins to dissipate heat as the coolant is pumped through the tubes and cool air rushing in at highway speeds. At lower speeds and at idle, the belt-driven fan forces air over the tubes and fins to achieve the cooling. The coolant is then pumped back to the engine block to pick up more heat from the engine and carry it back to the radiator.

COOLANT

Tap water was used for the first engine coolant, but water freezes and boils away too easily, and also has a tendency to be corrosive. So regardless of the weather conditions in the areas where the auto is being used, the cooling system should be maintained at least to -20 degrees Fahrenheit to provide adequate corrosion protection and proper temperature indicating light operation.

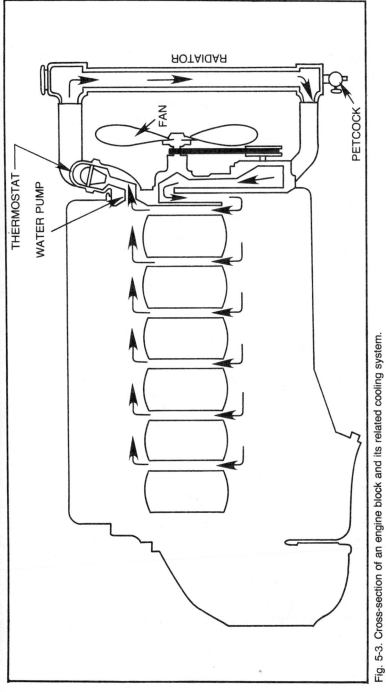

Fig. 5-3. Cross-section of an engine block and its related cooling system.

RADIATOR

FAN

THERMOSTAT

WATER PUMP

PETCOCK

93

This calls for an adequate amount of permanent-type glycol base coolant added to a fresh solution of water.

Every two years the cooling system should be serviced by flushing with plain water, then completely refilled with a fresh solution of water and a high-quality, inhibited glycol base coolant to provide protection at least to -20 degrees Fahrenheit. A high-quality cooling system inhibitor and sealer should also be added at the time of servicing 'and also every fall thereafter. The inhibitor and sealer retards the formation of rust or scale and is compatible with aluminum components.

COOLING SYSTEM CARE

The coolant level should be checked in the radiator at least as frequently as engine oil changes, but never remove the radiator cap when the coolant is hot and under pressure. The level should be at the bottom of the radiator filler neck when the system is cold. If the coolant is below this level, coolant should be added, using a 50/50 mixture of high-quality *ethylene glycol* anti-freeze and water.

Most water-cooled engines have cooling systems pressurized with a 15 pound pressure cap which permits safe engine operation at cooling temperatures of up to 256 degrees Fahrenheit with a 33 percent glycol solution. When the radiator cap is removed or loosened, the system pressure drops to atmospheric, and the heat which had caused water temperature to be higher than 212 degrees Fahrenheit will be dissipated by conversion of water to steam. Inasmuch as the steam may form in the engine water passages, it will blow coolant out of the radiator upper hose and top tank, necessitating coolant replacement. Therefore, always allow the engine to cool and the pressure to drop before removing the pressure cap.

COOLING SYSTEM CHECKS

Restrictions in the radiator can be checked by first warming the engine up and then turning the engine off and feeling the sides of the radiator. The radiator should be hot along the left side and warm along the right side with an even temperature rise from right to left. Any cold spots found indicate clogged sections.

Water pump operation may be checked by running the engine while squeezing the radiator upper hose. A definite pressure surge should be felt if the pump is operating correctly. If not, check for a plugged vent-hole in the pump.

A defective head gasket may allow exhaust gases to leak into the cooling system where the gases will combine with the water to form acids harmful to both the radiator and engine. To check for exhaust leaks, drain coolant from the system until the coolant level stands just above the top of the cylinder head. Then disconnect the radiator upper hose and remove the thermostat and fan belt. Start the engine and quickly accelerate several times noticing—at the same time—any appreciable water rise or the appearance of bubbles which are indicative of exhaust gases leaking into the cooling system. This can also be done with a radiator pressure tester.

PERIODIC MAINTENANCE

As mentioned previously, the cooling system should be maintained for protection to at least -20 degrees Fahrenheit to provide adequate corrosion protection—regardless of the climate. In areas where temperatures lower than -20 degrees Fahrenheit may occur, a sufficient amount of an *ethylene glycol* base coolant should be used.

Every two years the cooling system should be serviced by flushing with plain water, then completely refilled with a fresh solution of water and inhibited glycol base coolant. A good cleaning solution should be used to loosen the rust and scale before reverse flushing the system.

Drain all coolant from the cooling system, including the cylinder block. Check shop or owner's manual for the location of block drain plugs for the car being serviced. Remove the thermostat, but replace the thermostat housing before adding the cooling system cleaner. Then fill the cooling system with water to a level of about 3 inches below the top of the overflow pipe. Cover the radiator and run the engine at moderate speed until the engine coolant temperature reaches 180 degrees. Continue running the engine and remove the radiator cover. Run the engine for another 20 minutes, but avoid boiling. At the end of this time, stop the engine, wait a few minutes and then open the engine block drain cocks as well as the lower hose connection to the radiator.

The radiator should also be blown free of dirt and bugs with compressed air. Blow from the back of the radiator core and be careful not to bend any of the radiator fins.

REVERSE FLUSHING THE COOLING SYSTEM

Once the system has been thoroughly cleaned as out-lined above, the system should be reversed flushed. This is accomplished through the system in a direction opposite to the normal flow of coolant. This action causes the water to get behind the corrosion deposits and force them out.

To reverse flush the cooling system, remove the upper and lower hoses from the radiator and replace the radiator cap. Attach a piece of hose to the top inlet opening to lead the water away from the engine and radiator and then attach a new piece of hose at the radiator outlet connection and insert the flushing gun in this hose. Or use a standard garden hose with the openings around the hose tightly clogged. If the flushing gun is used, connect the water hose of the flushing gun to a water outlet and the air hose to an air line. Turn the water on and when the radiator is full, turn on the air in short blasts, allowing the radiator to fill between blasts of air. Continue this flushing until the water from the top hose runs clear.

The cylinder block and cylinder head as well as the heater core should be flushed out at the same time. With the thermostat still removed, attach a lead-away hose to the water pump inlet and a length of new hose to the water outlet connection at the top of the engine. The heater hose should be disconnected and plugged at the engine when reverse flushing the engine.

Insert the flushing gun in the new hose, turn on the water and air and when the engine block is full, apply short blasts of air. Continue this flushing until the water from the lead-away hose runs clean.

With the hose still disconnected from the engine, insert the flushing gun and flush out the heater core, but be careful of too much pressure as the core may be damaged.

CHECKING THE THERMOSTAT

While the thermostat is out, it can be checked by first observing its temperature range which is usually stamped on the thermostat itself. The lower temperature is the point at which it should begin to open, and the higher temperature marks the full-open position.

Place a pan of water on a stove or heater and insert a thermometer. When the thermometer reads 15 to 20 degrees below the lowest thermostat setting, put the thermostat in the water and continue heating. If the thermostat opens early, it should be replaced. If it does not open fully at its highest temperature, it should also be replaced.

When replacing the thermostat (either the existing one or a new one) use a new seal and coat the seal with a gasket sealing compound to insure a leak-proof fit. Tighten the fitting and replace the coolant.

FAN BELT DIFFICULTIES

A loose fan belt means slippage, and the fan may not produce enough air at slow and idle speeds to sufficiently cool the coolant in the radiator. Test the tension of the fan belt with a finger as shown in Fig. 5-4. A typical fan belt should depress from ½ to ¾ of an inch

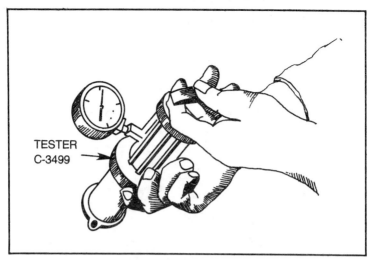

Fig. 5-4. Method of testing tension of fan belt with finger.

when pressed midway between pulleys. If the belt depresses more than this, the belt is too loose. Another indication of a loose fan belt is a squeak or wail during acceleration.

Inspect the fan belt for a glazing condition, cracks, oil and frayed places. Make adjustments according to instructions in the owner's manual.

The radiator cap should be washed with clean water and pressure checked at regular tune-up intervals with a pressure testing instrument as shown in Fig. 5-5. If the cap will not hold the pressure or does not release at the proper pressure, replace the cap.

WATER PUMP PROBLEMS

Water pump problems can be detected by rattling noise coming from the front of the engine compartment and also a visible leak at the pump. To check for worn out bearings, turn off the engine and try moving the fan back and forth. Any motion between the fan and water pump indicates that the bearings in the pump are worn and the pump should be replaced.

With all of the many accessories driven by the engine, the removal and installation of a new water pump can be a time-consuming operation. Begin by first draining all coolant from the radiator and then break loose the fan pulley bolts. Disconnect any hoses (radiator, heater, by-pass, etc.) at the water pump and then remove the fan belt, fan bolts, fan and pulley. Remove the water pump and gasket from the engine.

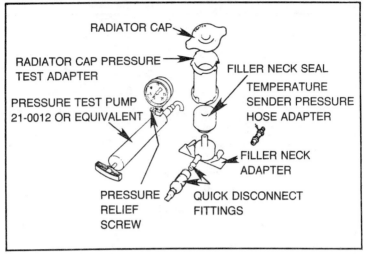

RADIATOR CAP

RADIATOR CAP PRESSURE
TEST ADAPTER

FILLER NECK SEAL

TEMPERATURE
SENDER PRESSURE
HOSE ADAPTER

PRESSURE TEST PUMP
21-0012 OR EQUIVALENT

FILLER NECK
ADAPTER

PRESSURE
RELIEF
SCREW

QUICK DISCONNECT
FITTINGS

Fig. 5-5. The radiator cap should be pressure checked at regular tuneup intervals with a pressure testing instrument.

When installing a new pump, use a new sealer coated, pump-to-block gasket and tighten bolts securely. Install the pump pully and fan on pump hub and tighten bolts securely. Connect all hoses and fill the system with coolant as discussed previously. Finish by installing the fan belt and adjust to the proper tension before starting the engine and checking for leaks.

TROUBLESHOOTING THE COOLING SYSTEM

If the cooling system looses coolant, check all connections in the cooling system for evidence of leakage. This inspection should be done when the engine is cold and the system filled completely with coolant. Small leaks which may show dampness or dripping can easily escape detection when the engine is hot, due to the rapid evaporation of coolant.

Check for cracks in the engine block that could have occurred during accidental freezing of the coolant. Also pull the engine oil dip-stick to check for water in the crankcase. Continue by removing the rocker arm covers and checking for cracked cylinder heads. Then remove the cylinder heads and check gaskets. While heads are off, check for cracks in the heads or block.

If overheating of the engine is frequent, check to see that the radiator cap seats in the radiator filler neck and releases at specified pressure (usually 15 psi). Check the coolant level, the temperature sending unit or gauge, the engine thermostat, and the fan belt for excessive looseness. Thoroughly check the radiator for punctures, ruptured or disconnected hoses, a loose pressure cap or use of low boiling point antifreeze. These conditions prevent the cooling system from maintaining proper pressure.

Clean debris from the radiator and/or condenser as described previously and also check the engine operation to see if a tuneup is needed. Improper timing may cause overheating.

Driving conditions may be the reason for constant overheating. Prolonged idling, start and stop driving in long lines of traffic on hot days, climbing steep grades on hot days, etc., will occasionally cause coolant to boil.

Clean the cooling system, backflush, and if the problem is still not solved, the cylinder heads will have to be removed and the water passages in the heads and block checked for obstructions.

The temperature sending unit may be at fault and give a false heat reading. The device can be found on either the manifold or cylinder head and will have an electric wire coming from it. The unit should have a plug-like fitting, and can be easily removed with a wrench and replaced by a new one.

Chapter 6

Fuel System

A typical automotive fuel system consists of fuel tank(s), fuel-vapor separator, fuel lines, fuel pump, fuel filter and an accelerator-linkage. The fuel pump draws gas from the tank and forces it through the filter into the carburetor where it is metered and injected into the air stream. This air-fuel mixture is then drawn into the engine by the vacuum created by the pistons. A diagram of such a system for late-model cars is shown in Fig. 6-1.

Automotive vehicles manufactured in the United States in recent years are also equipped with a variety of emissions control systems. The mechanic should note that any modification or adjustment of these systems so as to *render them inoperative* constitutes a violation of federal law.

THE FUEL TANK

Cars with the engine mounted in the front almost always have the fuel tank mounted in the rear of the vehicle beneath the luggage compartment (trunk). In cars having the engine in the rear, the tank is positioned in or under the forward compartment.

Fuel tanks with in-tank venting are provided with a vapor space above the gasoline level in the fuel tank to permit adequate breathing space for the tank vapor valve. This space is sufficient for all static and most dynamic conditions.

All fuel tank vapor valves make use of a small orifice that tends to allow only vapor and not fuel to pass into the line running forward to the vapor storage canister. This assembly mounts directly to the

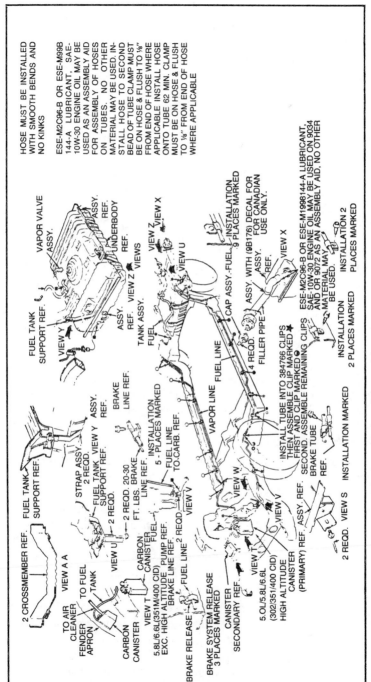

Fig. 6-1. Diagram and components of the fuel system for a late-model car.

fuel tank using a rubber grommet. Fuel vapors trapped in the sealed fuel tank are vented through the orificed vapor valve assembly in the top of the tank and leave the assembly through a single vapor line which continues to the charcoal canister in the engine compartment. The vapors are stored in this canister until such time as they are purged to the engine.

In vehicles equipped with fuel/vapor return lines, vapor generated in the fuel supply line is continuously vented back to the fuel tank. This action prevents engine surging from unwanted fuel enrichment and assists in hydrocarbon emission control.

Some older cars have the vent in the gas cap, and if you're in doubt about the kind of venting system on the vehicle you are working, examine the fuel tank to see if there is a vent line. You must use the proper cap for the type of system. For example, placing a vented cap on a system with a separate vent line will not usually cause any major operational problem, but the effectiveness of the fuel-evaporation control system will be reduced. On the other hand, a nonvented cap used on a fuel tank that should be vented can cause the fuel pump to deliver an insufficient amount of fuel. The walls of the tank could collapse also.

The easiest way to identify the correct gas cap for vehicles with a separate vent line is to check for the words *pressure-vacuum* on the inside of the cap. Also check for proper gas gap fit. On vehicles requiring a vented cap, an audible suction sound can be heard as the cap is removed should a nonvented cap be mistakenly placed on the filler neck. This is the sound of air rushing into the tank.

Cleaning Fuel Systems

If there is evidence of fuel tank contamination, it can usually be cleaned unless the tank is rusted internally. If the latter condition exists, the tank should be replaced. In some cases—like when a replacement tank is not readily available—a sloshing compound is sometimes used to clean the tank and retard the rust until such time as the tank can be changed.

The fuel tank must be drained first. If the fuel tank does not incorporate a drain plug, it will be necessary to siphon fuel from the tank. The following procedure is recommended.

1. Disconnect the fuel tank gauge unit wire or else the battery negative cable. Then disconnect the battery and ignition coil primary wire (+ wire on ignition coil).

2. Use approximately 10 feet of ⅜ inch inside diameter hose and cut a flap-type slit 18 inches from one end and in the direction of the shorter end of the hose.

3. Insert a small pipe nipple with an outside diameter of about ½ inch into the opposite end of the hose.

4. Insert the end with the nipple into the fuel tank filler neck with the natural curl of the hose pointed down. Continue pushing until the nipple is heard striking the bottom of the tank.

5. With the opposite end of the hose in a suitable container, insert an air hose in the downward direction in the flap-type slit to trigger the flow of fuel.

6. Remove the fuel tank by first unclamping the filler neck, vent tube hose and also the gauge unit hose.

7. Support the tank so it doesn't fall, and remove all support straps. Lower the tank gradually until the gauge unit wiring can be removed. Then remove the entire fuel tank.

To continue the cleaning operation, remove the fuel inlet filter at the carburetor and inspect for contamination. If the filter is plugged, it should be replaced. Leave the fuel line disconnected at this point.

Always keep the gas tank away from heat, flame or other sources of ignition while working on it or while in storage. At a safe place, remove the fuel gauge unit and inspect the condition of the filter. Replace the filter if it is contaminated. The tank can now be completely drained by rocking it back and forth and allowing fuel to run out of the tank unit hole.

When completely drained of all fuel, purge the tank with running hot water for five or 10 minutes; steam may also be used. Pour water out of the tank unit hole—again rocking the tank back and forth to assure the complete removal of all water. There could still be some fuel vapor within the tank, so *don't use any heat or flame on the tank or filler neck.*

The fuel lines should be cleaned at this time by disconnecting the fuel lines at the fuel pump and using air pressure to clean. The pressure should be applied in the direction fuel normally flows through the lines. A low air pressure should be used to clean pipes on the tank unit.

A new filter should be installed at this time if required. The fuel tank unit should be installed with a new gasket and then the entire fuel tank can be installed. Connect the tank unit wires first and then all fuel lines except the pump to carburetor line. In other words, the tank is installed just the opposite from removing the tank.

Finish the cleaning operation by connecting a hose to the fuel line at the carburetor. Insert the other end of this hose into a one gallon fuel can. Connect battery cables, but make sure the ignition coil primary wire (+ terminal) is disconnected. *This is extremely important.* Now pour six gallons of clean fuel in the tank and operate the starter to pump two quarts of fuel into the fuel can. This will purge the fuel pump. You may then remove the hose from the can and connect the fuel line to the carburetor. Also connect the coil primary wire and the operation is completed.

Fuel Tank Leak Test

If a fuel tank is known to leak, but the leak cannot be readily found, drain and remove the tank as discussed previously. Visually inspect the interior cavity of the tank. If any fuel is evident, drain again before moving the tank to a suitable flushing area like a wash rack.

Once at the wash rack, purge the tank by pouring a gasoline emulsifying agent and water solution into the tank and agitate the mixture for two to three minutes, wetting all interior surfaces. Follow directions on the can for the correct amounts of emulsifying agent to water ratio.

Continue the purging by filling the tank with water to nearly its full capacity and agitate again. Then empty the contents into a floor drain or other suitable drain.

When the tank is empty from the previous operations, refill the tank with water until it overflows to completely flush out the remaining mixture. Empty the tank.

If any vapor is present, repeat the gasoline emulsifying agent and water treatment and again flush with water until there is no evidence of fuel vapor. Dry the tank with compressed air and then test for leaks.

First plug all outlets. Use a good pressure-vacuum filler cap for the filler neck. Install the tank unit and plug the fuel line and all but one vent tube by using a single short piece of fuel line hose. A short piece of fuel line hose should be installed on the remaining open vent tube.

Apply air pressure to the tank through the open vent tube by using extreme caution to prevent rupturing the tank. To prevent this, listen very carefully for air escaping from the filler neck cap. When this is heard, pinch the fuel line hose to retain pressure. Now test for leaks by submersion or with a soap solution. If a leak is noted, make the repair and retest.

FUEL LINES

Fuel lines should be inspected occasionally for leaks, kinks or dents. If evidence of dirt is found in the carburetor, fuel pump or on disassembly of the line, they should be disconnected and blown out.

Most fuel lines are not replaceable as assemblies. Rather, they must be cut, squared and formed out of rolls of fuel system service tubing. They should be spliced into the line by means of connecting hoses and retaining clamps. Therefore, all replacement hoses must be cut to a length that will assure proper clamp retention beyond the flared ends of the connecting tubing.

To install, drain the fuel from the gas tank. Disconnect the line at the fuel gauge sender unit and the fuel pump. Then remove the lines from all holding clips along the underbody and all damaged hose sections and tube sections.

Cut a new section of tubing to approximately the same length as the section to be replaced. Remember to allow extra length for flaring the ends of the tubing. Square the ends of the cut tubing with a file. The inside edges should be reamed with the reamer blade on the tube cutter to make sure that all metal chips are removed. Couple flare the ends of the cut tubing as required.

Using the old tubing as a template, bend the new length of tubing to the same contour as the old. Connect the hose couplings to the tubing and install the retaining clamps.

Finish the installation by positioning the lines in the underbody clips and tighten. Connect the line to the fuel gauge sender unit and the fuel pump. Fill the tank and check for leaks

FUEL PUMP

There are two kinds of fuel pumps currently being used on American-made cars—mechanical and electrical (Fig. 6-2). Of these two types, the single action fuel pump (mechanically operated) is the type most widely used. This type of pump is actuated by an eccentric located on the engine camshaft. On in-line engines, the eccentric actuates the rocker arm, while a push rod actuates the pump rocker arm on V-8 engines. In both cases, suction is created inside the pump by the pushing and relaxing of the rocker arm. This suction draws gasoline from the fuel tank and pushes it to the carburetor.

Incorrect fuel pump pressure and low volume are the two most likely fuel pump troubles that will affect engine performance. Low pressure will cause a lean mixture and fuel starvation at high speeds. Excessive pressure will cause high fuel consumption and carburetor flooding. Low volume (capacity of flow rate) will cause fuel starvation at high speed.

To determine the operating condition of the fuel pump, tests for both fuel pump pressure and fuel pump capacity (volume) should be performed. These tests are performed with the fuel pump installed on the engine and the engine at normal operating temperature and at idle speed.

Begin the test by removing the air cleaner assembly and disconnecting the fuel inlet line or the fuel filter at the carburetor. Then connect a pressure gauge, a restrictor and a flexible hose between the fuel filter and the carburetor. Position this hose and the restrictor so the fuel can be discharged into a suitable, graduated container.

Start the engine and let it run for about 30 seconds while you open the hose restrictor and allow the fuel to discharge into the graduated container. At least one pint of fuel should have been discharged within this time period. If not, repeat the test using an auxiliary fuel supply and a new fuel filter. Then, if the correct amount of fuel is produced, check for a restriction in the fuel supply from the tank and for improper tank ventilation.

To test for pressure, operate the engine at a constant speed between 450-1000 rpm and vent the system into the container by opening the hose restrictor momentarily. Then close the hose restrictor to allow the pressure to stabilize, and note the reading. For an exact test, refer to service manuals for fuel pump pressure specifications. For a rule of thumb, the pressure should be between 5.0 to 8.0 psi. If the pressure reading is too low, too high, or varies significantly at different speeds, the pump should be replaced.

Replacing Fuel Pumps

Always double wrench the fittings to avoid possible damage and disconnect fuel inlet and outlets pipes at the old fuel pump. Then remove the fuel pump mounting bolts, the pump and gasket. Discard the old gasket.

Before installing the new pump, remove all the old gasket material from the mounting pad. Apply an oil-resistant sealer to both sides of the new gasket before positioning it on the pump flange and mounting the new pump. At this point, make sure the rocker arm or rod is riding on the camshaft or intermediate shaft eccentric. Press the pump tight against the pad, install the attaching bolts and alternately torque them to specifications found in the owner's service manual available from the car manufacturer.

Connect the fuel inlet and outlet lines and make certain that all connections are firmly secured. Again, double wrench the fittings to avoid damage to the lines or the new fuel pump. Operate the engine and check for fuel leaks.

Electric Fuel Pumps

Electric fuel pumps are used on some American-made cars and many imported cars. An in-tank fuel pump is used on all Ford 7.5L

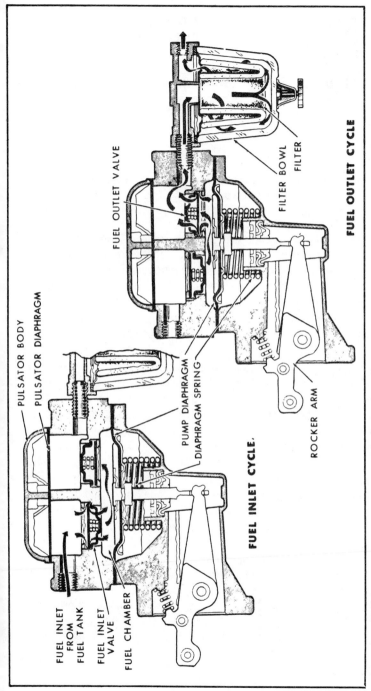

PULSATOR BODY
PULSATOR DIAPHRAGM

FUEL OUTLET VALVE

FILTER BOWL
FILTER

FUEL OUTLET CYCLE

PUMP DIAPHRAGM
DIAPHRAGM SPRING

ROCKER ARM

FUEL INLET CYCLE.

FUEL INLET
FROM
FUEL TANK

FUEL INLET
VALVE

FUEL CHAMBER

Fig. 6-2. Basic cycles of the fuel pump (courtesy Ford Motor Company).

107

(460 cubic inch displacement) police interceptor V-8 equipped vehicles. The electric circuit provides an interlock system that performs the following functions.

1. It provides power to the fuel pump during starting through a contact of the starter relay.
2. It provides reduced operating voltage during normal operation.
3. It provides full battery voltage during wide open throttle operation.
4. Should the engine oil pressure be lost during operation, the fuel pump is automatically disconnected from the electric circuit.

Electric fuel pumps are wired carefully. When the ignition switch is in the *off* position, current is fed to the ignition switch only. The vacuum, relay and oil pressure switches are all closed. When the ignition switch is turned to the *start* position, current flows through a fuse, diode, and the windings of the fuel pump to the tank ground. The diode is required to prevent current supplied to the pump during normal operation from activating the starter relay.

When the starter switch is returned to the *run* position, current is supplied through the ignition module connector and the windings of the fuel pump to the tank ground. If the engine is not running when the switch is turned to the *run* position, current will flow through the windings of the relay and through the closed contacts of the oil pressure switch to ground, opening the operating path of the fuel pump at the contacts of the relay.

At wide open throttle, the vacuum operated switch closes its internal contacts, allowing fuel pump operating current to bypass the voltage-dropping resistor. An additional diode is required to prevent current flowing in the *engine* warning lamp circuit from operating the relay A and cutting off the operating path of the fuel pump in the event of engine overheating.

Some models are equipped with an oil pressure gauge instead of or in addition to the *engine* warning lamp. A "Y" fitting is then required in the cylinder block, with one branch used for the oil pressure gauge sender and the other branch for the oil pressure switch.

The procedure for replacing a mechanical fuel pump—discussed previously—may be used with some variation to replace an electric fuel pump.

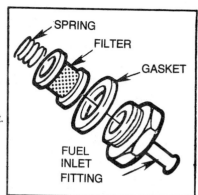

Fig. 6-3. Typical carburetor fuel filter utilizing a replaceable element.

Electric Fuel Pump Diagnosis

The following tests should be performed on inoperative electric fuel pumps. Check the fuel tank for an adequate fuel supply; the fuel level gauge may be wrong. If this checks out okay, remove the fuel line at the carburetor fuel filter and install a fuel pressure gauge with a range of 0-15 psi between the line and the carburetor. Turn the ignition switch to *start* for a second or two. If no fuel pressure is present during this test, check for a blown in-line fuse in the wiring harness (consult owner's handbook or service manual for the exact location).

Disconnect the lead wire to the oil pressure switch, turn the ignition switch to run position and watch for fuel pressure. If no fuel pressure is present, check for 12 volts at the relay controlling the oil pressure switch. If no current exists, check the circuit all the way back to the source to find the problem. However, if current does show at the relay, the relay is defective and should be replaced.

Once the relay has been replaced, check wire connectors to the taillight wiring harness and also the power lead at the fuel pump connector. If 12 volts is present on all of these connectors, the fuel pump is defective in most cases.

If the engine will start, but runs for only a short time—like a minute or two—check engine oil pressure. Also check the operation of the oil pressure sender as an inoperate oil pump or switch will activate the relay, stopping current flow to the fuel pump. When the problem is found, remove test gauge and reconnect fuel line to the fuel filter.

FUEL FILTERS

The fuel filters used on most engines are either of the in-line or internal type, and most cannot be cleaned. They must be replaced.

Problems caused by a partially or totally clogged filter include a noticeable lack of power and failure of the engine to start.

A typical carburetor fuel filter utilizing a replaceable element type filter is shown in Fig. 6-3. Inside this one-piece filter is a magnet to trap metallic particles which might be present in the fuel.

To change fuel filters, remove the air cleaner from the top of the engine. Loosen (screw-type) or remove (spring-type) the fastenings securing the inlet hose to the fuel filter line. If the filter is located in the line, loosen or remove the outlet hose clamps. Unscrew the fuel filter from the carburetor on those models so equipped. Then disconnect the fuel filter hose from the metal line and discard the clamps, filter and hose.

Install new clamps on a new inlet hose and connect the hose to the filter and line. Thread the filter into the carburetor inlet part if so equipped, and then tighten the filter.

Position the fuel line hose clamps and tighten the clamps securely as shown in Fig. 6-4. Finish by starting the engine and checking for fuel leaks.

CARBURETORS

A carburetor is a metering device which mixes fuel with air in the correct proportion and delivers the mixture to the engine cylinders for combustion. Its purpose is to meter, atomize, and distribute the fuel throughout the air flowing into the engine. These functions are designed into the carburetor and are carried out by the carburetor automatically over a wide range of engine operating conditions, such as varying engine speeds, load and operating temperature.

The carburetor also regulates the amount of air-fuel mixture which flows to the engine. It is this mixture flow regulation which gives the driver control of the engine speed.

Atomization

Before gasoline can be used as fuel for an engine, it must be atomized, which means breaking the fuel into fine particles so that it can be mixed with air to form a combustible mixture. Contrary to popular belief, gasoline in its liquid state is not combustible; only gasoline vapor will burn and then only when oxygen is present to sustain combustion. Vaporization is the act of changing from a liquid to a gas. This change of state occurs only when the liquid absorbs enough heat to boil.

In a carburetor, gasoline is discharged into the incoming air stream as a spray. The spray is then atomized, forming a mist. The

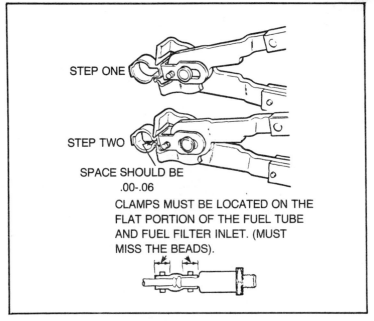

STEP ONE

STEP TWO

SPACE SHOULD BE
.00-.06

CLAMPS MUST BE LOCATED ON THE
FLAT PORTION OF THE FUEL TUBE
AND FUEL FILTER INLET. (MUST
MISS THE BEADS).

Fig. 6-4. Method of installing crimp-type clamps.

resulting air-fuel mixture is drawn into the intake manifold. At this point, the change of state occurs and the fuel *mist* vaporizes as the result of several factors.

Since the pressure in the intake manifold is far less than the atmosphere's, the boiling point of the gasoline is lowered considerably. At this reduced pressure, latent heat absorbed from the many air particles surrounding each fuel particle causes some vaporization, which is further aided by heat on the intake manifold floor.

Combustible mixtures in an engine are also limited by ratios of air to gasoline. Eight parts air to one part gasoline is the richest mixture that will fire regularly. A mixture of 18½ parts air to one part gasoline is the leanest mixture that will fire without missing in an engine. The most desired ratios are a mixture that will produce the most power per pound of gasoline and one that will provide the best economy or most miles per pound of fuel with the least exhaust emissions.

Metering

Good combustion demands a correct mixture ratio between fuel and air. To release all possible energy by combustion, the right amount of fuel must be mixed with a given amount of air. The metering job of the carburetor is to furnish the proper air-fuel ratio for all conditions, so that the engine operation will neither be too lean for power requirements nor too rich for economy. It still must meet prime requirements of low emission.

Distribution

For good combustion and smooth engine operation, the air and fuel must be thoroughly and uniformly mixed, delivered in equal quantities to each cylinder and evenly distributed within the combustion chamber.

Good distribution requires good vaporization. A gaseous mixture will travel much more easily around corners in the manifold and engine, while liquid particles, being relatively heavy, will try to continue in one direction. The particles will hit the walls of the manifold or travel on to another cylinder. The carburetor's principal job in distribution is to break up the fuel as finely as possible and furnish a uniformly vaporized mixture to the manifold.

Cleaning and Inspection

Carburetor overhaul kits are available for most makes and types of carburetors. All parts and gaskets included in the repair kit should be installed when the carburetor is assembled and the old gaskets and parts should be discarded. The cleaning and inspection of those parts not included in carburetor overhaul repair kits are covered here.

Dirt, gum, water or carbon contamination in the carburetor or the exterior moving parts of the carburetor are often responsible for unsatisfactory performance. Efficient carburetion depends upon careful cleaning and inspection.

Wash all the carburetor parts (except the accelerating pump diaphragm, the enrichment valve, the choke pulldown diaphragm, and the anti-stall dashpot assembly) in clean commercial carburetor cleaning solvent. If a commercial solvent is not available, lacquer thinner or denatured alcohol may be used. Rinse the parts in kerosene to remove all traces of the cleaning solvent; then dry them with compressed air. Wipe all parts that can not be immersed in solvent with a clean, soft, dry cloth. Be sure all dirt, gum, carbon, and other foreign matter are removed from all parts.

When cleaning any carburetor, never use a wire brush, drill or wire in any of the openings or passages in the carburetor as any of these devices may enlarge the passage, changing the calibration of the carburetor.

Check the choke shaft for grooves, wear and excessive looseness or binding. Inspect the choke plate for nicked edges and for ease of operation, and free it if necessary. Make sure all carbon and foreign material has been removed from the automatic choke housing and the piston. Check the operation of the choke piston in the choke housing to make certain it has free movement.

Look at throttle shafts in the bores for excessive looseness or binding and inspect the throttle plates for burrs which prevent proper closure. Inspect the main body, throttle body, air horn, nozzle bars and booster venturi assemblies, choke housing and thermostatic spring housing, enrichment valve cover and accelerating pump cover for cracks.

Check metallic float(s) for leaks by holding them under water that has been heated to just below the boiling point. Bubbles will appear if there is a leak. Shake the float to watch for the entry of fuel or water. If a float leaks, replace it. Replace the float if the arm needle contact surface is grooved. If the floats are serviceable, polish the needle contact surface of the arm with crocus cloth or steel wool. Replace the float shafts if they are worn, all screws and nuts that have stripped threads, and all distorted or broken springs.

Inspect all gasket mating surfaces for nicks and burrs. Repair or replace any parts that have a damaged gasket surface.

Troubleshooting Carburetor Operation

Proper carburetor operation is dependent upon the fuel supply, linkage and emission control systems, engine compression, ignition system firing voltage, ignition spark timing, secure intake manifold, engine temperature and carburetor adjustments. Any problems in these areas can cause many operating problems.

The following data are arranged so that the problem is listed first. Then the possible causes of this problem are listed in the order in which they should be checked. Finally, solutions to the various problems are given, including step-by-step procedures where it is felt they are necessary.

Problem A: Engine Cranks, but
Will Not Start Or Starts Hard When Cold

1. Add fuel. Check fuel gauge for proper operation. Perhaps there is no fuel in the tank.
2. Check to see if proper starting procedure is used, as outlined in the owner's manual.
3. Adjust the choke thermostatic coil in case the choke is not closing sufficiently when cold—or closing too tightly.

4. If the choke valve or linkage is binding, realign the choke valve or linkage as necessary. If caused by dirt or gum, clean with automatic choke cleaner.

5. If there is no fuel in the carburetor, proceed with the following:

   • Remove fuel line at the carburetor. Connect hose to the fuel line and run it into a metal container. Remove the high tension coil wire from the center tower on distributor cap and ground. Crank over the engine. If there is no fuel discharge from the fuel line, check for kinked or bent lines. Disconnect fuel line at the tank and blow out with an air hose. Reconnect the line and check again for fuel discharge. If there is none, replace fuel pump. Check pump for adequate flow, as outlined in the service manual.

   • If fuel supply is okay inspect fuel filters. If plugged, replace. If filters are okay, remove the air horn and check for a bind in the float mechanism or a sticking float needle. If okay, adjust float as specified.

6. Check for engine flooding by removing the air cleaner, with the engine off, and look into the carburetor bores. Fuel will be dripping off the nozzles and/or the carburetor will be very wet. The following may eliminate carburetor flooding.

   • Remove the fuel line at the carburetor and plug. Crank and run the engine until the fuel bowl runs dry. Turn off the engine and connect fuel line. Then re-start and run the engine. This will usually flush dirt past the carburetor float needle and seat.

   • If dirt is in the fuel system, clean the system and replace fuel filters as necessary. If excessive dirt is found, remove the carburetor unit. Disassemble and clean.

   • Check the float needle and seat for proper seal. If a needle and seat tester is not available, apply mouth suction to the needle seat with needle installed. If the needle is defective, replace with a factory matched set.

   • Check float for being loaded with fuel, bent float hanger or binds in the float arm.

   • Adjust float.

Problem B: Engine Starts and Stalls

1. Check and re-set the fast idle setting and fast idle cam because the engine probably does not have enough fast idle speed when cold.

2. The choke vacuum break may not be properly adjusted. Proceed as follows.
   - Adjust vacuum break to specification.
   - If adjusted okay, check the vacuum break for proper operation. On the externally mounted vacuum break unit, connect a piece of hose to the nipple on the vacuum break unit and apply suction by mouth to apply vacuum. Plunger should move inward and hold vacuum. If not, replace the unit.

3. The choke coil rod may be out of adjustment, so adjust.

4. If there is evidence of the choke valve and/or linkage binding, clean and align choke valve and linkage; replacement may be necessary. Re-adjust if part replacement is necessary.

5. Adjust idle speed to specifications on the decal in the engine compartment or obtain data from owner's manual.

6. The carburetor may not have enough fuel. Check fuel pump pressure and volume, and also for a partially plugged fuel inlet filter. Replace if dirty. Remove the air horn and check float adjustments.

7. For carburetor flooding, check float needle and seat for proper seal. If a needle and seat tester is not available, mouth suction can be applied to the needle seat with needle installed. If the needle is defective, replace it with a factory matched set. Also check float for being loaded with fuel, for a bent float hanger or for binds in the float arm. If excessive dirt is found in the carburetor, clean the fuel system and carburetor. Replace fuel filters as necessary.

A solid float can be checked for fuel absorption by lightly squeezing between fingers. If wetness appears on the surface or the float feels heavy, replace the float assembly.

Problem C: Engine Idles Rough and Stalls

1. Re-set idle speed per instructions in owner's manual.

2. Check all vacuum hoses leading into the manifold or carburetor base for leaks or being disconnected. Install or replace as necessary.

3. If the carburetor is loose on intake manifold, torque carburetor to manifold bolts (10 to 14 foot pounds).

4. Check for loose intake manifold or defective gaskets by spraying kerosene around manifold legs and carburetor base. If engine rpm changes, tighten or replace the manifold gaskets or carburetor base gaskets as necessary.

5. If the carburetor utilizes a hot idle compensator, it should be closed when engine is running cold and open when engine is hot. Replace if defective.

6. If inspection shows evidence of carburetor flooding, solve by procedure (7) in Problem B.

Problem D: Engine Hesitates on Acceleration

1. Remove air horn and check pump cup. If cracked or distorted, replace the pump plunger.

2. Check the pump discharge ball for proper seating and location. The pump discharge ball is normally located in a cavity next to the pump well. To check for proper seating, remove air horn and gasket and fill cavity with fuel. No *leak down* should occur. If it is, restake and replace the ball. Also make sure the discharge valve assembly is properly installed.

3. Clean and blow out pump passages and pump jet with compressed air to remove any dirt.

4. Check for sticking float needle or binding float. Free up or replace parts as necessary. Check and reset float level to specifications in ship manual.

5. If there's evidence of leaking air horn to the float bowl gasket, torque the air horn to the float bowl using proper tightening procedures.

6. If carburetor is loose on manifold, torque carburetor to manifold bolts (10 – 14 foot-pounds).

Problem E: No Power On Heavy Acceleration Or At High Speed

1. Adjust throttle linkage to obtain wide open throttle in carburetor.

2. A dirty or plugged fuel filter could be causing the problem, so replace with a new filter element.

3. Check power piston for free up and down movement, and if sticking, check for dirt or scores in the cavity. Check power piston spring for distortion and replace if necessary.

4. Adjust the metering rod according to manufacturer's specifications.

5. If the main metering jets are plugged or dirty, the carburetor should be completely disassembled and cleaned. Then check the jet rod for the correct one, by checking the manufacturer's parts list.

Problem F: Engine Starts Hard When Hot

1. The most logical fault is the choke valve not opening properly. Check for binding in the choke valve and/or in the linkage. Clean and free-up or replace parts as necessary, but do not oil the choke linkage. Also check and adjust choke thermostatic coil according to manufacturer's recommendations.
2. If engine is flooding, see procedure under Problem A.
3. If no fuel is present in the carburetor, run pressure and volume test on the fuel pump. Also check the float needle for sticking in seat or binding float.
4. Fill bowl with fuel and look for leaks in the float bowl.

Problem G: Engine Runs Uneven

1. Check all hoses and fuel lines for bends, kinks or leaks as fuel restriction is the most probable cause. Check fuel filter and if plugged or dirty, replace.
2. If there are signs of dirt or water in fuel system, clean fuel tank and lines as described earlier in this chapter.
3. Check for proper fuel level in the carburetor; that is, check for free float and float needle valve operation.
4. Remove the air horn and gasket on the carburetor and adjust the metering rod. Replace if the rod is bent or is the incorrect part.
5. Free up or replace a power valve or piston which might be sticking in the up position.
6. It is absolutely necessary that all vacuum hoses and gaskets are properly installed with no air leaks. The carburetor and manifold should be evenly tightened to specified torque.

Problem H: Poor Fuel Economy

There are many reasons for poor fuel economy, but this section will cover only those directly related to the fuel system. Other causes can be found in other chapters.

1. This problem could be caused by an out-of-tune engine. Check engine compression, spark plugs, engine point dwell, and reset ignition timing. Clean and replace the air cleaner element if it is dirty. Check for a restricted exhaust system. Also, watch the intake manifold for leakage. Make sure all vacuum hoses are correctly connected.

2. Clean the choke valve and free up linkage. Then check the choke coil for proper adjustment; reset if necessary.
3. Check fuel tank, lines and pump for any fuel leakage.
4. Remove carburetor air horn and gasket and adjust the metering rod. If the rod is bent, replace.
5. Free up or replace the power valve or piston if necessary.
6. Check for dirt in the needle and seat. Test using suction by mouth or a needle seat tester. If defective, replace needle and seat assembly with a factory matched set. Check for loaded float and re-set carburetor float to specifications. If excessive dirt is present in the carburetor bowl, the carburetor should be cleaned.
7. If there's evidence that fuel is being pulled from the accelerator system into the venturi through the pump jet, run the engine at an rpm where the nozzle is feeding fuel. Observe the pump jet. If fuel is feeding from the jet, check the pump discharge valve for proper seating by filling the cavity above the valve with fuel to the level to the casting. No leak down should occur with the discharge valve in place. Re-stake or replace leaking check valve assembly. Clean carburetor or overhaul as necessary.

Chapter 7

Electrical System

The electrical system is the most universal system in most automobiles and controls most automotive functions from the proper ignition to the operation of the automobile radio. Whereas other automotive systems will usually cover only a small portion of the total automotive operation, the electrical system is found throughout the automobile from the headlights to the vehicle's rear.

THE BASIC ELECTRICAL SYSTEM

The heart of the electrical system is the automobile storage battery which is normally rated at a nominal 12-volt DC output for most American-made automobiles. As power is drawn from this device, the stored energy begins to drop, and the alternator is called upon to restore this energy. The alternator is driven by the operation of the engine and will charge the battery at engine revolutions of almost any speed.

Once the engine has been started, the storage battery is no longer required to maintain proper engine operation. The alternator is now under power and can supply the potentials required for all electrical needs, except in periods of heavy electrical load when the battery may be called on to supply the additional electrical needs.

The Storage Battery

Storage batteries have progressed through the years to highly efficient devices which can deliver large amounts of current under conditions of severe wear and tear. Until recently, the storage battery remained little-changed from the days of the first automobile. It consisted of a hard, rubber case with a sealed cover with two terminals for connection to the automobile electrical system. The old, six volt batteries contained three, separate two volt cells connected in series. The 12 volt models had six of the same type of cells. The internal connections of these cells caused circuit resistances which, eventually, would cause an unused battery or a little used battery to slowly discharge. The many cells needed regular maintenance checks to assure an appropriate amount of electrolyte in each compartment. The water in these cells dissipated rapidly and had to be watched carefully to prevent burnt cells which dictated replacement of the entire battery.

Today, most batteries are made from polypropylene which is a lightweight, sturdy substance. These cases are much stronger and impact resistant than the rubber boxes of a few years ago and much more easily handled and installed. Many of these modern batteries are sealed at the factory and never need refilling. Other types need only water to activate the cells. The acid is internally contained and is activated by the water which is poured into the case just prior to installation.

Battery ratings have confused many motorists and mechanics alike for years, but now simplified ratings are being universally used and are stated or printed on the battery cases. The rating which is most meaningful is the zero cold test rating which states the amount of DC amperes the battery will deliver for a period of 30 seconds at a temperature of 0 degrees Fahrenheit, while maintaining a voltage of sufficient value to start the automobile. A good rule of thumb for choosing a battery by using the zero cold test ratings is to select one which gives an ampere rating equal to or greater than the cubic inch displacement of the engine. A 305 cubic inch engine should have a storage battery with a zero cold test rating of at least 300 or 305 amperes for best results.

Other battery ratings which are not as helpful as the zero cold test rating include the amp-hour rating. This states the number of amperes the battery will deliver for a 20 hour period continuously. A battery which will deliver five amperes for a 12-hour period will have an amp-hour rating of 60. This rating means little to an individual purchasing a battery, because operation of a battery in an automobile usually is for short periods of time at high current demands, or for longer periods of time at moderate current demands of 10 amperes or more (while driving at night with the headlights and radio on for example). A new rating of reserve capacity is now used in place of the amp-hour rating and tells the buyer how long the battery will deliver a current of 25 amperes. Another rating which is sometimes used is the peak watts rating, which tells about how much energy the battery will deliver for a short period of time. This is sometimes known as the *cranking power* rating and states the amount of current that may be drawn from the battery for short duration periods when the automobile engine is in the process of being started. Sometimes, as much as 200 amps are required to drive the starting motor.

Alternator

Most modern automotive electrical systems now use alternators where, only a few years ago, the generator was universally used. Generators are not as efficient as alternators and not as practical because they would provide an output to charge the storage battery and run the electrical system only when the engine was operated at moderate to high rpm rates. During slow speed or engine idle conditions, no charging current would be delivered by these devices. Alternators utilize the generator principle coupled with modern, solid-state electronics to produce an automobile component which will deliver relatively high charging rates at almost any motor speed. Generators are devices that utilize brushes and a computator to convert AC to DC, while an alternator utilizes solid-state rectifier diodes to convert AC into usable DC for the automotive electrical system.

Alternators may cause problems due to mechanical failures of specific moving parts or due to electrical failure of the non-moving solid-state components. Their charging rate is such that the nominal voltage present in a typical automotive electrical system is approximately 13.8 - 14.8 volts. A system of this type is normally referred to as a 12 volt system and 12 volts of DC potential will usually be present when the motor is shut down and the alternator is not in operation. This is the voltage that is read directly from the storage battery not under charge.

Alternators which are malfunctioning may not charge the storage battery adequately or to the correct voltage potential. They cause erratic electrical operation of other parts of the system due to abnormal voltage outputs. Each alternator accomplishes the charging procedure in three steps: AC generation, rectification of AC to direct current, regulation of DC output to a 13.8 to 14.8 volt level (Figs. 7-1 and 7-2). If any one of these three stages ceases to operate or operates erratically, the charging operation will be hindered. The charging rate will cease if the first two steps of this procedure fail. Should failure occur in the voltage regulator section, a

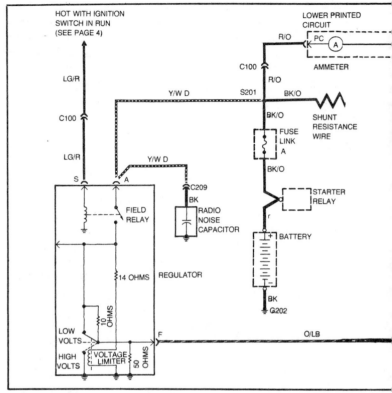

Fig. 7-1. Charging system with the electronic regulator and warning lamp indicator.

charging voltage which is higher than the nominal 13.8 - 14.8 volts DC may present itself and, if allowed to continue, may damage the storage battery and other parts of the electrical system.

Although alternators are used in the majority of automobiles manufactured today, generators still see some usage although, more and more, the alternator is taking its place. A generator is normally heavier than the alternator and since alternators weigh less, they are more easily installed and serviced.

Most modern alternators convert the original AC output to DC by using solid-state rectifiers which are small, efficient and relatively inexpensive. Older models accomplish the rectification process by using selenium rectifiers which are larger and, generally, less efficient. Both types of rectifiers, however, will be found from time to time and usually cease to operate when subjected to conditions of voltage or current overload. These devices are dependable and operate through all types of weather and vibration conditions, but

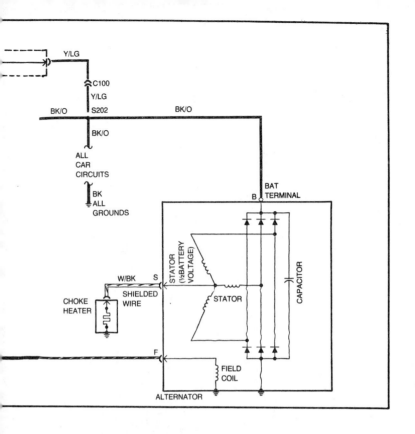

only a fraction of a second of electrical overload can cause permanent and complete damage. Fortunately, their replacement is usually a simple and inexpensive procedure.

Starters

The third major component of the automotive electrical system is the starter system which consists of the starter or cranking motor and the motor control circuits (Fig. 7-3). The starter motor is a device which requires tremendous amounts of current from the storage battery in order to turn the crankshaft of the engine to accomplish initial firing, a process which used to be done by hand in the very early years of the automobile. Depending on the size of the engine, up to 200 amperes may be required to operate the starter motor at a speed which will cause primary ignition. Although this current demand lasts for only a few seconds most of the time, this is where most of the wear and tear on the automobile storage battery is

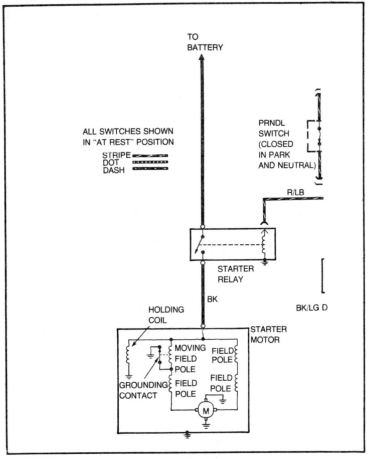

Fig. 7-2. Wiring diagram of a typical charge system.

found. Truck engines may require large starters that draw more than 200 amperes while starting.

The main parts of the starter motor are the drive mechanism, frame and field assembly, armature and brush assembly and the starter switch assembly. The starter accomplishes the job of turning the crankshaft by being specially designed to produce a very high horsepower rating for a limited period of time while operating under conditions of great overloads during the period when the starting switch is engaged. Due to these conditions, the starter motor should not be engaged for periods of longer than 30 seconds at a time without a pause of two to three minutes between each attempt. This allows for the dissipation of heat which builds up in the motor windings while the starter motor is cranking the engine.

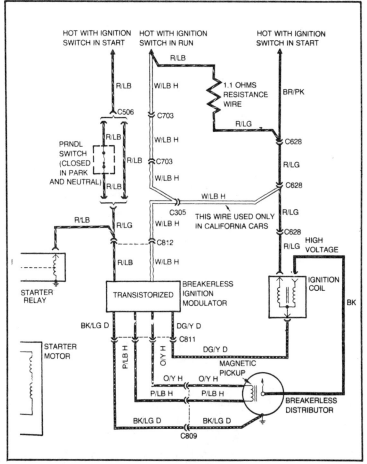

HOT WITH IGNITION SWITCH IN START

HOT WITH IGNITION SWITCH IN RUN

HOT WITH IGNITION SWITCH IN START

R/LB

R/LB

W/LB H

1.1 OHMS RESISTANCE WIRE

BR/PK

C506

C703

R/LB

W/LB H

R/LG

C628

PRNDL SWITCH (CLOSED IN PARK AND NEUTRAL)

R/LB

R/LB

C703

R/LG

C628

R/LB

W/LB H

W/LB H

THIS WIRE USED ONLY IN CALIFORNIA CARS

C305

R/LG

C628

R/LB

R/LG

W/LB H

C812

R/LG

HIGH VOLTAGE

R/LB

W/LB H

STARTER RELAY

BREAKERLESS IGNITION MODULATOR

TRANSISTORIZED

IGNITION COIL

BK

STARTER MOTOR

BK/LG D

DG/Y D

C811

P/LB H

O/Y H

DG/Y D

MAGNETIC PICKUP

O/Y H

O/Y H

P/LB H

P/LB H

BREAKERLESS DISTRIBUTOR

BK/LG D

BK/LG D

C809

Fig. 7-3. Wiring diagram of a typical start/ignition circuit.

The power or torque of the starter motor is transmitted to the engine through the drive mechanism by use of a flywheel gear which turns as the motor armature rotates. The drive mechanism serves two purposes. It must first engage the flywheel of the engine to provide the cranking torque for the starting process. And it must disconnect the starter from the flywheel after the engine has been started. If this latter procedure were not accomplished, the engine would turn the armature at a tremendous rate of speed causing damage to the windings.

The starter drive mechanism usually exhibits an approximate turning ratio of 20 to one over the automobile engine. This means that the starter must turn over 20 times for a single turn of the engine. In normal starting conditions, the automobile engine turns at a rate of approximately 100 revolutions per minute. This means that the starter armature is revolving at an approximate rate of 2000 rpm. Fortunately, the engine usually starts in just a few seconds and the starter motor turns for only a few hundred revolutions.

Most late model automobiles have completely enclosed starter switch assemblies to prevent road grime from entering the mechanism and fouling the operation. Just a small amount of oil or grease can completely stop the desired operating process.

Many starters are engaged to the flywheel and put into operation by an actuating solenoid. When cranking has started in a solenoid-equipped starter, a component known as an assist spring aids the solenoid in overcoming the return spring force and starts the drive mechanism moving toward the flywheel. When the solenoid circuit is open, the shift lever return spring will push on the lever which also exerts pressure on the armature through its associated linkage. The brush end of the armature is then pushed against a leather washer which acts as a brake to slow down the free speed of the armature when the drive mechanism has been disengaged.

PREVENTIVE MAINTENANCE

Many of the problems associated with the automotive electrical system can be overcome or, at least, delayed through a process of proper preventive maintenance. In any electrical circuit, parasitic resistance is always a major operation problem which gets worse with age. Parasitic resistance is simply poor contact between two or more electrical connections. These connections are not solid enough, electrically, to allow for the proper flow of current. When current passes through a contact point which presents an undue amount of resistance, heating occurs and the voltage increases at this point within the circuit reducing the available voltage at the starter. This is a problem which is inherent in all electrical circuits, but is most commonly found on a regular basis in circuits which pass large amounts of current. The automotive electrical system is one of the highest current handling circuits found in the presence of everyday usage. For example: a resistance factor of one ohm is not considered to be very high, but at 200 amperes of current, this small resistance will cause the voltage to drop to zero. In other words, the circuit will fail to operate. Even at smaller current levels, a small resistance will cause the voltage to drop at the starter to a value which is less than nominal. This can cause erratic or unreliable operation of many electrical circuits within the chassis of the automobile.

High resistance circuits are caused by grime and corrosion building up around electrical contacts. This foreign material forms an insulating layer between the contacts and hinders or completely blocks the flow of current through the system. Vibration can cause further hampering of electrical operation when contacts or wire connecters become loose. Road grime buildup can more easily creep into these loose fitting contacts also.

A regular maintenance procedure which involves only examination of electrical contacts and components, cleaning, and in some cases, tightening of connections is all that is required to maintain the proper operation of the electrical system. Periodically, a visual inspection of all electrical parts should be made, especially after periods of continued driving in conditions where rain, snow, and other bad weather conditions existed. Snow generally brings salt into the underframe of the automobile where roads have been treated to prevent ice buildups. This can quickly corrode not only electrical contacts but the car body as well.

The visual inspection should start at the very front of the automobile at the horn and headlights. Any device which has an electrical conductor or wire connected to it should be examined. Each wire should be lightly pulled and watched for any signs of looseness or breakage. The electrical component itself, should be checked to see that the protective case is intact and free from even small cracks and unusual openings.

If all checks out well at this point, move back through the engine compartment, starting with the battery. The main contacts should be cleaned of all buildup. Even if they appear to be clean, the connections should be removed and both the terminals on the battery and the connecting lugs scraped and cleaned and then fitted together again with tight connections. Check the contact which is made between the negative terminal of the storage battery and the frame of the automobile. This is a large nut and bolt type of arrangement and does not usually present any problems, but a high resistance condition at this point will cause a low-voltage condition within the electrical system and will probably create a condition where the battery will be unable to receive the charge. This condition has led many people to suspect a burnt cell or other type of battery defect, because the condition existed when the battery terminals actually were clean and making good contact. The problem was not readily discerned and corrected.

A further examination should be made of the spark plug connecting wires and at all points around the starter control mechanism, the voltage regulator and alternator. Any signs of loose connections when the wiring is pulled or moved should be corrected immediately. Examine the wiring which passes through the fire wall. Sometimes the protective grommets which are fitted through the holes in the firewall to prevent cutting of the wiring insulation will slip through. The insulating material on the elctrical wiring may be rubbed and eventually cause a short circuit.

The underframe of the automobile should be given a very close inspection. The wiring which passes under the automobile gets the most wear and tear and this portion of the electrical system is the most difficult to properly examine, parly due to its location and partly to the fact that the cables are generally dirty and insulation breaks are hard to discover.

Be certain to check for any signs of wiring harness breaks, especially in the small clips or connectors which hold the wiring firmly against the automobile chassis. When these break, the wiring is allowed to hang free and rub against sharp metal edges causing an abrasive condition to the insulation.

The final check of the electrical system can be made at the rear of the automobile in the trunk at the connections to the rear lights. Sometimes the plastic light covers develop small holes or may allow water to enter the lighting compartment around the cover edges. This can cause short circuits in the electrical system which are often hard to trace and to correct. Any signs of cracking or breaking of these protective covers should be corrected by replacement of the offending cover.

The external portion of the electrical system has now been thoroughly checked. The internal portion or the part of the electrical system which lies within the automobile cockpit may now be examined. The wiring in this section does not receive the same abuse that the external wiring does, but it is not as rugged as the external wiring and problems can exist.

Wet weather conditions contribute to internal electrical problems, because water is often brought into the cockpit when doors are opened and passengers enter with wet shoes and garments. Most of the internal wiring is located under the dash panel where all of the wet shoes usually end up sooner or later.

The first point of examination should be the fuse block which is normally located on the driver's side of the cockpit to the left of the steering wheel. Many of these compartments now have protective covers, but many do not. Fuses can be accidentally kicked out of place causing a ceasing of operations in one or more circuits within the electrical system. Connecting wires which attach to the fuse block can also be pulled free or their insulation scraped. Also check the block to make certain that a firm mechanical connection to the firewall exists. The screws or bolts which hold the block to this point can work loose and vibrate or move while the vehicle is being operated and cause wiring breakage.

If all appears in order at the fuse block, examine the other wiring which is run for the instrument lights and the various accessories offered on the automobile. Remember, any connection, no matter how minor, which may eventually present a short or a high resistance joint can cause the entire system or a major part of it to fail, and in some instances, fires can even be started. At the very least, a more expensive repair job will exist if the problem is allowed to continue to a point of inoperation.

After this portion of the inspection is completed, any other obvious inspection points not covered in the discussion should be checked. Broken or worn wiring insulation can be easily repaired by using all-weather electrical tape. Connectors which are broken or fit loosely can be replaced with parts from a local automotive store. Every part in the automobile electrical system is always connected in some way with all of the others and malfunctions can create problems for all of the other components. Do not allow any part or point in the electrical system to go unexamined or unrepaired. Think of the system as one large continuous loop and any break or change in the loop will terminate the loop's operation.

Replacement connectors and harness fasteners should be only of high-quality construction and intended for automotive type uses. Components of this type must be able to withstand extreme conditions. Failure of a component could mean expensive repairs at the least and, in a worst case example, dangerous operating conditions for the occupants of the automobile.

When one type of component is substituted for another, make certain that this is an acceptable substitution. Common sense may be all that is needed in making the decision on many substitutions, but when in doubt, check with the maker or supplier of a particular component as to its use in the mode intended. If doubt still exists, use the specified component.

There is always a danger factor to be considered when working with automobile storage batteries. Hydrogen sulfide is produced by the acid interior of many batteries and can explode under certain conditions. Never smoke around a storage battery especially when the fill caps have been removed. Avoid undue generation of electrical sparks in the area of the battery also. The explosion which can result from the stored gases in the average storage battery can be of a nature which is powerful enough to literally blow the front end out of the automobile. Use the proper caution a device of this type demands.

TROUBLESHOOTING

Here are seven electrical system problem examples and steps to take in finding solutions. Don't be discouraged if you don't find the trouble immediately. There are many possible causes for electrical system difficulties.

Problem A: Starter Motor Refuses To Operate

1. Determine where the problem lies by observing instrument lights. If the alternator generator indicator light is operative but dims or goes out completely when the starter switch is engaged, the problem may lie in dirty or faulty battery connections. Place the transmission in reverse temporarily. If the alternator or engine temperature indicator lights dim or go out, due to the current drawn to operate the backup lights, this practically assures that the problem is the battery connections.

2. Remove the battery clamps from the terminals and thoroughly clean the posts and the connectors until the respective surfaces are shiny. Replace these connections and tighten them securely. Attempt to start the engine.

3. If step number two fails, inspect the battery cables from their connections at the battery to the connection points on the engine and the car chassis, respectively. Tighten these connections and clean any suspiciously dirty or corroded points. If the engine fails to start at this point, the battery may be suspect or a defective switch could be the problem with the starter motor. The fact that the panel lights dim or go out when the electrical system draws heavier currents, however, almost always points to a minor, high-resistance problem at the battery.

Problem B: Fuse Blows Instantaneously When Replaced

1. Determine what accessories or components are on the circuit in which the fuse is located by referring to the wiring diagram of the automobile or by observing which portions of the electrical system fail to operate. Printing on the fuse block will often identify the circuit.

2. Make certain that the fuse used as a replacement was of the correct size and type for the circuit.

3. Make certain that no additional accessories or modifications have been added to the original circuits. Additional electrical components could draw more current than the circuit was intended to safely handle.

4. If all seems correct at this point, a short circuit exists somewhere in the circuit. This problem may be caused by a *hot* wire with bare insulation coming in contact with the chassis or may even be caused by a defective electrical component such as a radio, tape player, etc. If any components have been acting erratically, these should be examined first.

5. Inspect all wiring coming from the fuse block to the components on the circuit. Signs of bare insulation, burnt marks or other discolorations should be examined closely and repaired.

6. If fuse failure still occurs, various electrical components may be temporarily removed from the circuit. To continually test the circuit by replacing fusing and waiting to see if they blow when the circuit is activated can become expensive, so an ohmmeter may be brought into service. The leads of the ohmmeter are placed across the hot side of the fuse block and the automobile chassis or negative lead. During conditions of a dead short, the reading should be less than one ohm and will probably read zero. As components are removed from the circuit, the ohmmeter readings are noted. When the reading suddenly increases, the defective component or trouble area has been found. Replacing or repairing the defective part or defective conductor will completely cure the problem and a fuse may be inserted and operation continued as usual.

Note: This procedure is to be used only when the fuse blows immediately upon being placed in the activated circuit. Sometimes, defective components can cause fuse failure after a few minutes of, apparently, normal operation. This condition points to a component and completely precludes the possibility of its being any problem in the actual wiring. When a condition such as that just described exists, the electronics of the automobile are most suspect and the problem can be found by removing these components, one at a time, from the circuit. The defective electronic component should be repaired immediately. Never attempt to remedy this or any other overload problem by replacing the blown fuse with one of a higher ampere rating. This could cause circuit overloading and is the main cause of automobile fires in the United States.

Problem C: Headlight Blinks On and Off While Vehicle Is In Motion

1. Raise the hood and examine the connection at the back of the headlight which is operating erratically. A loose connection at this point is most likely the problem. Shake this connection to test for any excess play. If the connection appears to be tight, pull it loose from the headlight and examine it and the headlight connections for any signs of dirt, corrosion or other foreign materials which might create a high resistance connection.

2. If the problem still persists, suspect a faulty fuse block or wiring connection leading to the headlight. On many automobiles, the headlight fuse is located a short distance from the light inside of a line fuse holder. If the spring in the holder has been damaged, the intermittent connection problem may be originating from this point. Examine the connectors and the fuse holder for any signs of undue looseness. Often, if a fuse of the wrong length is placed in this type of holder, intermittent operation can result.

3. If the first two steps do not solve the problem, suspect a defective piece of wiring between the light and the switch. This problem must occur at a point which involves only the wiring to the one headlight since the problem being discussed is common to only one headlight.

4. Any further problems indicate a defective headlight which should be replaced immediately.

Problem D: Headlamps Are Dim or
Switch Intermittently From Bright To Dim

This problem does not involve lights switching from low-beam to high-beam or vise-versa, but is indicated by a slight to moderate dimming of the normal lamp brilliance.

1. This problem is often caused by a dirty or defective connector at the headlights involved. Examine the connectors and make certain that they are making good, tight connections with the mounting pins on the headlights. Make certain that no dirt or foreign matter is caked on any of these connection points.

2. A loose ground wire is often responsible for a problem such as this and all ground connections for the lighting and the light circuit should be examined and corrected as problems are discovered.

3. A defective headlight will rarely cause a problem such as the one described, but if all else fails, replacement of the lamp or lamps involved may remedy the problem.

4. If the problem only occurs during wet-weather conditions, poor insulation or component casing cracks may be a cause. Problems such as these allow moisture to seep into the component connectors and the wiring associated with the lighting circuit. Unusual problems such as the dimming discussed may result.

Problem E: All Headlights Are Completely Inoperative

1. Make certain that other electrical circuits in the automobile are operative such as the cockpit lights, radio, starter motor, etc. Failure of these devices to operate properly will usually indicate a defective or discharged storage battery or other problem related to this area of the electrical system. If the problem lies here, the procedures specified in problem A should be followed.

2. Check all connections at the fuse block or in-line fuse connector and examine all associated wiring coming from the main headlight circuit from the point where the wiring splits to connect both sets of lamps. Make certain the fuse is intact and making proper contact with the associated wiring.

3. Closely examine all wiring connections at the light switch and at the dimmer switch. Signs of burned contacts at these switches can indicate a defective or malfunctioning switch or a possible short circuit at these points. An ohmmeter can be used to determine whether or not these switches are working properly, but a voltmeter or the voltmeter position on your measuring instrument may be effectively used to determine whether or not current is being delivered past the switches.

4. If all switches are operating as required, the voltmeter should be used to trace the path of the current which will be indicated by a voltage reading of about 12 volts when the engine is not operating—13.8 to 14.8 volts during operation.

5. A break which is found in the circuit can be repaired with a wiring connector of the squeeze-lock type which may then be wrapped with an insulating tape of the weather-proofed variety.

6. An alternate method of checking a problem when speed is of the utmost necessity and no switch problems are suspected is to activate the headlight switch and begin the troubleshooting procedure by taking voltage measurements at the headlights. Continue taking these readings throughout the system back toward the source voltage or storage battery until the problem is discovered.

7. Once a problem is found and repaired, proper operation may still not be obtained. Headlamps draw relatively large amounts of current. When a short or other problem occurs, several points in the circuit may be rendered inoperative or damaged. Often, repairs will be required at several points along the headlamp circuit before correct operation is restored. An initial repair of a shorted switch may create partial operation of the lights or operation which is very dim. Continued checking and repair of the system will bring about correct operation. When the main problem of no operation whatsoever has been corrected and a dimming condition or other improper operation exists, simply refer to the problem in this text which comes closest to describing the condition which remains and follow that procedure. For example: if complete inoperation is the problem, follow the procedures in the discussion under problem E of this chapter until the condition stated "complete inoperation" is corrected. If normal operation is the result, no further work is required, but if the lights are, for instance, operating only when on dim, refer to the discussion under problem D. In this manner, complete restoration of correct headlight operation will be the end result.

Problem F: Dimmer Switch Inoperative

1. This is a very simple problem to troubleshoot because the trouble will almost always lie in the switch or in the associated wiring between the switch and the headlights. First, check the switch with a voltmeter. If no voltage is indicated, the switch is defective, either in the high-beam or low-beam position and should be replaced.

2. If no problem is indicated at the switch, the wiring from that component to the headlights is not connected properly or has become shorted or corroded at some point in the circuit. Visually inspect this wiring and, if the problem is not apparent, take readings between the switch and the

headlights with an ohmmeter. Note: when an ohmmeter is used to check the resistance in an electrical circuit, no power should be applied to the circuit at the time of measurement. A high or infinite resistance between the switch and the headlight indicates a broken wire or a poor contact. Examine all connectors and clean any suspicious looking areas until operation is restored.

3. Any problems, no matter how minor, with the dimmer switch should be corrected immediately. Even though improper operation may be occurring only on rare occasions, it must be remembered that if this switch suddenly becomes completely inoperative, all headlight operation may cease. Replace any suspicious switches or other components at the first sign of improper operation.

Problem G: Lamps Burn Out Frequently

1. Make certain that the correct lamps are being used. Refer to the owner's manual.

2. Make certain that all lamps involved are not subject to intermittent operation. Constant switching from on to off can severely shorten the life of light bulbs.

3. Using a DC voltmeter, measure the voltage at the input to the lamps in question while the engine is running. Observe this voltage reading. Rev the engine to rpm rate which is equal to the average rpm encountered in normal driving. Observe this reading on the meter. If excessively high voltage is present during any of these readings, the voltage regulator is probably defective and should be replaced or repaired. Nominal voltage readings should not be in excess of 15 volts while the engine is running.

4. If none of the above steps correct the problem, examine the mounting brackets and housing of the lamp or lamps in question. Severe vibration can be created when one of these mounts becomes loose or defective. This type of vibration can cause the delicate filaments in the lamps to open up and fail to operate on a regular basis.

OTHER PROBLEMS AND THEIR CURES

Following are three more common electrical system difficulties and steps to take in rectifying them.

Engine Misses and is Hard to Start During Wet-Weather Conditions

The problem is due to water or moisture particles entering the electrical system. Replace spark plug wires if defective. Make certain the distributor cap is sealing properly (Fig. 7-4). Examine entire ignition system for any signs of worn insulation or obvious cracks in components.

Courtesy Lights Flicker And Operate Intermittently

A defective switch which is located in the door channel or a dirty or corroded lamp base or socket are the most likely causes. Examine the lamp base and socket and clean these points until they are smooth and shiny. Make certain that the contact which lies inside the socket shell is also free of foreign matter. If the problem persists, the switch should be removed and examined for signs of breakage or bad or broken contacting wires. A break may also have occurred in the conductors leading to the switch from the battery or in the conductors leading to the lamp. Make certain that a good ground connection is being obtained as a corroded ground wire may also cause a problem. If all else fails, try replacing the lamp. This works in only a small percentage of cases, but may sometimes be depended upon to effect a cure.

Electrical Noise is Present in Radio

This is a very difficult problem to solve in many instances because many factors may be contributing to the trouble. Make certain that the electrical system is in good physical condition, with all wiring secure. The electronic device may have a noise suppressor already installed which has become defective, so if the problem suddenly presents itself, the radio should be operated in another location which is known to be noise free. Examine the alternator for any signs of defects. Alternator trouble or noise will be heard in the radio as a whine which changes with the rpm rate of the engine.

Another noise problem is heard as a static crack in the speaker every few seconds and can be caused by ground differentials within the automobile chassis. Often, a loose tailpipe will swing back and forth making contact with parts of the chassis and cause this type of problem. Bonding the tailpipe to the chassis will quickly rectify this problem. Other loose metal parts which vibrate severely when the vehicle is in motion may cause the same difficulty.

Another noise problem is heard in the speaker as a frying sound only when the vehicle is moving. This problem occurs only on paved roads and is not present when traveling over gravel, mud or any

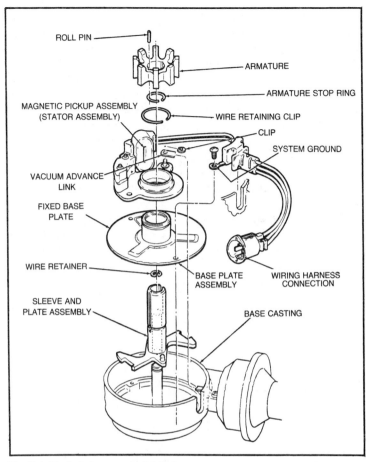

Fig. 7-4. Typical dura spark distributor.

other unpaved surface. The noise is created by a static build-up on the tire which is conducted to the axle of the automobile. Many automotive stores carry a type of anti-static powder which is injected into the tires through the air valve and will alleviate this problem.

Many problems which are not directly covered in this discussion can be solved by performing the preventive maintenance required and by following a set of procedures which are used to correct a similar situation. While the discussion on lamp failures dealt mainly with the headlights, problems with brake, tail, or back-up lights should be solved in the same manner.

A good point to remember when solving electrical problems in an automobile is not to discount a mechanical malfunction as well. When all logical procedures for correcting apparent electrical trouble have been tried and it still exists, mechanical housings and connections should be considered. The steps offered in this text present a practical and logical method for troubleshooting and solving electrical problems. If these steps do not correct the problem, the analysis you have used may be incorrect. It should be remembered, however, that very unusual situations can develop which are rare and almost never encountered. These may tax the troubleshooting abilities of the repairman, but by using common sense and proper troubleshooting techniques offered here, these special cases will be eventually solved.

Always remember the safety aspects when working on the electrical system. High voltages are generated in the ignition system and, while these voltages rarely cause any direct accidents, they have been known to cause repairmen and mechanics to pull away from accidental contact and do harm to themselves by slamming into lifts, cables and even other persons. Then, too, the battery is subject to explosion should a match or other flame ignite the gases created by the electrolyte in the case. Use the proper techniques, take the proper precautions and this job is as safe as any other automotive troubleshooting.

Chapter 8

Exhaust Systems

When the exhaust valve opens just before the piston completes the power stroke, pressure in the cylinder at this time causes the exhaust gas to rush into the exhaust manifold. The upward movement of the piston on its exhaust stroke then expels most of the remaining gas. This exhaust gas then is routed through exhaust pipes and muffler and is expelled through the tail pipe.

When installing a new exhaust system, care should be taken to have the correct alignment and relationship of the components to each other. Particular care should be given to the installation of the exhaust pipe and crossover pipe assembly on V-8 engine single exhaust systems. Incorrectly assembled parts of the exhaust system are frequently the cause of annoying noises and rattles due to improper clearances or obstructions to the normal flow of gases. Leave all clamp bolts and muffler strap bolts loose until all parts are properly aligned and then tighten, working from front to rear.

New packings and nuts should always be used to install the exhaust pipe to the manifold. Be sure to clean the manifold stud threads with a wire brush before installing the new nuts.

SERVICE DIAGNOSIS

Excessive exhaust noise is one of the most common problems that occurs to exhaust systems. Begin troubleshooting the exhaust system by inspecting all pipe joints for leaks. Tighten clamps at all leaking joints. Move to the muffler and examine for burned or blown out muffler. Most modern mufflers are made of long-life aluminum or stainless steel and most last as long as the average car. However, some do blow occasionally, and these should be replaced.

Check for a leaking exhaust pipe at the manifold flange. If a leak is found, install a new gasket and tighten the exhaust pipe flange nuts to about 35 foot-pounds—using a torque wrench. While examing the manifold, look for cracks or broken places. A new manifold will have to be installed if any cracks are found. If a leak between the manifold and cylinder block is detected, tighten manifold to the cylinder block nuts to about 30 foot-pounds or as specified in the manufacturer's shop manual.

Leaking exhaust gases occur at joints, damaged or improperly installed gaskets, or if there are restrictions in the muffler or tail pipe. Examine all of these locations, tighten clamps at any leaking joints, replace gaskets as necessary, and remove any restrictions if possible; if not, replace the muffler.

When an engine is hard to warm up or it will not return to normal idle, the heat control valve could be frozen in the open position. To correct, free up the manifold heat control valve vent with a suitable solvent.

An unusual noise in the manifold could be an indication of a broken thermostat or a weak, broken or missing anti-rattle spring. In either case, the defective parts should be replaced.

In general, the exhaust system must be free of leaks, binding, grounding and excessive vibrations. These conditions are usually caused by loose, broken or misaligned clamps, shields, brackets or pipes. Therefore, if any of these conditions exist, check the exhaust system components and alignment. Adjust or replace as necessary to maintain the specified clearances by referring to illustrations of each part in the manufacturer's service (shop) manuals.

DESCRIPTION AND APPLICATION OF EXHAUST SYSTEMS

Factory-installed single exhaust systems on modern vehicles consist of a catalytic converter, inlet pipe assembly, muffler and supporting hangers as shown in Fig. 8-1. Dual exhaust systems used with some V-8 engines consist of two one-piece catalytic converters and inlet pipe assemblies connecting the exhaust manifolds to the muffler inlet pipe, which is connected to the muffler. Some dual systems are equipped with a resonator while some are not. Fig. 8-2 shows a typical dual exhaust system.

Exhaust shields are not subject to repair other than replacing missing or damaged attaching parts such as clamps or screws, and removing debris that may collect in the shield area. If an exhaust

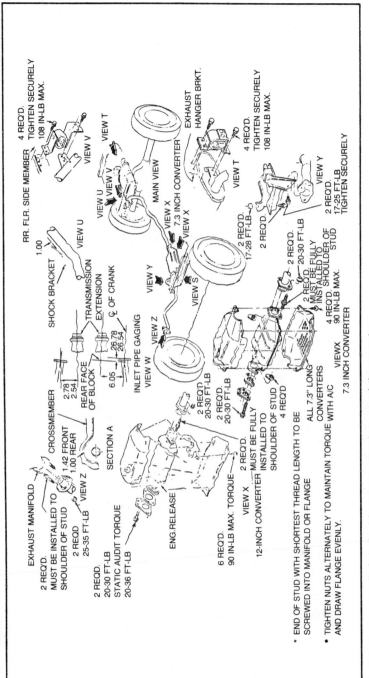

Fig. 8-1. Factory-installed single exhaust system using a catalytic converter.

141

shield is damaged or shows evidence of deterioration, it should be replaced rather than repaired.

Removal/installation procedures are, in most cases, a matter of removing the shield attachments and shield; installing is the reverse process using new parts. The illustrations found in most shop manuals indicate the types and proper positioning of exhaust shields and clamps.

Catalytic converters need not be replaced just because they have broken studs, stripped threads or loose nuts. The following is recommended for repairing these fasteners:

Converters With Threaded Flanges. Remove damaged studs and install new studs or a bolt of suitable length. If the flange thread has minor damage, retap the hole with the proper size tap. If the flange thread cannot be repaired, resize the hole with a drill and use a new diameter bolt of suitable length and a locking nut.

Converters With Loose Clinch Or Weld Nuts. Remove the loose nut and dress the flange surface upon which the bolt and washer will rest. Fasten the joint with a suitable bolt, lock nut and flat washer between the bolt head and the dressed flange surface.

I-4 SINGLE EXHAUST SYSTEM

All four-cylinder I-4 engines such as those used for Ford Pinto, Bobcat, etc., use a single-pipe type exhaust system. Factory installed exhaust systems have two pieces for a non-converter system and three pieces for a converter system. The non-converter system has an inlet pipe which connects to the engine exhaust manifold, and a muffler inlet pipe, muffler and tailpipe all welded together. On catalytic converter systems, the converter assembly is a bolt-on unit connected between the inlet pipe and the muffler. Flat flange connections are used between the inlet pipe and the converter, while ball joint connections are used between the converter and the muffler.

The exhaust system is usually serviced in three pieces for a non-converter system and four pieces for a converter system. The rear section of the muffler inlet pipe is furnished separate from the muffler in most cases.

V-6 SINGLE EXHAUST SYSTEM

Most V-6 engines are equipped with a single exhaust system as shown in Fig. 8-3. This system consists of a welded "Y" pipe, one catalytic converter and either a muffler assembly or muffler and resonator assembly. The exhaust system is serviced in separate

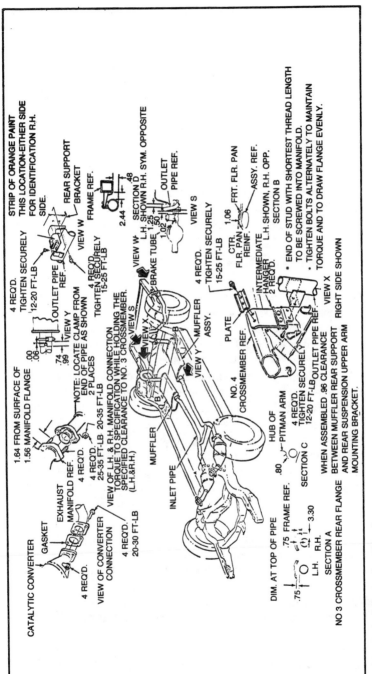

CATALYTIC CONVERTER

GASKET

EXHAUST MANIFOLD REF.

1.64 FROM SURFACE OF
1.56 MANIFOLD FLANGE

4 REQ'D.

4 REQ'D. 25-35 FT-LB 20-35 FT-LB

VIEW OF L.H. & R.H. MANIFOLD CONNECTION
TORQUE TO SPECIFICATION WHILE HOLDING THE
SPECIFIED CLEARANCE TO NO. 3 CROSSMEMBER.
(L.H.&R.H.)

NOTE: LOCATE CLAMP FROM
END OF PIPE AS SHOWN
2 PLACES

VIEW OF CONVERTER
CONNECTION

4 REQ'D.
20-30 FT-LB

4 REQ'D.
TIGHTEN SECURELY
12-20 FT-LB

OUTLET PIPE
REF.

VIEW Y

.00
.06
.74
.99

REAR SUPPORT
BRACKET

STRIP OF ORANGE PAINT
THIS LOCATION-EITHER SIDE
FOR IDENTIFICATION R.H.
SIDE.

FRAME REF.

VIEW W

4 REQ'D.
TIGHTEN SECURELY
15-25 FT-LB

SECTION D
L.H. SHOWN R.H. SYM. OPPOSITE

2.44
.48

OUTLET
PIPE REF.

VIEW W

BRAKE TUBE

VIEW S

1.25
1.02
.50

VIEW S

VIEW X

MUFFLER
ASSY.

PLATE

VIEW Y

B

4 REQ'D.
TIGHTEN SECURELY
15-25 FT-LB

FRT. FLR. PAN

1.06

CTR.
FLR. PAN
REINF.

ASSY. REF.

L.H. SHOWN, R.H. OPP.
SECTION B

INTERMEDIATE
HANGER
2 REQ'D.

* END OF STUD WITH SHORTEST THREAD LENGTH
TO BE SCREWED INTO MANIFOLD.
• TIGHTEN BOLTS ALTERNATELY TO MAINTAIN
TORQUE AND TO DRAW FLANGE EVENLY.

VIEW X
RIGHT SIDE SHOWN

MUFFLER

INLET PIPE

NO. 4
CROSSMEMBER REF.

.80

HUB OF
PITMAN ARM

SECTION C

4 REQ'D.
TIGHTEN SECURELY
12-20 FT-LB-OUTLET PIPE REF.

WHEN ASSEMBLED .96 CLEARANCE
BETWEEN MUFFLER REAR SUPPORT
AND REAR SUSPENSION UPPER ARM
MOUNTING BRACKET.

DIM. AT TOP OF PIPE

.75 FRAME REF.

(†) 3.30

.75 L.H. R.H.

SECTION A
NO 3 CROSSMEMBER REAR FLANGE

Fig. 8-2. Typical dual exhaust system.

143

pieces consisting of an inlet pipe, catalytic converter, resonator and inlet pipe assembly.

SIX-CYLINDER ENGINES

All I-6 (L-6) engines have basically the same type of single muffler exhaust system. These systems have a resonator inlet pipe, resonator, resonator outlet pipe and a muffler. On some systems, a catalytic converter is used between the resonator inlet pipe and the resonator.

V-8 SINGLE EXHAUST SYSTEMS

The basic single exhaust system used with most V-8 engines consists of a muffler, a resonator and/or diffuser. This basic system is subject to the addition of one or two catalytic converters.

V-8 DUAL EXHAUST SYSTEMS

The dual-pipe exhaust systems—without resonators—are all of the same basic design. The H-shaped inlet pipe on most factory installations is a welded assembly.

Normal service parts procedure is to furnish the H-pipe as a single, welded assembly. The muffler and outlet pipe are serviced separately and assembled with clamps.

Dual exhaust system with resonators consists of a welded H-pipe assembly connected to two welded muffler-resonator assemblies. Two catalytic converters are also connected to most dual exhaust systems on modern vehicles. These converters are located between the exhaust manifold and the inlet "H" pipe.

For service replacement, the H pipe is furnished as a single welded assembly, but the muffler/resonator and outlet pipe are available separately.

EXHAUST MANIFOLD

To remove the exhaust manifold for inspection or cleaning, disconnect spark plug cables from spark plugs and remove any other components that are in the way of the manifold; the alternator on Chrysler products is one example. Disconnect the exhaust pipe at exhaust manifold flanges and then remove the nuts that hold the exhaust manifolds to the cylinder heads. Slide the manifolds off studs and away from cylinder heads.

Clean exhaust manifolds in solvent and then blow dry with compressed air before inspecting for cracks and distortion. Also check the heat control valve for free operation. If it's necessary to

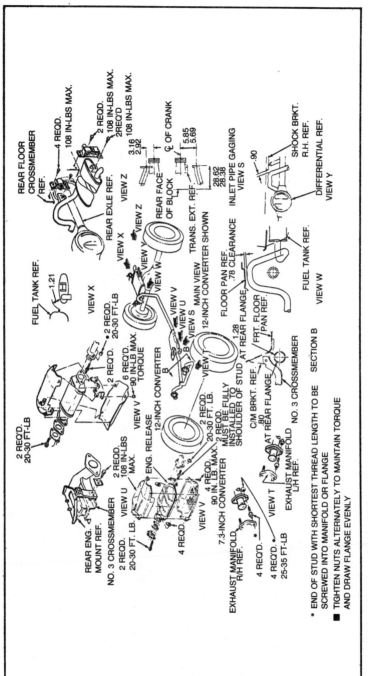

Fig. 8-3. Single exhaust system for V-6 engine.

free up the valve, apply a suitable manifold heat control valve solvent to both ends of the valve shaft. Be sure the manifold is cool before solvent is applied and then allow the solvent to soak a few minutes to dissolve deposits. Then work the valve back and forth until it turns freely.

To reassemble, note whether the studs came out with the nuts when the manifold was removed. If so, new studs should be installed with sealer applied on the coarse thread ends. If this precaution is not taken, water leaks may develop at the studs.

Continue by connecting the manifolds to the cylinder heads. No gaskets are needed, but the stud nuts should be tightened to 30 foot-pounds. Install any equipment or components removed during disassembly, and then reconnect spark plug wires.

The general servicing for intake manifolds includes the cleaning of the manifold in solvent and then blowing dry with compressed air. Inspect exhaust crossover passages and pressure test for leakage into any of the intake passages. Inspect mating surfaces for parallelism and use new gaskets when reinstalling intake manifolds.

Operation of the manifold heat control valve in exhaust manifolds should be inspected periodically. With the engine idling, accelerate momentarily to wide open throttle. The counterweight—found on many models—should respond by moving perhaps as much as ½ inch and then returning to its original position. If no movement is observed, the shaft is binding due to accumulation of deposits or the thermostat is weak or broken.

The application of a suitable manifold heat control valve solvent, every six months, to both ends of the manifold heat control valve shaft at the bushings, will keep the valve working freely. The solvent should be applied when the engine is cool and allowed to soak a few minutes to dissolve the deposits. Then, work the valve back and forth until it turns freely.

GENERAL SERVICE PROCEDURES

To remove exhaust pipes, muffler, and tail pipes from most vehicles, the vehicle must first be raised on a hoist and then the nuts and bolts should be lubricated with penetrating oil to loosen rust and corrosion. Remove clamps from exhaust pipe, muffler and tail and disconnect all ball joint connections in the exhaust pipes. Disconnect the exhaust pipe at exhaust manifolds and remove the exhaust pipe. Remove muffler, extension pipe and tail pipe assembly. If only the muffler is to be replaced, cut the extension at the muffler with a hack saw or cutter, as it is not necessary to remove this pipe. The replacement muffler can be installed, using a clamp at the front of the muffler.

Chapter 9

Clutch And Transmission System

A means of delivering engine torque to the wheels is achieved by the transmission. The rotational speeds of the engine are modified in a controllable way in the transmission before this power is delivered to the drive wheels.

Both automatic and standard transmissions are gear-boxes fitted with gears which are designed to deliver various ranges of speeds to the vehicle's drive shaft. Each set of gears forms a pair—a driving gear which comes from the crankshaft of the engine, and a driven gear which is connected to the driveshaft. The first gear is designed to operate at relatively low vehicle speeds. This combination will consist of a small driving gear and a driven gear which is almost three times the diameter of the first. Many rotations of the drive gear—attached to the crankshaft—are required to cause the driven gear to rotate only once. In this manner, engine speed is increased to turn the driveshaft and wheels of a vehicle throughout the initial low speeds involved in the beginning of movement. In a vehicle equipped with a manual transmission, this example will correspond to the first gear.

As the gearing advances from first to second and so on, the ratio of the drive gear to the driven gear becomes smaller and less crankshaft rotations are required to cause wheel or drive rotation for the automobile. Figure 9-1 depicts a cross-section of a typical transmission.

Many components make up the transmission and clutch mechanisms in an automobile. In this discussion, each of the major parts will be dealt with as to its function in the drive train.

THE CLUTCH

Vehicles equipped with a manual transmission need some control to transfer the torque from the engine to the driveshaft. The device used is called a clutch (Fig. 9-2). Clutches depend on friction for their operation, whether it be solid friction as in the conventional clutch, or fluid friction and inertia as utilized in the fluid coupling and torque converter. The fluid coupling serves the same purpose as the conventional clutch, but the difference in the principle of operation makes it necessary to discuss the two mechanisms separately.

In general, a clutch in an automotive vehicle provides a means of connecting and disconnecting the engine from the power transmission system. Since the internal combustion engine does not develop a high starting torque, it must be disconnected from the power train and allowed to operate without load until it develops enough torque to overcome the inertia of the vehicle when starting from rest. The application of the engine power to the load must be gradual to provide smooth engagement and to lessen the shock on the driving parts. After engagement, the clutch must transmit all the engine power to the transmission without slipping. Furthermore, it is desirable to disconnect the engine from the power train during the time the gears in the transmission are being shifted from one gear ratio to another.

The transmission of power through the clutch is accomplished by bringing one or more rotating drive members secured to the crankshaft into gradual contact with one or more driven members secured to the unit being driven. These members are either stationary or rotating at different speeds. Contact is established and maintained by strong spring pressure controlled by the driver through the clutch pedal and suitable linkage. As spring pressure increases, the friction increases and less slippage occurs until, when the full spring pressure is applied, the speed of the driving and driven members is the same. All slipping has stopped and there is, in effect, a direct connection between the driving and driven parts.

Clutch Components

The principal parts of a clutch are: the driving members, attached to the engine and turning with it; the driven members, attached to the transmission and turning with it; the operating members, which include the spring or springs; and the linkage

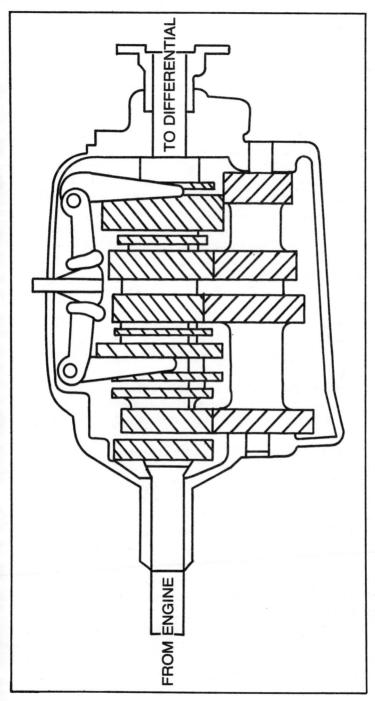

Fig. 9-1. Cross section of a typical automotive transmission.

149

required to apply and release the pressure holding the driving and driven members in contact with each other (Fig. 9-2).

The driving members of a clutch usually consists of two iron plates which are machined and ground to a smooth finish. One of these surfaces is usually the rear face of the engine flywheel, and the other is a comparatively heavy flat ring with one side machined flat and smooth. This part is known as the pressure plate and is fitted into a steel cover which also contains some of the operating members, and is bolted to the flywheel.

The driven member is a disc with a splined hub which is free to slide lengthwise along the splines of the clutch shaft, but which drives the shaft through these same splines. Grooves on both sides of the clutch driven plate lining prevent sticking of the plate to the flywheel and pressure plate due to vacuum between the members on disengaging. The clutch driven plate is usually made of spring steel in the shape of a single flat disc consisting of a number of flat segments. Suitable frictional facings are attached to each side of the plate by means of brass rivets. These facings must be heat resistant since friction produces heat. The most commonly used facings are made of cotton and asbestos fibers woven or molded together and impregnated with resins or similar binding agents. Very often, copper wires are woven or pressed into material to give it additional strength.

In order to make clutch engagement as smooth as possible, the steel segments attached to the splined hub are slightly waved, which also causes the facings to make gradual contact as the waved springs flatten out.

The driven member of the clutch is usually provided with a flexible center to absorb the torsional vibration of the crankshaft, which would be transmitted to the power train unless it were eliminated. The flexible center usually takes the form of steel compression springs placed between the hub and the steel plate. This arrangement permits the plate to rotate slightly backward as the springs decompress. This slight backward and forward rotation permitted by the springs allows the clutch shaft to rotate at a more uniform rate than the crankshaft, thereby eliminating some vibration from the crankshaft and preventing the vibration from being carried back through the transmission.

The driving and driven members are held in contact by spring pressure. This pressure may be exerted by a one-piece conical or diaphragm spring or a number of small helical springs located around the outer portion of the pressure plate. In the diaphragm design clutch, the throwout bearing moves forward against the spring

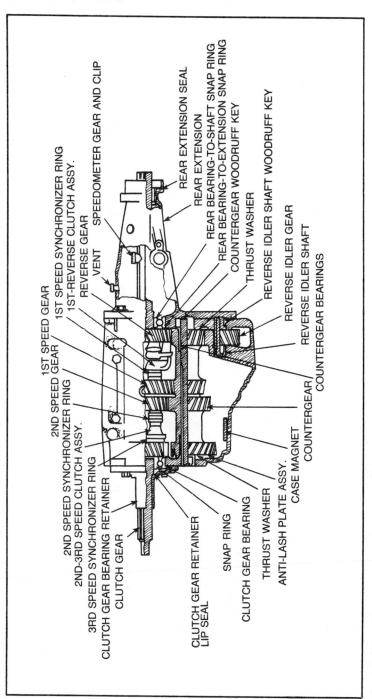

Fig. 9-2. Manual transmission and clutch arrangement.

REAR EXTENSION SEAL
REAR EXTENSION
REAR BEARING-TO-SHAFT SNAP RING
REAR BEARING-TO-EXTENSION SNAP RING
COUNTERGEAR WOODRUFF KEY
THRUST WASHER
REVERSE IDLER SHAFT WOODRUFF KEY
REVERSE IDLER GEAR
REVERSE IDLER SHAFT
COUNTERGEAR BEARINGS
REVERSE GEAR BEARINGS
COUNTERGEAR
CASE MAGNET
ANTI-LASH PLATE ASSY.
THRUST WASHER
CLUTCH GEAR BEARING
SNAP RING
CLUTCH GEAR RETAINER LIP SEAL
CLUTCH GEAR
CLUTCH GEAR BEARING RETAINER
3RD SPEED SYNCHRONIZER RING
2ND SPEED SYNCHRONIZER RING
2ND-3RD SPEED CLUTCH ASSY.
2ND SPEED GEAR
1ST SPEED GEAR
1ST SPEED SYNCHRONIZER RING
1ST-REVERSE CLUTCH ASSY.
REVERSE GEAR
VENT
SPEEDOMETER GEAR AND CLIP

151

fingers, forcing the diaphragm spring to pivot around the inner pivot ring and dishing the fingers toward the flywheel. The outer circumference of the spring now lifts the pressure plate away from the driven disc through a series of retracting springs placed around the outer circumference of the pressure plate. In the helical-spring clutch, a system of levers pivoted on the cover forces the pressure plate away from the driven disc and against the pressure of the springs, thus performing the same function as the dish-shaped diaphragm spring.

The clutch release (throw-out) bearing is a ball-thrust bearing contained in the clutch housing, mounted on a sleeve attached to the front of the transmission case. The release bearing is connected through linkage to the clutch, and is moved by the release fork to engage the release levers and move the pressure plate to the rear. Clutch driving members are thus separated from the driven member when the clutch pedal is depressed by the driver. A return spring preloads clutch linkage, removing looseness due to wear. The clutch free pedal travel, therefore, will increase with linkage wear and decrease with driven disc wear. The free travel felt at the clutch pedal is throw-out bearing lash.

Clutch Operation

In diaphragm spring type clutches, a diaphragm is used instead of coil springs. It is a conical piece of spring steel punched to give it greater flexibility. The diaphragm is positioned between the cover and the pressure plate so that the diaphragm spring is nearly flat when the clutch is in the engaged position. The action of this type of spring is similar to that of the bottom of an ordinary oil can. The pressure of the outer rim of the spring on the pressure plate decreases as the flat position is passed. The outer rim of the diaphragm is secured to the pressure plate and is pivoted on rings approximately 1 inch in from the outer edge. The application of the pressure at the inner section will cause the outer rim to move away from the flywheel and draw the pressure plate away from the clutch disc, releasing or disengaging the clutch. When the pressure is released from the inner section, the oil-can action of the diaphragm causes the inner section to move out, and the movement of the outer rim forces the pressure plate against the clutch disc, thus engaging the clutch.

Coil springs are sometimes used in automotive clutches instead of a diaphragm spring. In this type of clutch, the driven disc is firmly clamped between the flywheel and the pressure plate by the pressure of the springs when the clutch is fully engaged. When the driver disengages the clutch by depressing the pedal, the release fork is moved on its pivot, and the pressure is applied to the release bearing. The rotating race of the release bearing presses against the clutch release levers and moves them on their pivot pins. The outer ends of the release levers, being fastened to the cover, move the pressure plate to the rear, compressing the clutch springs and allowing driving members to rotate independently of the driven member. The release fork moves only on its pivot, which contacts the clutch fork ball stud. All parts of the clutch, except the release bearing and collar, rotate with the flywheel when the clutch is engaged. When the clutch is disengaged, the release bearing rotates with the flywheel, but the driven plate and the clutch shaft rotate as dictated by the transmission gear range and vehicle speed.

CLUTCH PRELIMINARY INSPECTION

There are many things which affect good clutch operation. Therefore, it is necessary, before performing any major clutch operations, to make a preliminary inspection to determine whether or not the trouble is actually in the clutch.

1. Check the clutch pedal and make sure that the pedal has at least ¾ to 1 inch free travel.
2. Check the clutch pedal bushing for wear and for sticking on the shaft or loose mountings.
3. Lubricate the pedal linkage.
4. Tighten all front and rear engine mounting bolts. Should the mountings be oil-soaked, it will be necessary to replace them.

CLUTCH REMOVAL

The following clutch removal procedures are for most General Motors vehicles. However, the exact procedures may vary from vehicle to vehicle, so be sure to consult the manufacturer's shop manual before performing the operation.

1. Remove transmission as outlined in a later section of this chapter.
2. Disconnect clutch fork push rod and pull back spring.
3. Remove clutch and flywheel housing.
4. Remove the clutch fork by pressing it away from its ball mounting with a screwdriver, until the fork snaps loose from the ball. Remove the ball stud from rear of clutch housing. Remove throwout bearing from clutch fork. The retainer may be removed from the fork by prying out with a small screwdriver.

5. Before removing clutch from the flywheel, mark the flywheel, clutch cover and one pressure plate lug so that these parts may be assembled in their same relative positions, as they were balanced as an assembly.
6. Loosen the clutch attaching bolts one turn at a time to prevent distortion of clutch cover until the diaphragm spring is released.
7. Remove clutch pilot tool and clutch assembly from the vehicle.
8. Inspect the flywheel for cracks, heat checking, flatness and other defects.

DRIVE SHAFT AND DIFFERENTIAL

The majority of automobiles in use today utilize standard, rear-wheel drives. In this type of drive, power from the transmission is applied to the drive shaft. Normal driving presents certain stresses on a drive shaft which is directly coupled to the drive mechanism due to twists and bends that would be encountered. Therefore, the drive shaft is attached to flexible joints called universal joints. The differential contains these joints and is a metal housing which is normally located near the center of the rear wheels. The differential is basically a box of gears that directs power from the drive shaft to each wheel. When cornering, the wheel on the outside of the turn must rotate faster than the wheel located on the inside. The differential is designed in such a manner as to engage side gears which allows for the uneven rotation. This prevents the outside wheel from being dragged while negotiating a turn. The differential provides a 90-degree shift in drive angle as is presented by the drive shaft.

MANUAL TRANSMISSIONS

Since an internal combustion engine cannot develop appreciable torque at low speeds, a transmission is necessary to provide a means of varying the gear ratio between the engine and the rear wheels. The transmission also enables the engine to propel the vehicle under adverse conditions of load and furnishes the driver with a selection of vehicle speeds while the engine is held at speeds within the effective torque range. It furthermore allows disengaging and reversing the power flow from the engine to the wheels. Therefore, the transmission provides the driver with a selection of gear ratios between engine and wheels so that the vehicle can operate at best efficiency under a variety of driving conditions and loads.

Before attempting to repair the clutch, transmission or related linkages for any reason other than an obvious failure, the problem and probable cause should be identified. A large percentage of clutch and manual transmission problems are manifested by shifting difficulties such as high shift effort, gear clash and grinding or transmission blockout. However, the following checks and adjustments should be performed in the presented sequence before removing the clutch or transmission for repair.

Clutch Adjustment

1. The clutch free pedal travel adjustment should be made by adjusting the free play of the clutch pedal to ⅞-1 ⅛ inch. This is done by changing the length of the link between the throwout lever rod and the bell-crank assembly on most six cylinder and V8 engines.
2. Check clutch linkage for lost motion caused by loose or worn swivels, deflection of mounting brackets or damaged shaft.
3. Run the engine at a normal idle with transmission in neutral and clutch engaged. Disengage the clutch and wait about 10 seconds before shifting the transmission to reverse. No grinding noise should be heard. A grinding noise indicates incorrect clutch adjustment, lost motion clutch alignment, or internal problems such as failed dampers, facings, cushion springs, diaphragm spring fingers, pressure plate driver straps and the like.

Shift Linkage Adjustment

1. Remove the shift control rods from the column levers.
2. Check shift effort at the shift control lever knob. If an effort of more than two pounds is felt, adjust the steering column lower bearing as described in the shop manual for the particular vehicle.
3. Lubricate all rod and swivel connections and recheck shift effort after adjusting or replacing the lower bearing.
4. If shift linkage is free from binding, the column levers should be checked for end play with a .005 feeler gauge. This gauge should fit between the levers and control lever.
5. Connect control rods and check steering column control levers for alignment. In neutral, the column control lever tangs should line up with the slot in the main control lever.

All swivels, rods and mountings should be checked for lost motion and repaired or replaced as necessary. Transmission control levers should be checked for wear and repaired or replaced as necessary.

Transmission Shift Effort

1. Remove the shift rods at the transmission and align the sleeve, blocker ring and gear by shifting into the offending gear and then back into neutral.
2. Check the torque required to shift into gear with an inch pound torque wrench on the shift lever attaching bolt. Check the shop manual for the vehicle under test to determine the specified torque. If more than specified, the transmission shift lever should be checked for rust or dirt binding the lever.
3. Clean levers, lubricate and recheck the torque value. If the condition still exists, squirt an anti-chatter lubricant into the transmission through the filler plug.

When the above procedures have been checked and the problem still exists, the transmission will have to be removed and disassembled for further diagnosis. There are three basic types of transmission internal problems reflected by shifting effort: hard shifting, blockout and clash.

Cleaning and Inspection

When the transmission has been removed as described in the shop manual for the vehicle under diagnosis, wash all parts except the ball bearings and seals in a suitable cleaning solution. Brush or scrape all foreign matter from the parts, but be careful not to damage any parts with the scraper.

Rotate the ball bearings in a cleaning solvent until all lubricant is removed, and then dry it with compressed air. Lubricate the bearings with an approved transmission lubricant and warp them in a clean, lint-free cloth or paper until ready for use. The magnet in the bottom of the case should be cleaned with kerosene or mineral spirits.

When all parts are clean, inspect the transmission case for cracks, worn or damaged bearing bores, damaged threads, or any other damage that could affect the operation of the transmission.

Inspect the front face of the case for small nicks or burrs that could cause misalignment of the transmission with the flywheel housing. Remove all small nicks or burrs with a fine stone on cast iron cases, or with a fine file on aluminum cases.

Replace any cover that is bent or distorted and make certain that the vent hole in the cover is open. Check the condition of the shift levers at this time and also the forks, shift rails and the lever and shafts. Inspect the ball bearings and replace any that are broken, worn, or rough.

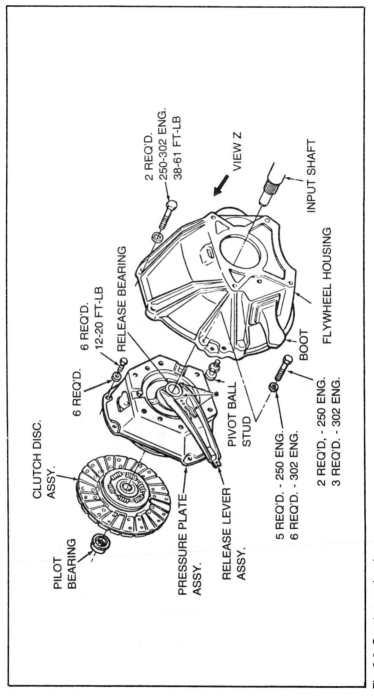

2 REQ'D.
250-302 ENG.
38-61 FT-LB

VIEW Z

INPUT SHAFT

6 REQ'D.
12-20 FT-LB
RELEASE BEARING

6 REQ'D.

CLUTCH DISC.
ASSY.

FLYWHEEL HOUSING

BOOT

PIVOT BALL
STUD

2 REQ'D. - 250 ENG.
3 REQ'D. - 302 ENG.

PRESSURE PLATE
ASSY.

RELEASE LEVER
ASSY.

5 REQ'D. - 250 ENG.
6 REQ'D. - 302 ENG.

PILOT
BEARING

Fig. 9-3. Countergear bearings.

157

Check the countershaft gear and if the teeth are chipped, broken, or worn, replace the defective part. Replace the countershaft if it is bent, scored or worn.

Replace the reverse idler gear or sliding gear if the teeth are defective and replace the idler gear shaft if bent, worn or scored. Also replace the input shaft and gear if the splines are damaged or if the teeth are chipped, worn or broken. If the roller bearing surface in the bore of the gear is worn or rough, or if the cone surface is damaged, replace the gear and the gear rollers. Replace all other gears that are chipped, broken or worn.

Check the synchronizer sleeves for free movement on their hubs. Make sure that the alignment marks (if present) are properly indexed. Continue by checking the synchronizer blocking rings for widened index slots, rounded clutch teeth and smooth internal surfaces. With the rocker ring on the cone, the distance between the face of the blocker ring and the clutch teeth on the gear must not be less than 0.020 inches (Fig. 9-3).

Replace the speedometer drive gear if the teeth are stripped or damaged and replace the output shaft if there is any evidence of wear or if any of the splines are damaged. Inspect the bushing and the seal in the extension housing, and replace if worn or damaged.

Replace the seal in the input shaft bearing retainer and then replace the seals on the cam and shafts.

AUTOMATIC TRANSMISSIONS

A typical automatic transmission consists primarily of three-element hydraulic torque converter and two planetary gear sets. Four multiple-disc clutches, two roller clutches and an intermediate overrun band provide the friction elements required to obtain the desired function of the two planetary gear sets.

The three-element torque converter consists of a pump, turbine and a stator assembly, the latter of which is mounted on a one way roller clutch which will allow the stator to turn clockwise, but not counterclockwise.

The torque converter is filled with oil and is attached to the engine crankshaft by a flywheel and always rotates at engine speed. The converter pump is an integral part of the converter housing; therefore, the pump blades rotating at engine speed set the oil within the converter into motion and direct it to the turbine—causing the turbine to rotate. As the oil passes through the turbine, it is traveling in such a direction that if it were not redirected by the stator, it would hit the rear of the converter pump blades and impede its pumping action. So at low turbine speeds, oil is redirected by the stator to the converter pump in such a manner that actually assists the converter pump to deliver power, or multiply engine torque.

When turbine speed increases, the direction of the oil leaving the turbine changes and flows against the rear side of the stator vanes in a clockwise direction. Since the stator is now impeding the smooth flow of oil, its roller clutch releases and it revolves freely on its shaft. Once the stator becomes inactive, there is not further multiplication of engine torque within the converter. At this point, the converter is merely acting as a fluid coupling as both the converter pump and turbine are being driven at approximately the same speed.

A hydraulic system pressurized by a gear type pump provides the working pressure required to operate the friction elements and automatic controls. External control connections to the transmission are:

1. *Manual Linkage*—to select the desired operating range.
2. *Engine Vacuum*—to operate the vacuum modulator.
3. *Cable Control*—to operate the detent valve.

A vacuum modulator is used to automatically sense any change in the torque input to the transmission. The vacuum modulator transmits this signal to the pressure regulator, which controls line pressure, so that all torque requirements of the transmission are met and smooth shifts are obtained at all throttle openings.

The detent valve is activated by a cable that is connected to the accelerator lever assembly. When the throttle is half open, the valve is actuated causing throttle downshift at speeds below 50 mph. When the throttle is fully open, the detent valve is actuated causing the transmission to downshift.

Troubleshooting the automatic transmission is simplified by using the proven method of diagnosis. One of the most important things to remember is that there is a definite procedure to follow. Never try to take shortcuts or take for granted that someone else has done the critical checks of adjustments.

The following procedures are recommended for checking and/or verifying that the various components are adjusted and operating properly.

Linkage Check

Check for wide open carburetor and linkage travel at full throttle. The carburetor full throttle stop must be contacted by the throttle linkage and there must be a slight amount of movement left in the downshift linkage. Be sure the downshift linkage return spring is connected and the downshift lever returns to a closed position.

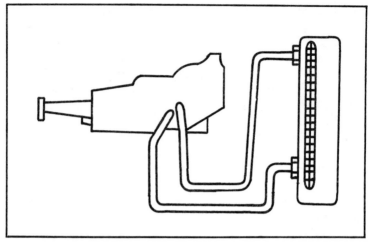

Fig. 9-4. Some transmissions cool their oil in the radiator.

The adjustment of the manual linkage is a very critical adjustment. Be absolutely certain the "D" detent in the transmission corresponds exactly with the stop in the steering column or console. Hydraulic leakage at the manual valve can cause delay in engagements and/or slippage while operating if the linkage is not correctly adjusted.

Fluid Level Check

Most automatic transmissions are designed to operate with the oil level between the *add* and *full* mark on the dipstick, at an operating temperature of 150 degrees Fahrenheit to 170 degrees Fahrenheit. Fluid level should be checked under these temperatures. Obtain this temperature by driving 15 to 20 miles of city-type driving with the outside temperature above 50 degrees Fahrenheit.

When the desired temperature has been reached, place the transmission in *park* (P) and let the engine idle. Then with the foot brake applied, move the transmission selector lever through each range—allowing time in each range to engage the transmission. Return the selector to *park*, but do not turn off the engine during the fluid level check.

Clean all dirt from the transmission fluid dipstick cap and then pull the dipstick out of the tube, wipe it clean, and replace in the tube. Be sure it is fully seated. Pull the dipstick out of the tube again and check the fluid level. It should be between *full* and *add*. If fluid is needed, be sure that the correct type will be used. If in doubt, check the vehicle certification label affixed to the car.

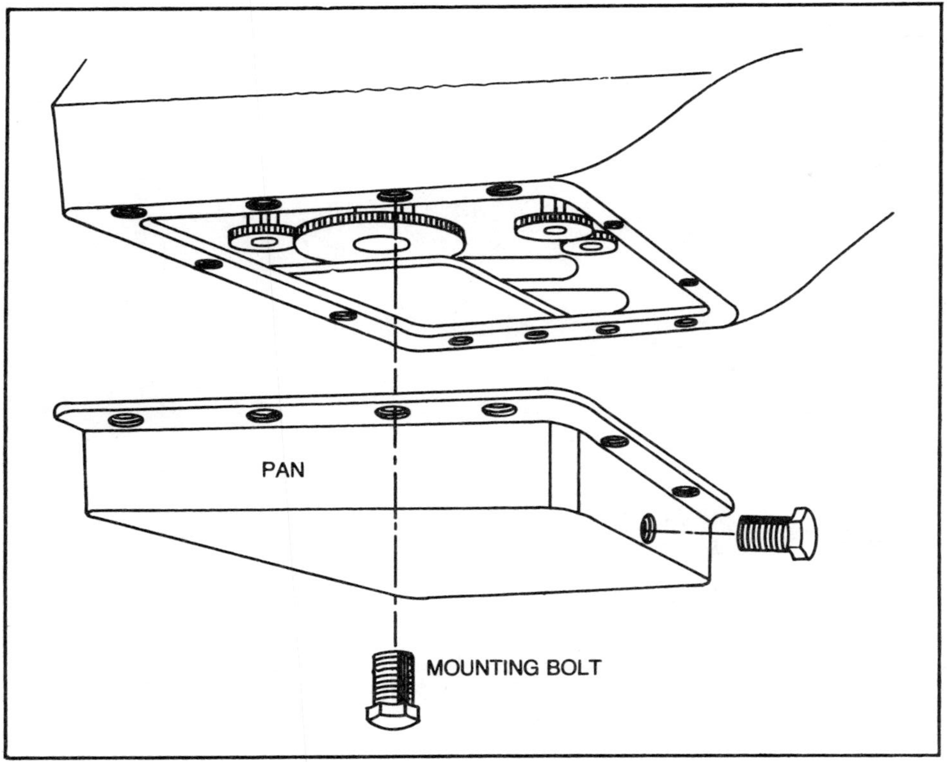

Fig. 9-5. Bottom of automatic transmission where fluid is discharged.

MOUNTING BOLT

PAN

While making the fluid check, observe the color and odor of the fluid. It should be red, not brown or black. Odor can sometimes indicate that there is an overheating condition or clutch disc or band failure. Continue the check by using a white paper like kleenex to wipe the dipstick. Examine the stain for evidence of solids and for anti-freeze signs. If specks are present in the oil or there is evidence of antifreeze, the transmission oil pan must be removed for further inspection (Figs. 9-4 and 9-5). If fluid contamination or transmission failure is confirmed by further evidence of coolant or excessive solids in the oil pan, the transmission must be disassembled and completely cleaned and repaired. This includes cleaning the torque converter and transmission cooling system. It would be a waste of time to perform any further checks before cleaning and repairing the transmission.

During disassembly and assembly, all overhaul checks and adjustments of clearance and end play must be made. After repairs have been made to the transmission, all diagnosis tests and adjustments listed must be completed to make sure the problem has been corrected.

Chapter 10

Steering

There are two types of steering systems normally used on American-made autos—manual and power steering. The manual steering gear is designed to provide easy steering with a minimum of friction in the steering gear by transmitting forces from the wormshaft to the pitman shaft through the use of ball bearings. The wormshaft and ball nut assembly are supported in the gear housing by an adjustable ball thrust type upper and lower bearing. The lower bearing cup is pressed into the gear housing, and the upper bearing cup is pressed into the wormshaft bearing adjuster.

The cross shaft is integrated with the sector gear which meshes with the rackteeth on the recirculating ball nut. Adjustment at this point is controlled by the cross shaft adjusting screw which extends through the housing cover.

The steering column is connected to the steering gear by a flexible coupling with incorporates a capturing strap—designed to prevent column-to-coupling deflection from exceeding the length of the coupling alignment pins.

TROUBLESHOOTING MANUAL STEERING SYSTEM

The following are some typical problems occurring on vehicles with a manual steering system. Solutions to the problems are given to determine the possible cause and how to correct them.

Hard Steering

Low and uneven tire pressure is one of the major causes of hard steering. The problem can easily be solved by inflating all tires on the vehicle to recommended pressures. However, if correcting the tire air pressures does not better the situation, the mechanic will have to check the lubricant in the steering gear housing or in the steering linkage. Lubricate as necessary. Also check the steering gear shaft as the adjustment may be too tight. Front wheels may be out of line and should be aligned for proper steering. The final and less likely problem is a misaligned steering column. Consult the shop manual for alignment procedures for the particular make of car.

Vehicle Pulls To One Side

Again, incorrect tire pressure could be causing the problem, but also check wheel bearings for proper adjustment. Check for dragging brakes and for grease, dirt, oil or brake fluid on the brake linings.

Improper caster and camber as well as incorrect toe-in could be causing the problem. Check and correct according to standard front wheel alignment procedures. Also check for front and rear wheels out of alignment, broken or sagging rear springs, or a bent suspension part. Repair or replace as necessary.

Wheel Trap

As before, incorrect tire pressure could be causing excessive vertical motion of the wheels and should be checked. In fact, for any steering problem, always check the tire air pressure and inflate (or deflate) to recommended pressures as suggested by the car manufacturer. Continue by checking for improper balance of tires, wheels and brake drums; balance as necessary.

If the wheels or tires seem okay, check for loose tie rod ends or steering connections. These should be corrected immediately. Finish the diagnosis by checking for worn or inoperative shock absorbers and replace as required.

Excessive Play Or Looseness In The Steering Wheel

The most probable causes of this problem are a loose or worn steering linkage or steering gear shaft. In either case, replace worn parts and adjust according to manufacturer's instructions.

Continue the check for wheel tramp by checking the front wheel bearing for improper adjustment and correct according to manufacturer's instructions. Also check for loose gear housing attaching bolts and for loose steering arms at steering knuckles. Tighten according to specifications and then check the ball joints. If worn, replace.

POWER STEERING SYSTEMS

The hydraulic power steering system consists of a pump, an oil reservoir, a steering gear, a supply hose and a return hose. The integral power steering gear may be either constant ratio or variable ratio. The integral power steering gear has an open center, rotary type three-way control valve, which directs oil to either side of the rack piston. The rack piston converts hydraulic power into mechanical output.

Power Steering Gear

The power steering gear consists of a gear housing containing a gear shaft with sector gear, a power piston with gear teeth broached into the side of the piston, which is in constant mesh with the gear shaft sector, and a wormshaft connecting the steering wheel to the power piston through a U-joint type coupling. The wormshaft is geared to the piston through recirculating ball contact. The steering valve, mounted on top of the steering gear, directs the flow of fluid in the system.

Fluid is supplied to the steering gear by an engine driven constant displacement slipper type pump through a pressure hose. Oil is returned to the pump reservoir from the steering gear through a return hose.

TROUBLESHOOTING POWER STEERING SYSTEMS

The following are typical problems occurring on vehicles with power steering systems. Possible causes are given as well as corrections or solutions to the problems.

Hard Steering

This problem is frequently attributed to improperly inflated tires and is certainly the simplest to check. Make sure all tires are inflated to recommended pressures before any further tests are made for hard steering of a vehicle. Once the system has been tested, and improper inflation does not seem to be the problem, continue with the following tests.

1. Check oil level in pump reservoir.
2. Check for a loose pump belt.
3. Check for improper caster and camber.
4. Perform pump pressure and pump flow tests to determine whether power steering output is low.
5. Check steering linkage for binding and repair and lubricate as necessary.

6. Check for malfunctions of steering gear—that is, gear shaft adjustment too tight, faulty or damaged valve lever, etc. Adjust or repair as necessary.

Poor Recovery From Turns

As with any steering problem, check the tires for proper inflation before proceeding with the following diagnosis.

1. Check for binding steering linkage and improper wheel alignment. Repair and lubricate as necessary.
2. Check for damaged steering tube bearing.
3. Check steering wheel column jacket and steering nut for proper alignment.
4. Check for steering malfunctions such as improper gear shaft adjustment, loose column support spanner nut, damaged valve lever, improper worm thrust bearing adjustment, etc. To check, remove steering gear and then repair as necessary.
5. Check for a worn or damaged cylinder head worm seal ring or faulty worm piston ring.
6. Check for burrs or nicks in the reaction ring grooves in the cylinder head or column support.
7. Dirt or chips in the steering gear unit may be causing the trouble; remove steering gear, disassemble completely, clean in a clean solvent, inspect and make repairs as necessary.
8. Check for a rough or catchy worm in the piston assembly and replace if necessary.

Car Leads To Either Side

1. Inflate tires to recommended pressures and then check the front wheel alignment.
2. If the vehicle leads to the left, move the steering valve housing down on the steering housing. If the vehicle leads to the right, move the steering valve housing up on the steering housing.
3. Check the valve lever for damage and replace or repair as necessary.
4. Check for loose column support spanner nut and repair as necessary.
5. If coupling is not centered, refer to manufacturer's shop manual and adjust.

166

Excessive Steering Wheel Free-Play

1. Check for improper gear shaft adjustment.
2. Check for loose column support spanner nut and repair as necessary.
3. Check for improper worm thrust bearing adjustment.
4. Check for loose coupling on the worm shaft.

Lack of Assist

Remove the steering gear, disassemble, and inspect for oil leaking past the worm shaft oil seal ring; replace the parts as necessary. Also check for broken or worn ring on worm piston and for a loose piston end plug. If the reaction seal is missing, remove the steering gear and repair as necessary.

Should lack of assist occur in both directions, check for pump belt slippage and then perform a pump pressure and flow test. As for lack of assist in one direction, check for a broken or worn ring on worm piston and for a loose piston end plug. If there is leakage in the steering gear valve body, replace the steering gear valve body assembly.

Temporary Increases In Effort When Turning Steering Wheel To The Right Or Left

The chief causes of this condition are low oil level in pump reservoir, loose pump belts, oil on pump belt or binding steering linkage. To correct, either replace or adjust the belts and lubricate and repair the linkage as necessary. The engine idle may be too slow or there might be air in the system. If the latter is suspected, work the steering wheel from right to left until the air is expelled. Also check for low output on power steering pump as well as a gear malfunction.

Noises

A buzzing noise while the vehicle is in neutral and at stops when the steering wheel is turned is an indication of a noisy pump. Make pressure test and repair as necessary. Another cause could be damaged hydraulic lines of interference of the hoses with components attached to the fender shield. If air in the system is suspected, work steering wheel from right to left until the air is expelled.

A chucking noise is an indication of either an improper gear shaft adjustment, improper worm shaft thrust bearing adjustment, or a loose coupling on the worm shaft. To correct, check manufacturer's manual for gear shaft adjustment procedures. Remove the steering gear, disassemble, and inspect improper worm shaft thrust bearing adjustment; repair and reassemble. Continue by inspecting the worm shaft splines for wear. Inspect the coupling bolt for tightness and if loose, replace the bolt and inspect wormshaft and coupling. Check worm and piston assembly and replace if necessary.

If a metallic clatter or tapping noise occurs, replace back pressure valve cushion; a knocking condition indicates that the rubber stop is worn or missing from the pump bracket. Also check for a loose pump belt.

Exact details of disassembling the steering system varies from car to car, so the manufacturer's manual should be referred to for reference in all cases.

Chapter 11

Brakes

Automobile braking systems are crucial to safe operation, but they are not really complex in nature and are easily repaired by using relatively few special tools or parts. Disc brakes and the older drum brakes are sometimes used in conjunction on many autombiles and are easily reached and serviced. Disassembly is relatively simple and reassembly rarely gives even the newer mechanic much trouble.

Many American automobiles of recent manufacture contain brake warning lights which indicate when the brake lining wears down to a point which could be considered dangerous. Where light indicators are not used, spring steel-wear sensors are placed on the inboard brake shoe linings of many automobiles equipped with front disc brakes. When the lining wears down, the spring rubs against the rotor, setting up a squealing sound which means it's time to replace the linings.

Brakes must always be kept in excellent operating condition. Special attention should be paid to maintenance of automobile braking systems and the replacement of worn or defective parts at the first sign of any unusual operation or indication of pulling, fading or grabbing. Any of these conditions can cause an accident or prevent the operator from avoiding one.

BASIC COMPONENTS

All automobiles are now equipped with dual hydraulic brake systems which are actually a split system containing two, separate braking systems. When one of these systems fails, the other system

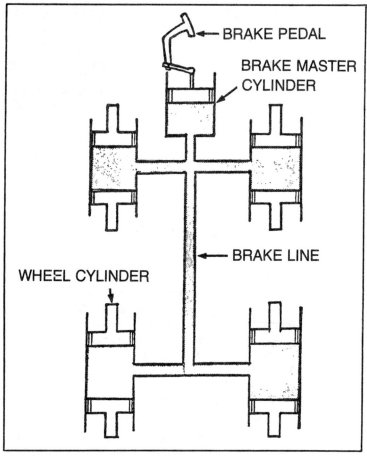

Fig. 11-1. Hydraulic brake system.

is adequate to bring the automobile to a complete stop. When one system is inoperative, the other system will probably increase the pedal pressure and brake pedal lash which is normally present on a properly operating braking system.

Figure 11-1 shows a representation of a hydraulic brake system which shows the master cylinder and the four wheel cylinders are all connected by the brake line.

The Master Cylinder

The master cylinder is designed with a separate hydraulic system for the front and rear brakes. This is accomplished by using two, separate reservoirs (Fig. 11-2). It can be seen that most master cylinders resemble an oval, deep cut with two containers.

The master cylinder should be checked periodically to make certain that the brake fluid level is satisfactory. Fluid is added at this point. The side of the master cylinder is usually marked with a fluid level line and both reservoirs should be filled to this point.

Drum Brakes

Figure 11-3 shows an example of the drum brake design which is used on the majority of American automobiles in connection with disc brakes on the front wheels, which will be discussed later in this text.

Drum brakes have a metal drum attached to the automobile wheel. Inside of this drum are two, half-moon components called brake shoes. Fluid which is pumped through the brake line from the master cylinder enters a small wheel cylinder. Inside of this cylinder are small pistons which are pushed outward by the pressure of the hydraulic fluid. This action causes the brake shoes to move outward and press against the brake drum. The friction created by this

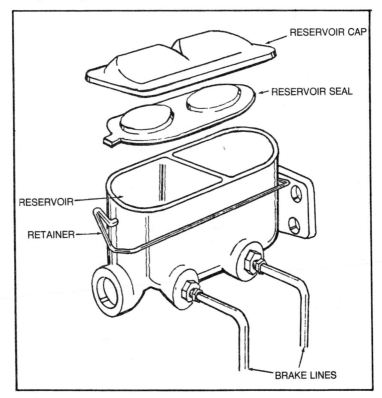

Fig. 11-2. Brake master cylinder.

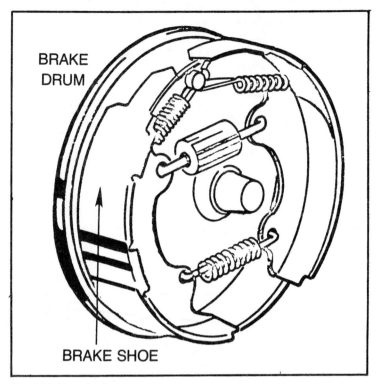

BRAKE
DRUM

BRAKE SHOE

Fig. 11-3. Drum brake.

rubbing effect slows the wheel and the braking action is completed. Figure 11-4 shows an example of this process. It follows the braking action from the initial depressing of the brake pedal through the master cylinder pressure action down to the wheel cylinder, and finally to the drum/shoe stopping action.

Wherever there is friction, there is also heat, and heat is a major problem with all types of brakes. Drum brakes are more subject to fade than disc brakes. Also drum brakes cause a steady decrease in braking power during a power stop, due to the heat buildup.

Disc Brakes

Because of the fade which is inherent in drum brakes during power stops, disc brakes were invented to better correct this situation and to provide more adequate braking power for longer periods of time and in all types of driving and braking conditions.

Figure 11-5 shows a drawing of a typical disc brake which consists of a steel disc connected directly to the wheel. A set of

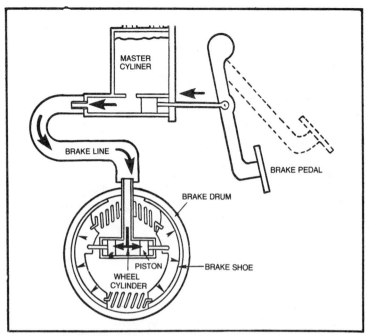

Fig. 11-4. Hydraulic brake system function using drum brake.

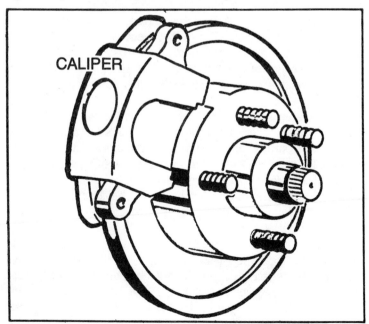

Fig. 11-5. Disc brake.

calipers are activated by the hydraulic fluid and grab the disc with padded jaws when braking action is initiated. This grabbing action is applied to both sides of the disc which causes friction for the stopping action, but this friction is applied to a much larger surface area at the disc than is the case with standard drum brakes. Because of this larger surface area, heat buildup is not as great. The heat is dissipated by the larger metal surface or heat sink provided. The final result of this type of brake design is consistent braking action for much longer periods of time than can be expected when using drum brakes. Generally, disc brakes also provide better stopping power than do drum brakes because of the greater friction generated.

While disc brakes stay cooler for longer braking periods, they can become heated to a point where serious fade does present itself. They are not immune to brake fade but withstand fading effects for longer periods of time than drum brakes.

The Hydraulic System

When fluid is contained in a closed system, and pressure is applied to any portion of it, the pressure is exerted equally in all directions throughout the closed system. This is known as *Pascal's Law* as is applied to the braking systems of all modern automobiles.

Figure 11-6 shows another representation of the hydraulic system, similar to one shown earlier. Here the various pressure points have been simulated as to the effect they have on braking action. Again, in a hydraulic system, pressure is equal at all points at all times. The applied pressure is introduced at the master cylinder and is immediately transferred to every other point in the hydraulic system.

The system shown in Fig. 11-6 is a typical system used on many American automobiles. The drawing represents a braking system which uses front disc brakes and rear drum brakes. Many foreign automobiles and vehicles used for high-speed touring and competition use disc brakes on all four wheels, but the cost of the latter type of brake is much higher than for the drum type. Using disc brakes only on the front wheels is more economical. Stopping power, however, is not quite as good.

One great advantage of the hydraulic system is the ability to apply unequal force where necessary. Although the pressure within the system is equal at all points, this does not mean that equal pressure is being applied to each wheel. The way that more force is applied to one wheel than another is found in the surface area presented to the hydraulic fluid. If the hydraulic system pressure is 10 psi (pounds per square inch), then a surface area of 10 square

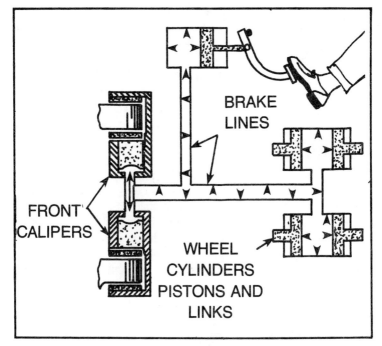

Fig. 11-6. Hydraulic system showing pressure distribution.

inches will be pushed by a force equal to 10 pounds, but if another area has 2 square inches of surface area exposed to the hydraulic fluid, 20 pounds of force will be applied overall. Pressure on the pistons or calipers is equal to the hydraulic system pressure times the amount of surface area exposed to the system by the driven elements such as pistons and calipers.

Using this formula, the braking power to the wheels can be altered by changing the surface area of the components which are exposed to the hydraulic fluid. For example, the wheel cylinder piston area can be increased for more braking power or decreased for less power. By knowing the typical hydraulic system pressure figure, accurate calculations may be made on how much surface area is required to deliver a specific amount of driving power from the system.

A reason for applying different braking power to different wheels is found when studying the weight transfer involved during normal braking action. Much of the vehicle weight is transferred to the front wheels by the inertia set up. This transfer of weight can be better balanced by the application of different braking forces at the front and rear wheels.

Hydraulic systems that are installed in automobiles are by no means perfect, textbook systems which exactly fit the hydraulic theory just discussed. In a practical system, pressures are not exactly equal at all points, because valves are normally used at points in the system which will slightly affect pressure values at various points. However, the theory is applied to all practical systems and will closely describe what will actually be encountered when working on modern braking systems.

PREVENTIVE MAINTENANCE

Because of the dependence which must be placed on the braking system, preventive maintenance and daily diagnosis are absolutely necessary each time the automobile is driven. Diagnosis is almost an automatic reaction with most drivers who may not even be aware of their testing of the brake pedal pressure each time they depress it. A lot of information can be obtained from the feel of the pedal along which, if correctly used, can prevent any serious decay of braking efficiency due to problems with the system.

Figure 11-7 shows the hydraulic braking system superimposed on an automobile chassis. Disc brakes are used on the front wheels while standard, drum brakes are located at the rear. The master cylinder can be seen mounted at a point just behind the place where the steering column would normally be found. The brake pedal is attached directly to the master cylinder by a short linkage arrangement. The emergency brake handle and lines to the rear drums are also indicated. This figure will be helpful in getting an overall picture of the braking system and its place in the automobile.

Regarding diagnosis through pedal pressure and operating traits, the free play of the pedal when it is operating in its normal travel range makes allowance for a certain amount of clearance between the brake drums and their contact. These friction points may be drums or linings, depending on the type of brake when the brakes are not engaged. If this play is not adjusted properly, especially where too little play is found, the brakes can become partially engaged during periods of normal driving and premature wear will result. Also, undue wear and tear on the engine will occur as it must supply much more power to propel the automobile at a specific speed due to the resistance created by this partial brake drag. Where a condition of too much free play exists, an indication of a possible faulty master cylinder should be suspected on newer automobiles with self-adjusting brakes. Older automobiles which have a low brake pedal may only need a simple adjustment to take up this free play.

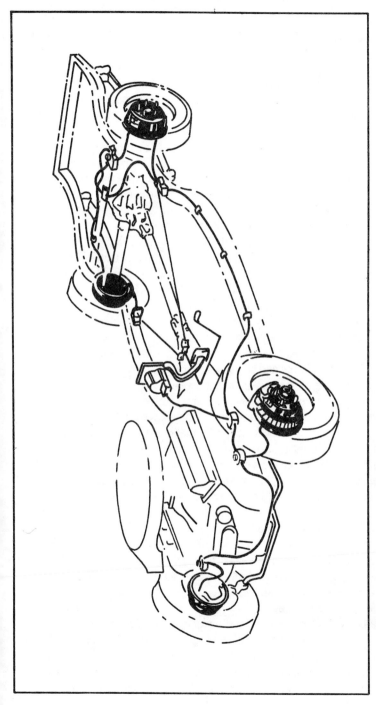

Fig. 11-7. Automotive braking system superimposed on chassis.

The amount of pressure required to depress the pedal is another good indicating signal as to the condition of the overall braking system. When more pressure than usual is required to stop an automobile with manual brakes, several problems may be indicated. The master cylinder may be defective and should be rebuilt or replaced. The pistons in the wheel cylinder may be sticking or grabbing. The hydraulic line may have a partial blockage or restriction. If this condition occurs on an automobile equipped with lower brakes, it could be an indication of trouble in the vacuum lines to the power brake cylinder or a defect in the cylinder itself.

Other problems associated with an increase in the pressure needed on the pedal to stop the automobile can involve grease or oil seeping into brake linings or brake shoes, which were not properly adjusted or were thrown out of adjustment.

Some conditions within the main system can cause the brake pedal to feel spongy when depressed. This is usually a sign of pressure problems within the hydraulic line and can be caused by air bubbles in the system with pressure differentials at points where the bubbles have amassed. This problem can be corrected by simply bleeding off the air within the system. Spongy pedal feel can also be caused by worn hydraulic hoses which have been stretched severely due to the internal pressure. This condition can eventually lead to a break in the system and should be corrected by examining the hoses and replacing those which appear worn.

Preventive maintenance on automotive braking systems includes the periodic examination of all visible parts and lines involved in this system. Hydraulic hoses should appear smooth and uniform. Any light-colored areas which have been created by stretching of the rubber material should be corrected by replacing the hose. Make certain that the master cylinder is filled to the proper level at all times. If fluid seems to be dropping on a regular basis, a small leak may have occurred in the system at some point and is slowly draining off the system's hydraulic fluid. The fluid in the master cylinder reservoir should remain at about the same level at all times. This is a closed system which is sealed from any possible condensation or loss. A problem with the brakes which is detected by the feel of the brake pedal may be further investigated, without the necessity of disassembling components in the braking system, by checking the master cylinder reservoir and observing the level of the fluid. Any leak in the brake system must be found immediately, no matter how small it may be before the vehicle is operated.

Brake fluid should always be used for replacement in the master cylinder. Never use any other type of fluid other than hydraulic fluid designed for use in the automotive braking system. Brake fluid must have special properties because of the vital demands placed upon its function in the hydraulic system. It has to be able to withstand the extreme heat which is caused when the brake shoes or calipers are engaged and the braking friction sets in heating up the entire area to extreme temperatures. This fluid must remain liquid at the temperatures encountered instead of changing to a gas which would lend the system inoperative. Brake fluid must also be non-corrosive to the metal surfaces and to the rubber hydraulic hoses it passes over. Brake fluid absorbs water from the air quite easily, so it should be stored only in containers which are rendered air tight. At the extreme temperatures encountered in the automotive braking system, water contaminates in the fluid will boil and the gases created will prevent the desired braking action from taking place or, possibly, prevent braking entirely, depending on the amount of contamination in the fluid.

Most brake linings are provided with indicators to warn the operator when they wear thin. This warning—as discussed earlier—may be a light or in the form of a scraping noise coming from the offending wheel. When this occurs, the lining should be replaced immediately. No preventive maintenance, other than sensible use of brakes while driving, will prevent this natural wear. The warning is an indication to repair the brake while some braking action is still left. If the condition is allowed to continue, grabbing and possibly failure will result.

TROUBLESHOOTING

Troubleshooting of brake systems usually is not difficult. Any problem that develops should be fairly obvious—that is, the automobile pulling to either left or right upon braking, a grinding noise when braking, etc. However, finding small hydraulic leaks when suspected can be difficult if the leak occurs in an area where the automobile chassis collects the dripping fluid and channels it to another area of the body before allowing it to drop to the surface below.

Drum Brakes Fade Quickly When Engaged

1. Brake fade is commonplace with braking systems when power stops are attempted several times in quick succession or when brakes are severely misused. The problem described indicates a fade during periods of normal to medium-severe brake use. The condition can be caused by

a brake lining which is out of alignment or a lining designed for the braking system other than the one on which it is being used. Examine the brake lining for any signs of improper placement or incorrect design. This situation can be corrected by replacing the lining or the shoe and lining assembly.

2. Dragging brakes is another reason for the condition described above. This condition is most often caused by improper adjustment of the brake pedal. Adjust the free play in the pedal for correction of the problem.

3. The next most common reason for the condition described is thin or worn brake drums. Inspect the drums and replace if necessary.

Drum Brakes Grab or Hold In Wet-Weather Driving

1. Grit or road grim may have built up on the brake shoes or on the lines causing poor friction connection. A thorough cleaning of these parts are necessary to correct the problem.

2. The type of brake linings used may be too sensitive to water for various reasons. Corrective methods call for replacement of the linings.

3. The brake drums could be damaged in some way. Inspect all parts and replace or re-condition if found to be defective.

The problem of brakes grabbing in wet weather usually applies only to drum brakes and may be noticed only at the rear wheels of most vehicles. The problem is caused by wet-weather driving of normal duration and conditions. When the wheels are subjected to deep pools of water which cover almost all of the brake drums surfaces, even properly functioning braking systems will not respond normally or fail altogether. This condition, however, will occur only when the wheel is completely covered in water.

Disc Brakes Feel Rough And Give Uneven Braking

1. Improperly adjusted wheel bearings is the most probable cause of this condition. The following procedure is suggested for adjusting the front wheel bearings.

• Raise the vehicle until the tire clears the floor and then remove the wheel cover and grease cap from the hub.

• Wipe excessive grease from the end of the spindle and then remove the cotter pin and nut lock.

- Loosen the adjusting nut three turns and rock the wheel, hub and rotor assembly in and out several times to push the shoe and linings away from the rotor.
- While rotating the wheel, hub, and rotor assembly, torque the adjusting nut to 17 to 25 foot-pounds to seat the bearing.
- Loosen the adjusting nut one-half turn, then retighten to 10 to 15 inch-pound (or as recommended by the manufacturer's specifications) using a torque wrench.
- Place the nut lock on the adjusting nut so the castellations on the lock are in line with the cotter pin hole in the spindle.
- Install a new cotter pin and bend the ends around the castellated flange of the nut lock.
- Check front wheel rotation. If the wheel rotates properly, reinstall the grease cap and wheel cover. If rotation is noisy or rough, follow the inspection, lubrication and replacement procedure given in the manufacturer's shop manual. Pump the brake pedal several times to restore normal brake pedal travel.

2. Uneven braking can be caused by out-of-round rear brake drums, although the condition may feel like it's originating from the front of the vehicle due to the imbalance. Check the rear drums for any signs of this condition or for scouring or wear. Replace if defective.

3. The thickness of the rotor may not be within specifications or may be out-of-round which causes uneven friction pressures. Have the thickness measured on a caliper and resurface if it is found to be outside of the specified dimensions.

4. Inspect calipers and general condition of the front wheel disc brakes—looking for any signs of unusual wear or friction heat breakdown. Replace any damaged parts and inspect the remainder of the components for signs of future breakdown.

Brake System Fails Completely

1. Inspect master cylinder for level of fluid. If fluid is low or completely absent, fill to proper levels and test brakes. Partial braking action may indicate a break in the line, air in the line, and perhaps both conditions if a complete drain of the hydraulic fluid is noted. Look for signs of fluid leaks throughout the entire hydraulic system. If a leak is detected around the master cylinder, it should be removed and repaired. Leaking hydraulic hoses should be com-

pletely replaced if they show signs of fatigue or wear. Check around the wheel cylinders as a leak could occur at these locations or else a line could be broken.

2. If the fluid level seems to be normal, check the area and linkage from the brake pedal to the master cylinder. This is a rare situation, but sometimes a break can occur here or a foreign object can become lodged in this area. Almost always the feel of the brake pedal will be strange and the problem is discovered immediately.

A complete failure of the braking system is rare, but such a condition does occur on occasion. Normally, however, brake failure will make itself known well in advance of a complete failure by partial or difficult operation. This is the time to take steps to correct the situation before a complete failure results.

Chapter 12

Wheels and Tires

American automobiles are equipped with a wide range of tube or tubeless tires and wheels selected according to the gross vehicle weight rating and type of service the vehicle is expected to give. Since these tires are manufactured for use on wheels of specific size, configuration and load carrying capacity, it is essential that replacement tires are used of the same size and load rating. The use of any other size of tire may seriously affect the ride, handling, ground clearance, tire clearance and even speedometer calibration.

Most autos use tubeless tires. This type of tire has an inner liner which, if punctured, tends to cling to the penetrating object, forming a partial seal until the object is removed from the tire. Some commercial vehicles are equipped with synthetic rubber tires and tubes—usually at the customer's request.

PUNCTURE INSPECTION AND REPAIR

At each lubrication (see Chapter 3), tires should be checked for foreign objects in the tread or breaks in the tread or sidewalls. Periodic pressure checks should also be performed in case imbedded objects have punctured the tire and a partial seal has been set up. If a puncture or other damage is found, the tire should be repaired immediately using one of the several repair kits available through tire outlets.

Tread wear should also be noted as there is a significant decrease in traction and anti-skid properties when the depth of the tread becomes 1/16-inch or less. The majority of flats and blow-outs

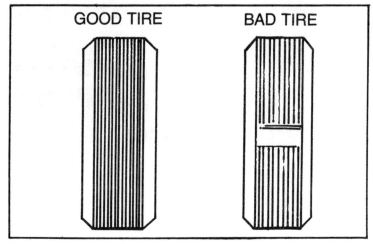

Fig. 12-1. Passenger-type car tread wear.

also occur in the last 10 percent of the tire life. Some passenger type tires incorporate built-in tread indicators to assist in judging when tires are worn out and should be replaced. These indicators are molded into the bottom of the tread groove and will appear as bands across the tread as a visual reminder that the tire should be replaced. See Fig. 12-1.

The wheel nut torques are very important to safe driving and should be checked at 100, 1000, and 6000 miles and every 6,000 miles thereafter when a wheel has been changed.

TIRE ROTATION

The rotation of tires will minimize tire trouble and produce longer tire life. With rotation, accelerated and irregular tire wear on any one particular tire will be spread out over the entire set, and replacement frequency will be reduced.

No definite tire rotation formula is applicable to all driving conditions, but certain fundamentals, mixed with experience and observation, will assist the driver in reducing tire costs. A rotation sequence that moves the front tires to the opposite rear side (Fig. 12-2) is a general recommendation. However, different manufacturers recommend different tire rotation patterns and you may want to abide by the recommendations given in the shop or owner's manual.

TIRE TREAD WEAR

Tire tread wear should be uniform over the entire surface that is in contact with the road. If wear is spotty, or concentrated on only one side of the tread, the problem lies with either the tire or the vehicle. The following failure signs are common and therefore correction procedures are given for each problem.

Heel And Toe Wear. This is a saw-toothed effect where one end of each tread block is worn more than the other. The end that wears is the one that first grips the road when the brakes are applied. This effect is more noticeable on the front tires than on rear tire, and in any case, a certain amount of heel and toe wear is normal.

The best remedy for excessive heel and toe wear is to use good driving habits (reduce high speed driving and cut down on excessive use of brakes) and interchange tires regularly.

Side Wear. This condition may be caused by incorrect wheel camber, underinflation, high cambered roads or by taking corners at too high a rate of speed. Camber wear can be easily identified since it occurs only on one side of the tire treads. If the condition occurs on both sides, the most probable cause is underinflation. Camber wear requires correction of the camber first and then interchanging tires.

Misalignment Wear. When tires revolve with a side motion and scrape the tread rubber off, the most probably causes are either toe-in or toe-out—that is, misalignment of the wheels. If the condi-

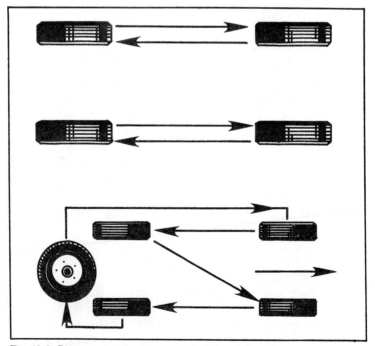

Fig. 12-2. Diagram showing recommended tire rotation sequence.

tion is slight, only one tire may be affected; if the condition is severe, perhaps both tires will be damaged. The remedy is readjusting toe-in, or rechecking the entire front-end alignment if necessary.

Uneven Wear. This condition is caused by such irregularities as unequal caster or camber, bent front suspension parts, out-of-balance wheels, brake drums out of round, brakes out of adjustment or other mechanical conditions. The remedy in each case consists of locating the mechanical defect and correcting it.

Cornering Wear. When a vehicle makes an extremely fast turn, the weight is shifted from an even loading on all four wheels to an abnormal load on the tires on the outside of the curve and a very light load on the inside tires, due to centrifugal force. When this happens, the rear tire on the inside of the curve may be relieved of so much load that it slips—grinding off the tread on the inside half of the tire at an excessive rate. The transfer of weight can also overload the outside tires to the point where they are laterally distorted—producing a type of wear like that caused by excessive camber.

Cornering wear often produces a fin or raised portion along the inside edge of each row in the tread pattern. The only rememdy is to check one's driving habits and take corners more slowly. Some normal cornering wear will also occur and rotating the tires will help offset this condition.

WHEEL AND TIRE BALANCING

It is desirable to maintain proper balance of wheel and tire assemblies to cut down on tire wear as well as to insure a good ride and ease of handling. Wheels and tires may be kept in balance by the use of either two types of balancing systems in current use—the *on the vehicle* type or *off the vehicle* type. The former is the more desirable in that all rolling components are included in the balancing procedure and thereby have any existing unbalance corrected.

To insure successful, accurate balancing, the following precautions must be observed:

1. Wheel and tires must be clean and free from all foreign matter.
2. The tires should be in good condition and properly mounted with the balancc mark on the tire (if any) properly lined up with the valve.
3. Bent wheels that have runout over 1/16-inch should be replaced.
4. Inspect tire and wheel assembly to determine if an eccentric or out-of-round condition exists. If this condition is severe, it cannot be *balanced out*.

5. When balancing wheels and tires, it is recommended that the instructions covering the operation of the wheel balancer being used are closely followed.

NOISE, VIBRATION AND HARSHNESS

A gradual appearance of a noise or vibration can indicate a deterioration of a tire or other item while a sudden appearance of such a condition could indicate a lost wheel balance weight or lost driveshaft balance weight.

Before testing, set tire pressures to recommended specifications. Then perform a road test, noting the following factors to properly isolate the condition.

1. At what road speed does the vibration occur? Low speed vibration is an indication of tire runout conditions while high speed—40 mph and up—vibration is an indication of tire imbalance.
2. At what engine rpm does the complaint occur?
3. Does the vehicle have a harsh ride quality? If so, the cause is tires or suspension.

Inspect tires for abnormal wear such as cupping on the outer tread rows. Also, check for bulges in the tread of sidewall areas which indicate a tread or body ply separation. These conditions may induce vibration in the vehicle.

Be aware of the characteristics of nylon tires. They have an inherent stiff ride quality, and will produce temporary flat spots when they have been setting for extended periods of time—such as overnight.

Over-inflated tires will give a hard ride quality, so make sure the tire pressures are set to the recommended levels. Have these pressures checked frequently.

Inspect tires for the correct size and type. For example, 8.45 ×15, four ply tires with an eight ply rating are intended for trailer towing. Tires of this nature produce a harsh ride when the vehicle is in an unloaded condition. Advise the customer of this situation.

The use of a set of test tires will be helpful in determining if the tires are the cause of the problem. Before installing the test set, however, mark the original tires and wheels as to location (right front—left front, etc.) and position to facilitate reinstallation. Then balance the test set on the vehicle before road testing.

Vibrations that occur at steady road speeds of 40 mph or above are usually attributed to tire and wheel imbalance. These vibrations can be felt in the steering wheel, floor pan and in the seat. Excessive tire and wheel runout can produce an effect similar to an unbalanced tire and wheel. The tire must be warm prior to balancing or checking the tire and wheel runout.

Check the tire and wheel balance as an apparent imbalanced tire can be caused by a lost wheel weight, a poorly balanced brake drum, excessive axle shaft runout, or by not being balanced properly. It is recommended that an *on the car* balance check of all four tire-wheel assemblies be performed. Then check the tire and wheel runout. Irregularities in the tire, axle shaft or wheel can cause excessive runout.

Next, use a dial indicator mounted on a stand, and check the *radial* runout of the tire and wheel assemblies on the car. This is done with the roller of the gauge running on the center tread of the tire and pointing to the center of the wheel for a radial runout check, and at the scrub rib for a lateral check as shown in Fig. 12-3.

If the radial runout on the center tread of the tire exceeds the service performance limit of .070 inch, measure the radial and lateral runout of the wheels. Wheel radial and lateral runouts are checked as shown in Fig. 12-3.

If the radial or lateral runout of the wheel exceeds .070 inch, remove the wheel and rotate it two studs on the drum. Re-measure the radial and lateral runout of the wheel and tire assembly. Continue rotating the wheel until runout is within the specifications or replace the wheel if required.

If the runout of the wheel-tire assembly is reduced to the proper specification or less, the unit should exhibit acceptable performance after re-balance. But if the total radial runout still exceeds the limits shown, match the highest radial point on the tire with the lowest radial point on the wheel and again measure the radial runout of the assembly on the car. If the wheel-tire assembly is still over the limit for either radial or lateral runout, and the wheel itself is within the runout specifications, the tire should be replaced.

A run-down or coast-down rumble noise in neutral may still be evident after a complete tire and driveline diagnosis on vehicles with rear coil springs. This condition could be the result of spring surge and can be dampened out by the use of a spring damper kit available at auto supply stores.

RADIAL PLY TIRES

Those not already familiar with radial ply tires and their advantages may question the under-inflated look, even though the pressure is to specification. This is a normal condition and is not detrimental to the tire.

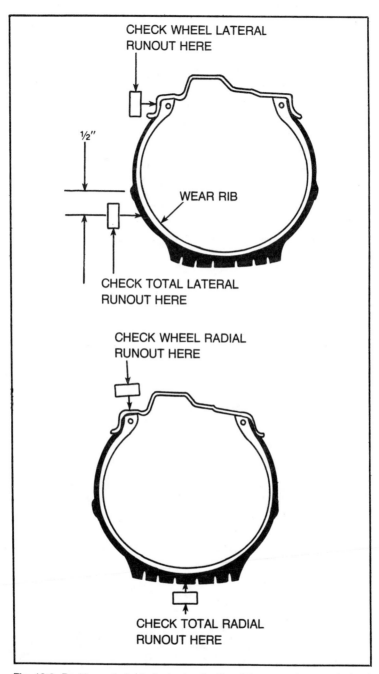

CHECK WHEEL LATERAL
RUNOUT HERE

½″

WEAR RIB

CHECK TOTAL LATERAL
RUNOUT HERE

CHECK WHEEL RADIAL
RUNOUT HERE

CHECK TOTAL RADIAL
RUNOUT HERE

Fig. 12-3. Positions of dial indicator to check radial runout of tire and wheel assemblies.

Certain road and loading conditions may cause a slight whine to be induced by the road gripping characteristic of the tread. In some instances, this whine may be misinterpreted as rear axle whine. However, rear axle whine will usually vary with a change from drive, cruise or float at a given speed. Tire tread noise will remain virtually constant under the same conditions. In the event this whine condition is experienced, be aware that this is a normal characteristic of the radial ply tire tread design.

The use of the new radial tire design with increased tire life, improved handling ability and improved stopping characteristics has resulted in increased tire noise. The *sizzle* noise is caused by reaction of the tire tread to the road surface.

Chapter 13

Body Maintenance

This chapter is designed to give information on maintaining the "new car" appearance on any vehicle. For best results, appearance maintenance should be performed at regular intervals by qualified experienced personnel using the recommended agents and established service procedures outlined in this chapter.

ROOF MAINTENANCE

Wash the top covering with mild soap and lukewarm water, lathering well with a soft brush, cloth or sponge. Avoid heavy brushing as this may scratch the surface and dull the appearance. Rinse all traces of suds away with clear water—including those that may drip on the paint finish. In no case should volatile cleaners or solvents be used on the top covering.

Although convertible tops are no longer made in this country, several older models have been restored and are becoming classics. Here are a few hints for maintenance on convertible tops.

Frequent brushing and vacuuming will keep the top free of abrasive dust and dirt. When washing, convertible top material should be thoroughly wet. Then scrub with a soft, natural bristle hand scrub brush. Use only warm water and naptha bar type soap as the cleaning agent. Do not wash in the direct sunlight. Scrub the top with soap suds, starting in the center and gradually working toward the edges. Rinse with plenty of clean water to remove all traces of soap and then allow the top to dry completely before lowering. If the top is lowered wet, dampness may cause formation of mildew, and damage to the fabric will result.

Most convertible top backlights (rear windows) are made from a flexible vinyl plastic material. This material should be rinsed with a cold water spray to remove dirt and grit before lathering the surface with suds of a mild soap—using the palm of the hand. Rinse thoroughly and allow to air dry. Do not use a towel, sponge or chamois to apply the suds or dry the window as the surface may be scratched.

If the procedure in the previous paragraph does not clean the window sufficiently, a solution of 40 percent rubbing alcohol and 60 percent clear water should be used. Again, apply this solution with the palm of the hand, rubbing the surface of the window with a circular motion. Use the rubbing alcohol and water solution generously.

To clean the top boot and well, remove all abrasive dust and dirt from the boot and well by brushing or vacuuming. For scrubbing, use only a soft, natural bristle, hand scrub brush. Use warm water and naptha type bar soap. Make certain the drain is open in the well and then rinse with plenty of clean water to remove all traces of soap. Use a soft absorbent towel to dry the material.

INTERIOR TRIM

Dust and loose dirt that accumulate on interior fabric trim should be removed frequently with a vacuum cleaner, whisk broom or soft brush. Vinyl or leather trim should be wiped clean with a damp cloth. Trim soilage, spots or stains can be cleaned with the proper use of trim cleaners available through automotove supply dealers.

Before attempting to remove spots or stains from upholstery, determine as accurately as possible the nature and age of the spot or stain. Some spots or stains can be removed satisfactorily with water or mild soap solution and for best results, they should be removed as soon as possible. Some types of stains such as lipsticks, some inks, certain types of grease, mustard, etc., are extremely difficult and, in some instances, impossible to completely remove. When cleaning this type of stain or soilage, care must be taken not to enlarge the soiled area as it is sometimes more desirable to have small a stain than an enlarged stain as a result of careless cleaning.

One word of caution: when cleaning interior soft trim such as upholstery or carpeting, do not use volatile cleaning solvents such as acetone, lacquer thinners, carbon tetrachloride, enamel reducers, nail polish removers, etc. Furthermore, such cleaning materials as laundry soaps, bleaches or reducing agents should normally not be used.

Most stains can be removed quite easily from fabrics while they are fresh and have not hardened and set into the fabric. An exception is mud or clay, which should be allowed to dry so that most of it can be brushed off. It is also very helpful, though often not possible, to know the nature of the staining matter so the correct cleaning agent may be used.

Use a piece of clean cotton cheesecloth about 3 inches square and squeeze most of the liquid from the fabric to prevent leaving a ring. Wipe the soiled fabric very lightly with a lifting motion, always working from the outside toward the center of the spot. Turn the cheesecloth over as soon as one side becomes stained to prevent working the stain matter back into the cleaned portion of the fabric. Use a new piece of cheesecloth as soon as both sides become stained.

Before starting any cleaning action, a test should be made for the type of material being cleaned. Sample material for testing can usually be found under the seat cushion, sun visor and dome light brackets, or in back of the trim panels. Natural cloth will burn like string, slow and smoky, while synthetic material such as nylon, burns fast and "balls up" into a hard mass. Another method of testing is to rub the back of a fingernail over the surface of the material. Synthetic materials appear to *whistle* when this is done.

Before cleaning entire seats, door panels, headliners, etc., remove as many individual spots as possible. Then wash the entire section after the spot has been removed to avoid water stains.

Use a pocket knife or putty knife to break up and remove any encrusted foreign matter; then vacuum thoroughly. Continue by applying the recommended spot removing agent with a clean cloth or sponge, working in a wide circle to prevent making a ring and then working toward the center.

TROUBLESHOOTING SPECIFIC SPOTS AND STAINS

Surface spots. Surface spots may be brushed out with a small hand brush, but exercise extreme care not to damage the fabric when brushing.

Deep Pentrating Spots. Work the spot removing agent in by brushing. When the spot is thoroughly worked and saturated, use high air pressure to blow the dirt down through material. In extreme cases the entire spot may not be removed and it will then be necessary to cover the area with a light application of dye.

Water Stains. Water stains in fabric materials can be removed with a cleaning solution made from one cup of ordinary table salt and one quart of water. Vigorously scrub the solution into the stain; then wash with clean water. Water stains in nylon and other synthetics should be removed with commercial type spot remover, compounded for the specific material being cleaned.

Mildew. Clean around mildew with warm suds. Rinse with cold water and then soak mildew area with solution of one part common table salt and two parts water. Finish by washing the area with the recommended upholstery cleaner.

Rust Stains. Dampen the stained area with water before applying a commercial rust remover solution, available at dry cleaning supply or chemical supply houses. When using, keep the rust remover solution away from the skin and wash hands immediately if they are exposed. Clean extra well under fingernails and always read instructions prior to using.

Sponge the area with clean water to clean rust from upholstery buttons. Wrap a small strip of cloth around each button to avoid leaving a ring on upholstery material. Moisten button with a few drops of water applied with a small piece of sponge or cloth. Apply one or more drops of rust remover before dry cleaning areas with heat lamps.

Chewing Gum and Tar. Avoid using spotting or cleaning solution that will dissolve or soften gum or tar. Place a cube of ice on gum or tar to harden it. Then remove as much of the gum or tar as possible with a dull knife when it is in this hardened state. Moisten the remainder with cleaning fluid and scrub clean. In some cases, soak with cleaning fluid and blow the stain through using high air pressure.

Ice Cream and Candy. Use a dull edged pocket knife or putty knife to remove as much substance as possible from the surface of upholstery. Be careful not to damage upholstery fibers. Most candy has a sugar base and can be removed by rubbing the area with a cloth wrung out in warm water. However, an oily type of candy—after using warm water—shoud be cleaned with an upholstery type cleaner that will emulsify with the oil. Rinse with water and remove the remaining stains with cleaning fluid.

Blood Stains. In removing blood stains, never use warm or hot water. Rather, use a clean cloth wrung out in cold water and rub the stain. If this does not completely remove the stain, use spot remover or vinyl cleaner and apply it with a brush.

Wine or Alcohol. Scrub the stain with a cloth moistened in lukewarm water. Avoid the use of soap as it has a tendency to set the stain. The remaining stains can be removed with a regular cleaning solution.

Shoe Polish. Scrub area with a cloth saturated with cold water. Remove wax base polishes by sponging with spot remover.

Grease, Oil, Lipstick and Related Stains. Use spot remover to avoid leaving a *ring*. Start the cleaning operation from outside the spot and work toward the center. When the spot has been removed, dry fabric with a clean cloth.

Headliners—Cloth Type. Mix a cleaning solution of water and a foaming type upholstery cleaner to produce thick suds. Use only foam when cleaning headliner as saturation with liquids may result in streaks, spots or shrinking.

On nap type headliners, lay down nap, usually left to right. Do not stop when washing a headliner. Complete the entire operation using the same solution.

Starting in the left rear corner, clean only one or two sections at a time. Thoroughly work suds into the cloth with a natural sponge. Use circular or short back and forth strokes to remove all the dirt. The amount of dirt determines the effort needed. When headliner appears clean and the sponge glides easily, leaving an even distribution of foam, finish cleaning with sweeping motions in one direction.

Headliners—Hard Board Type. Apply a solution of upholstery cleaner and water with a sponge. Use a circular or short back and forth stroke, wiping clean with a cloth. If this type of headliner is extremely dirty, wash with vinyl cleaner using the same procedure.

Headliners—Vinyl Type. Apply vinyl cleaner with a sponge and then wipe clean with a dry clean cloth. If the headliners are extremely dirty, first scrub with a brush.

Seats and Door Panels. Mix one pint of upholstery cleaner to one gallon of water. If seats or door panels are extremely dirty, add more upholstery cleaner to the mixture.

Apply cleaning solution with a scrub brush or sponge. Scrub thoroughly only one section at a time. Avoid oversoaking the material. Frequently stains that show when material is damp will disappear when dry. Use care not to injure the fabric being cleaned by attempting to brush out stubborn spots. Spots should be removed before washing. After each part has been scrubbed, remove loosened dirt by rubbing down the area briskly with a clean cotton towel or soft rag. Make final strokes in one direction.

For average cleaning on nylon or synthetic fabrics, use methods and materials as used in washing cloth upholstery. When the material is extremely dirty, use multi-purpose cleaner full strength and a stiff scrub brush. Scrub thoroughly in all directions, wiping off dirt and excess cleaner with a clean cotton towel or soft rag.

Leather or Vinyl Fabric. Use multi-purpose cleaner full strength and a stiff scrub brush. Apply to the surface to be cleaned and let it soak for two minutes before scrubbing thoroughly. Make sure to clean between all seams and in all cracks and underneath beading. Wipe dirt and excess material off with clean cotton toweling or soft rags.

Kick Pad Panels. Use multi-purpose cleaner full strength, using a stiff brush to apply the cleaner to the surface. Allow cleaner to set about two minutes and then scrub thoroughly. Clean all seams, cracks and beneath beading. Wipe dry with a clean soft towel or rags.

Glove Compartment. Vacuum thoroughly and then clean with upholstery cleaner or vinyl cleaner. Some glove compartment interiors are made of a cardboard type material, so make sure these don't become waterlogged.

Floor Covering—Rubber Mat. Vacuum thoroughly and then clean with upholstery cleaner or multi-purpose cleaner. Use towels or rags to wipe up dirt and excess cleaners.

Floor Covering—Carpeting. Thoroughly vacuum, then mix one pint of upholstery cleaner to one gallon of water. If the carpet is faded, discolored or spotted, add upholstery tint to this solution. To determine the right color shade, pour a small amount of tint at a time. Check by dipping a white rag into the solution, wring it out and then see if that is the right shade. Remember, the dye will dry a shade or two darker. With a stiff brush, use the solution to scrub the carpet vigorously. Lay the nap down in one direction. When the carpets dry, fluff them up by rubbing with a brush.

Salt Stains. These can be removed by first vacuuming the carpet thoroughly to remove as much salt and dirt as possible. Mix a solution of ordinary table salt and water—using a heavy concentration of salt. Soak the stained area to loosen the embedded salt—using a wire brush if necessary. Wash the entire carpet with the recommended cleaner. More than one washing may be necessary to effect a satisfactory result.

Luggage Compartment. Remove the spare wheel, tools, floor covering and all other items. Vacuum the area thoroughly. Use a steel brush to loosen rust and caked dirt. Wash with upholstery cleaner or multi-purpose cleaner and then wipe dry with clean toweling or rags.

Color Restoration or Change. In those instances in which stains persist, after cleaning, or a change in color is desired on trim material, dyes or tints can be applied. However, not all tints and dyes give satisfactory results. Use only those recommended for the exact material being worked on. To accomplish the "new car" look, tints and dyes should be applied by reliable experienced personnel.

Leather and Vinyl Sealers. These are used for repairing holes or tears on seats, arm rests, cargo areas of station wagons, etc. To repair, cut a piece of leather or vinyl about ½ inch larger than the area being repaired. Position the patch under the hole and apply sealer to the contacting areas. Place a piece of masking tape over the tear to hold the torn edges in place until the sealer dries. After the sealer dries, remove the tape and trim all visible rough edges. Fill any visible cracks with sealer. After sealer has thoroughly dried, sand lightly with #400 grade sandpaper until the surface is smooth. Apply the desired shade of color to the repaired area.

CARING FOR THE EXTERIOR

To retain the "new car" look of the car exterior surface, the acrylic finish should be polished at least twice a year to remove all film. When polishing, use one pad made from folded cheesecloth or an old "turkish" towel to apply the polish and another pad to remove the dried film. Test the polished area by rubbing with the fingers. If the surface is not thoroughly cleaned, smears of the polish will show where the fingers were rubbed.

Sand scratches, overspray, and other foreign material can be removed from the acrylic finish using the following procedure:

1. Oil sand the affected surface by hand with Number 600 grit paper and oleum spirits, mineral spirits or kerosene.
2. Remove all sanding sludge.
3. Machine polish the sanded surface using rubbing compound until the surface is completely free of sand scratch marks. Blend with adjacent areas.
4. Buff the surface with a clean wool pad using a liquid type final polish. If the appearance of the polished area is noticeably different than adjacent areas, completely buff the adjacent panels, and if necessary, the complete side or horizontal surfaces to assure uniform appearance.
5. Use a clean, soft, cotton cloth to hand clean all inaccessible areas, but do not use cheesecloth.
6. Remove all traces of polish or rubbing compound from moldings, medallions, nameplates or any other exterior ornamentation.

Bright metals such as bumpers, grilles, exterior moldings, wheel covers, mirrors and the like should be thoroughly cleaned at least twice a year to maintain a new look condition. The recommendations of the cleaner product manufacturer should always be followed. Remove all materials used to protect the bright metal. Use care not to allow the removing agent to come into contact with the acrylic finish. Clean the bright metal thoroughly and remove all traces of cleaner from corners, etc. After cleaning thoroughly, apply and rub out a coat of good body wax to the bright metal. During the winter months and in areas in which salt is used on the roads, do not rub out the wax.

Frequent washing of bright metals, by steam, will necessitate more frequent applications of the protective wax. When cleaning anodized aluminum, use care not to rub through the anodized coating.

TIRE CARE

White sidewall tires should be cleaned using a stiff bristle brush with white sidewall cleaner or multi-purpose cleaner. After washing, rinse with clean water. Do not clean tires with scouring powder, steel wool or other abrasive type cleaners. Scuff marks can be dressed down by sanding lightly with #400 sand paper.

GLASS

Interior glass surfaces should be thoroughly cleaned weekly to remove all traces of smoke and other films resulting from fingers, exhaust fumes, dusts, moisture, etc.

Exterior glass surfaces having an oily film are easily and best cleaned with the use of a commercially made cleaner compounded for that particular application. Do not scrape off smears from bugs, road tars or other similar objects. Rather, use warm water or the necessary type solvent to remove.

During the winter months, snow, ice and frost can be removed with a plastic or rubber type scraper, or a commercially made solvent. Do not remove ice or other objects from the glass by chipping. Furthermore, do not use putty knives, razor blades, steel wool or any other metal object to remove deposits from the glass.

DRAIN HOLES

Drain holes at the bottom of the cowl plenum chamber, doors and floor sills should be inspected regularly to insure drainage. Road tars, mud and similar other foreign matters should be removed immediately. Should bare metal be exposed, surface treat the metal and refinish as necessary.

The drain holes in the quarter panel well areas are sealed with a removable plastic plug on most cars. The plugs should only be

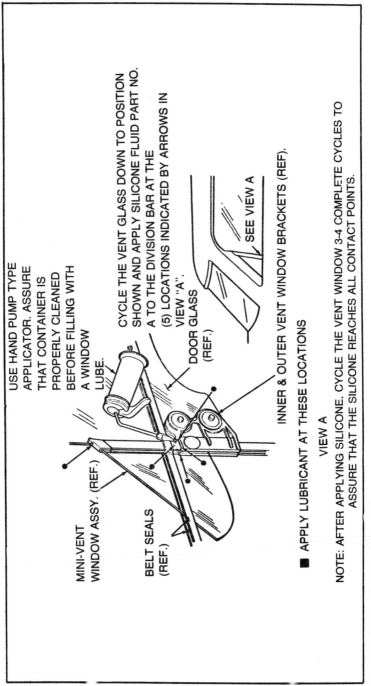

USE HAND PUMP TYPE APPLICATOR. ASSURE THAT CONTAINER IS PROPERLY CLEANED BEFORE FILLING WITH A WINDOW LUBE.

CYCLE THE VENT GLASS DOWN TO POSITION SHOWN AND APPLY SILICONE FLUID PART NO. A TO THE DIVISION BAR AT THE (5) LOCATIONS INDICATED BY ARROWS IN VIEW "A".

DOOR GLASS (REF.)

MINI-VENT WINDOW ASSY. (REF.)

BELT SEALS (REF.)

INNER & OUTER VENT WINDOW BRACKETS (REF.)

SEE VIEW A

VIEW A

■ APPLY LUBRICANT AT THESE LOCATIONS

NOTE: AFTER APPLYING SILICONE, CYCLE THE VENT WINDOW 3-4 COMPLETE CYCLES TO ASSURE THAT THE SILICONE REACHES ALL CONTACT POINTS.

Fig. 13-1. Mini-vent window lubrication.

199

removed whenever it is necessary to clean or drain fluids from the well area.

LUBRICATION

To maintain ease of operation, the hood, door, deck lid mini-vent windows and tail gate hinges should be lubricated at the recommended intervals with the recommended lubricants (Fig. 13-1). Refer to Chapter 3 for the type of lubricant to be used and the lubrication points.

Chapter 14

Auto Heating
And Air Conditioning

While heating systems in automobiles have been around for a long time, only a small percentage of the passenger cars manufactured in the United States before 1971 were equipped with air conditioning systems. Today, however, the percentage of air conditioning installations has increased tenfold and more than 80 percent of all autos manufactured are equipped with convenient heating and cooling systems. Even the few foreign automobiles which are not available with factory-equipped air conditioning can be fitted with add-on units.

This chapter will deal with troubleshooting the modern automotive heating and air conditioning system. A brief overview of the operation of each system is presented, followed by a diagnosis of the problems that commonly occur and finally, how to correct the problem. Much information is also presented on the care and maintenance of such systems.

THE HEATING SYSTEM

In typical, water-cooled engine configurations, automotive heaters work by passing a portion of the heated water in the cooling system through a heater core. When the core is heated to a satisfactory point by the water, which is pumped through the system by the water pump or a portion of the pump, a fan can be activated to blow air through the core. The warmed air is passed through vents and, finally, into the cockpit.

Water temperature is maintained at a constant temperature by the thermostat after the engine has reached a normal operating temperature. The input air to the cockpit is temperature regulated by a manual or automatic control which mixes the outside air at an intake with the heated air. Automatic systems control the mixture through the use of an internal thermostat, while manual models are directly controlled by the operator to suit individual comfort prefer-ences.

Any problem with the cooling system of the engine may have an adverse effect on the heater. Low water levels, defective water pumps, and pressure leaks can all cause heater malfunction.

Figure 14-1 shows a typical automotive heating system and the various hose attachments which are made to the engine, radiator, and water pump for circulation through the heater core. Specifics may vary from car to car, but the system depicted will give the reader a good, overall idea of just what is involved in the basic heating system. Cars equipped with air conditioning have a vacuum valve which channels the heated coolant through the core only when the heater switch is activated. Cars which are now air conditioned circulate the coolant through the core at all times, transferring heat to the passenger compartment when the electrical fan is actuated.

Again, the condition of the automotive cooling system will determine the condition, in many many instances, of the heating system. The hoses which connect to the heater core are much smaller than the major cooling hoses connected to the engine and the radiator. They are more easily blocked by materials such as radiator stop-leak, rust and other foreign matter in the cooling system.

Heating system preventive maintenance should include re-verse flushing of the heater core at the same time the cooling system is flushed. This is normally done once a year. Flushing usually involves the use of a plastic flushing tee which reverse flushes the radiator and engine block, but does absolutely nothing to the heater core. The proper method for flushing the heater core involves the removal of both hoses from the engine block. Jam a water hose into the heater outlet hose which is connected to the water pump hous-ing. When the water is turned on, it flows through the heater outlet hose and pours out of the inlet hose after passing through and flushing the heater core. When the water finally runs clear, the job is completed and the hoses may be refitted.

The actual disassembly of the heater core and related mechanisms for repair can be a very simple task on some makes of automobiles. For the great majority, it is one of those jobs that even very experienced automotive mechanics hate to do. The time con-

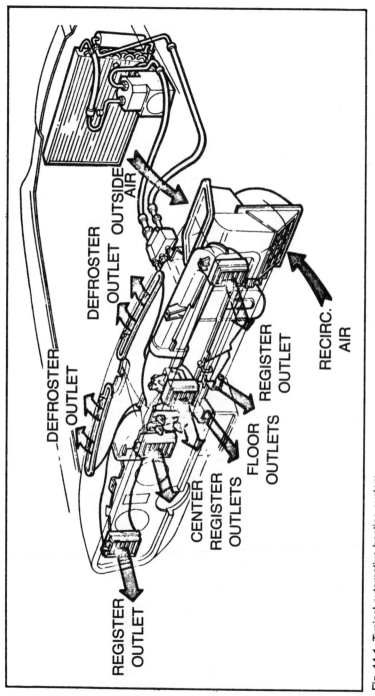

DEFROSTER
OUTLET

DEFROSTER
OUTLET

OUTSIDE AIR

RECIRC.
AIR

REGISTER
OUTLET

CENTER
REGISTER
OUTLETS

FLOOR
OUTLETS

REGISTER
OUTLET

Fig. 14-1. Typical automotive heating system.

sumed in just getting to the various parts is very substantial. The system is relatively simple and does not tax the abilities of even a neophyte mechanic, but the labor involved usually borders on the horrible. For this reason, proper preventive maintenance is absolutely essential.

PREVENTIVE MAINTENANCE

Monthly inspections should be performed to assure the proper operation of the heating system. Heater hoses should be checked for signs of hardening or any undue wear. When a heater hose breaks, gallons of expensive coolant is dumped in the road to say nothing of the inconvenience of a delayed trip or on-the-road repair. Whenever a hose is in questionable condition, it should be replaced with a similar hose designed for automotive heater requirements. Make certain that all clamps are secure and in a good state of repair. All of these maintenance procedures are, of course, in addition to the regular maintenance checks which should be performed on the automotive cooling system. Check hoses and clamps as well as other integral components.

Electrical maintenance procedures should be performed on a regular basis as well and usually involve the inspection of the wiring leading to the fan motor. Control wiring which leads from the fan switch on the console should also be examined. Many times the harness is connected to this switch by means of a plug and socket arrangement which can become partially dislodged after continued use. A simple shake will indicate whether or not a tight connection exits. If looseness is discovered, simply press the plug against the receptacle and it should snap back into place, which will be indicated by a minimum of movement when the plug is shaken.

Automotive heaters also serve as defrosters and often have a vent control which will direct the heated air into the passenger compartment through vents in the floor, the console or through defroster channels. The opening and closing of these vents will be a purely mechanical process in older automobiles, but in the newer models, air pressure valves and switches are used to open and close the ducts. Small plastic hoses are connected to a central air switch which is controlled by a knob on the heater panel. When a particular duct is called on to open by throwing the switch, compressed air from the engine is channeled through the proper hose which activated the vent. When these hoses become dislodged, and most are connected only by friction fittings, vents will not activate. Repair is effected by replacing the hose to the correct fitting connection.

One other preventive maintenance step, which is very simple to perform, should be done on a weekly basis to automobiles equipped with air conditioning as well as a heater. As was previously discussed, automobiles which are equipped with air conditioning do not circulate the heated coolant constantly through the heater core but, through the use of a vacuum switch, control the coolant flow. The coolant flows through the core only when the heater switch is activated. During the spring and summer months when the heater is no longer needed, the switch is not activated and the vacuum valve may tend to lock up from underuse. Also the heater core is empty and internal accumulations may concentrate in this core. The maintenance procedure to prevent these conditions from ever occuring involves the activation of the heater switch every week or so while the automobile is traveling at normal highway speeds. Activation for four or five minutes will open the vacuum valve and allow coolant to flow throughout the heater core, flushing any buildups throughout the entire cooling system where blockages are less likely due to the increased size of the main cooling hoses.

Naturally, vent openings should be kept free of objects which can block the flow of the heated air. Small objects which are placed above the console such as pencils, tie clips and the like often enter the de-froster vents causing air flow problems. Many of these objects can necessitate time-consuming removal. Keep all small, slender objects off of this area of the console.

TROUBLESHOOTING

In spite of all of the preventive maintenance techniques already discussed, problems do occur within the heating system and need to be analyzed just as is done in other automotive systems. Troubleshooting is not as difficult in the heating system as it is for other automotive systems due to the few components involved, but the actual repair work, although simple, may take many hours due to complexities in gaining access to the system on many makes of automobiles. An owner's manual for the make of automobile is practically mandatory for effecting repairs when the problem is located within the heating core, and these manuals will also aid in determining which hoses and cables may be suspect in attempting to diagnose a problem or problems with the system. Generally, no special tools are required to work on the heating system as would be the case with the air conditioning system. Standard shop tools should suffice in almost every instance.

Due to the hours involved in gaining access to most heating core installation, make certain that any problems that are diagnosed to originate in the core cannot be corrected by other methods such as flushing from the heater hoses. Also, attempting to repair hoses that are old and hardened and beginning to crack is not reccommended. Repairs of this nature can only be considered as temporary and will surely give way at some point in the near future.

Problem A: Temperature Of Output Air Is Lower Than Normal

1. Check the level of coolant in the radiator. A slightly low coolant level may limit the amount of circulation through the heating core and lower the temperature to which the core is allowed to heat up.
2. Referring to Fig. 14-1, make certain the engine thermostat has not locked or is operating erratically. Sounds of water boiling in the radiator or excessively hot engine temperatures may indicate a problem in this area.
3. On cars equipped with air conditioning, examine the vacuum valve. Figure 14-2 shows one of these valves and a method for checking for correct operation. If the inlet hose to the heater is not warm, remove the vacuum line, which is the small hose connecting to the middle of the valve, and examine both the hose and the valve port for any signs of blockage. Air suction should be felt at the end of the hose when the engine is in oepration. With the heater control in the high position and the engine at normal operating temperature, reconnect the vacuum line and feel the inlet hose for any signs of heating up. If the hose stays cool, the valve is defective and should be replaced. Note: any signs of corrosion showing on this valve indicates failure or a condition where failure is imminent in the near future. Replace the valve under these conditions.

Problem B: Total Absence Of Heated Air When Blower Is Activated

This problem assumes that air is being emitted in normal quantities from the heating ducts, but the temperature is that of the outside air.

1 . Look for signs of a break in the flow of coolant either in the heater hoses or the main cooling system hoses, which will be indicated by steam or water flowing out on the ground beneath the automobile.
2. Check the vacuum valve as was outlined in the previous problem.
3. Note the water level in the radiator. If very low, and no indications of a leak are present in the coolant systems

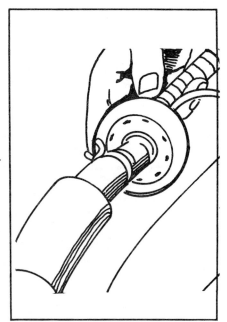

Fig. 14-2. Method of checking vacuum valve for proper operation.

hoses, the radiator itself may have a small leak which has caused the coolant to slowly drain out. An automotive pressure gauge inserted where the radiator cap is normally located will indicate whether a leak exists in the cooling system by reading any signs of a pressure loss. Stop leak may be used to temporarily seal radiator leaks, but this substance can also cause clogged heater hoses and heater cores. Radiator leaks should be welded for a permanent repair. All defective hoses should be replaced also.

4. If no obvious flaws are noted in the heating system, the problem may lie in a jammed or dislocated vent duct. While the switch may be in the passenger compartment heat position, the vents may be locked into the outside air position and the blower is simply delivering normal vent air under pressure. This problem may be corrected by replacing a dislodged vacuum line which is normally terminated at the vent selection control on the heater control panel. A vent may also be mechanically jammed due to a foreign object entering the ducting mechanism, or a hose which directs air from the fan to the vent port may be dislodged. The make of automobile will determine the correct service procedure for this last problem.

Problem C: Fan Motor Will Not Operate

1. Check the wiring leading to the fan motor for signs of breakage or short circuits. Repair any suspicious areas and measure the voltage on the line. For most automobiles, the measured voltage should be 13.8 volts while the engine is in operation.

2. Lack of voltage at this point indicates the possibility of a blown fuse which will usually be found on the fuse block on the driver's side of the passenger compartment. The fuse is normally marked "heater". Never depend on a mere visual examination to determine if a fuse is blown. When fuses open up, they usually can be located and diagnosed as bad on sight, but sometimes a small, hairline gap will be created in the element which will not be noticed. Check suspicious fuses with an ohmmeter. A reading of practically zero ohms indicates a good fuse. High readings indicate bad.

3. Check all wiring at the heater-blower switch for signs of looseness. Repair or replace bad connections. Check the operation of the switch with an ohmmeter to make certain that the switch is connecting and breaking properly. Replace a defective switch with a standard replacement part.

4. Finally, if voltage is indicated by a voltmeter and is being delivered to the fan motor, and electrical winding in the motor coil has probably broken and the motor will have to be rewound or replaced. A short circuit can also occur in the motor which will cause the fuse to blow each time the the circuit is activated. Rewinding or replacement of the component is again necessary.

Common sense and preventive maintenance plays a large role is repairing and keeping the automotive heating system. This system, traditionally, gets the least amount of care and preventive maintenance and is always sorely missed when it becomes inoperative. A relatively simple automotive system such as the heater is easy to maintain on a working basis, but when problems do develop, they can be costly, more to working hours than the cost of replacement parts. The few components of this system are relatively inexpensive and should be replaced at the slightest sign of wear or erratic operation.

Don't allow this system to be neglected as to maintenance and operation in the summer when its use is not needed. Keep the system operative on a weekly basis for a few minutes to assure proper operation the following winter.

THE AIR CONDITIONING SYSTEM

Temperatures in a parked automobile with the sun shining through the windshield can exceed 140 degrees Fahrenheit. But automotive air conditioning can bring that temperature down to a very comfortable level in just two to three minutes and maintain that temperature through almost all extremes of outside temperature conditions.

Comparing automotive air conditioning to the residential models indicate the differences in operating conditions which must be tolerated by the automotive variety and the extreme variations the latter unit will encounter and must properly operate under. Unlike most homes, offices and businesses, automobiles have virtually no insulation, the inside temperature will tend to equalize with the outside temperature in less than two minutes. Automotive air conditioning must cool an area which is composed of about ⅓ glass walls or windows to allow sunlight to enter as heat. This area is usually occupied by more than one person at all times. It must provide a steady output of cooling air at a noise level conducive to comfortable conversation at highway driving speeds. It must do all of this with compressor speeds which vary from about 450 to 5000 revolutions per minute. Efficiency at low speeds necessitates the use of an oversized compressor which may over-exceed the needed requirements when the speed is increased to a high level at higher engine speeds.

These adverse operating conditions hinder but do not stop the automotive air conditioning system from keeping the automobile occupants comfortable even on the hottest days, if properly maintained. Automotive air conditioners vary tremendously in capacity, which is dependent on the type or size of the compressor and other components used, the engine speed, the outside temperature, the interior temperature and other factors. Many systems can produce upwards of 25,000 BTU'S for a short period of time and often operate continuously in the 8000 to 10000 BTU range on a per hour basis.

AIR CONDITIONING COMPONENTS

Specialized tools, components and testing devices such as temperature and pressure gauges are needed for repair and maintenence of this system. Several types of refrigerants are available, but type R-12 is used for automotive purposes because it is best suited for rubber hoses and seals. It also operates well at relatively low pressures.

Automotive air conditioning systems are composed of many parts, but the major components will include the condenser, the compressor, the suction and discharge mufflers, the expansion valve, evaporator and a blower. Other components include the various liquid hoses and input valves.

Figure 14-3 shows a typical air conditioning system with the various components labeled, and will be helpful for referral throughout this discussion as to component placement in relationship to the engine and the other air conditioning components.

The Condenser

The air-conditioning condenser is normally mounted at the very front of the engine compartment in front of the radiator just behind the grill. The amount of air which flows through the condenser coils is directly dependent upon the speed of the automobile. The purpose of the condenser is to remove heat from the air conditioning system. Heat is conducted to the passing air by means of a coal configuration that may take two shapes. Figure 14-4 shows the two types of condenser coil configurations which are often used on American automobiles. One type resembles a radiator but consists of one, long continuous loop of flat tubing which runs back and forth over the aluminum frame. The other type depicted is made up of several rows of ⅜ inch tubing between a solid grid network for increased cooling capacities. Either may be encountered in different makes of automobiles.

The cooling refrigerant flows through the condenser under pressure as gas and is cooled to its liquid state again when the passing air drops the temperature of the gas to a certain level.

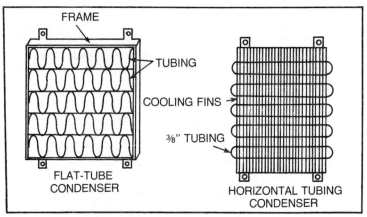

Fig. 14-4. Two types of condenser coil configurations.

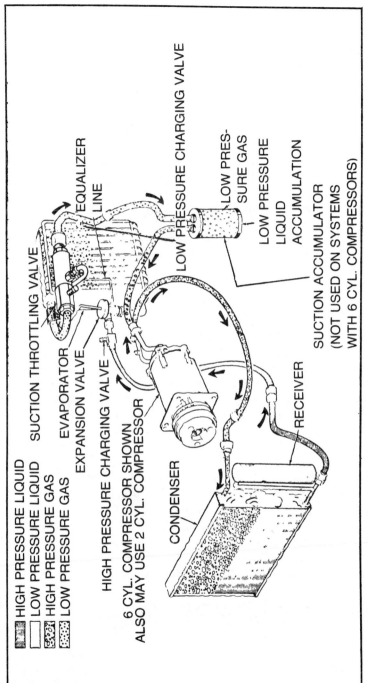

HIGH PRESSURE LIQUID
LOW PRESSURE LIQUID
HIGH PRESSURE GAS
LOW PRESSURE GAS

HIGH PRESSURE CHARGING VALVE

6 CYL. COMPRESSOR SHOWN
ALSO MAY USE 2 CYL. COMPRESSOR

CONDENSER

RECEIVER

SUCTION ACCUMULATOR
(NOT USED ON SYSTEMS
WITH 6 CYL. COMPRESSORS)

LOW PRESSURE
LIQUID
ACCUMULATION

LOW PRES-
SURE GAS

LOW PRESSURE CHARGING VALVE

EQUALIZER
LINE

SUCTION THROTTLING VALVE

EVAPORATOR

EXPANSION VALVE

Fig. 14-3. Basic automotive air conditioning system.

The Compressor

Compressors encountered in home air conditioners and refrigeration units are of the electric type. They are not suitable to automotive requirements because of the large amount of electrical current required. The most practical means of powering the air conditioning compressor is by the automotive engine itself. The hermetically sealed, closed type of compressor construction used in home units is replaced with an open construction model which has a shaft extending throughout the entire length of the compressor body and protrudes at one end to be driven by belt and pulley connections by the engine driveshaft. Shaft seals must be used to prevent severe leakage of the refrigerant and, at the same time, to allow the shaft to rotate to drive the compressor. In most systems, some leakage is always present; however, proper seal installations will minimize the loss to less than an ounce of refrigerant yearly.

Due to the means of drive, compressors create vibration. Shaft torque can be very high for the larger units and mounting brackets and connections must be examined periodically for signs of looseness or metal fatigue. Loose mounting platforms will eventually cause complete failure and, possibly, severe damage to the system. At the very least, seal connections will become loose and all of the refrigerant may be lost in a matter of seconds.

The compressor increases the temperature of the liquid refrigerant. This high-pressure vapor is channeled to the condenser through a rubber discharge line. The condenser pressure remains fairly constant throughout the process. The condenser action removes heat from the vapor which causes it to change to a liquid. This liquid refrigerant then enters the receiver-drier through the condenser outlet tubes. The receiver acts as a storage area for a reserve of refrigerant. From the receiver, the refrigerant flows to the expansion valve. This valve creates a pressure drop which, basically, causes the liquid to be sprayed into the evaporator. In the evaporator, the refrigerant is again placed under a lower pressure where it changes to gas. At this pressure, the liquid which originally enters the evaporator boils at a temperature of approximately 42 degrees Fahrenheit. This gas, which results from the boiling liquid, is returned to the compressor through the suction line. At the same time heat is removed from the evaporator coil, which delivers the coolness to a stream of air directed across it by the air conditioning fan. When the gas reaches the compressor again, it is put under a higher pressure once more and the process starts over.

The various other components in the liquid and gas circuit simply facilitate the flow of these gases and liquids throughout the system. Comparing the air conditioning system to the heating system discussed earlier in this chpater, the evaporator and the heater core are similar in function, but the heater core performs its function by heating up from the passing coolant. The evaporator performs its function, not by being cooled externally, but by having much of its ambient heat *removed* externally. The heater core conducts heat to its surface from the coolant. The evaporator does not connect coolness to it surface, but, rather, the heat is conducted away from the evaporator surface.

Other Air Conditioning Components

Figure 14-5 depicts a typical receiver-drier which is, basically, a storage tank for the liquid refrigerant. These components are usually not repairable and are replaced when foreign matter enters the system, clogging or damaging this element.

Figure 14-6 shows the evaporator unit's position in the automobile. In factory equipped systems, the evaporator is housed in the same basic compartment as the heat core. A selectable duct is used to channel air over the desired element, heat core or evaporator, when the switch is thrown to either the heater or air conditioning position.

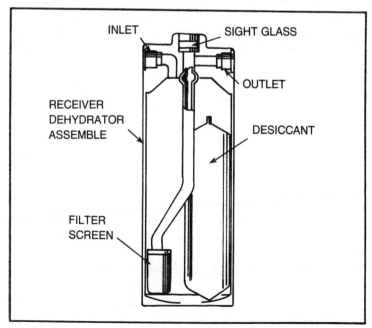

Fig. 14-5. Typical receiver-drier.

Figure 14-7 shows the internal workings of an expansion valve which is used in the system to change the pressure on the refrigerant as it enters this device. The operation of this valve is controlled by its feeler bulb, which is a device mounted to the suction line to sense the temperature of that line. The diaphragm has two different pressures applied to each side of its surface. The tube entering the pressure chamber at the point just below the diaphragm is connected to the evaporator just ahead of its outlet. Evaporator pressure presses upward on the bottom of the diaphragm.

Air conditioning systems are much more complex than the heating systems discussed in the earlier portion of this chapter. Air conditioning systems work on a completely different principle that used to change the temperature of air to a value higher than the ambient, outdoor temperature used when designing heating systems.

Components used for air conditioning systems are numerous and relatively complex. Many of the components are not serviceable but must be replaced when found to be defective. By properly maintaining the working air conditioning system, repair time and costs can be kept to a minimum. As with the heating systems, the air conditioner should be activated periodically during the winter months in order to keep all seats sealed and to prevent a type of severe aging that can set in on this system if not used for long periods of time. This is a sealed system with only minor refrigerant leakage around the shaft seal on the compressor. A break in the system can mean the loss of the refrigerant and the need to replace components such as the receiver-drier. As was the case with the engine cooling system, the air conditioning system must be kept completely sealed at all times.

MORE TROUBLESHOOTING

Servicing of air conditioning systems can only be accomplished with the correct tools and diagnostic equipment. There are also certain hazards that should be noted when working around the refrigerant and the high-pressure systems encountered.

The refrigerant normally used is the R-12 variety is one of the safest varieties to work with. Make certain that if refrigerant must be replaced in a system, the R-12 type intended solely for automobile recharging purposes is used. R-12 is used for other purposes as well, but only R-12 which is labeled for recharging of automotive air conditioners is pure enough to work in the system without causing problems.

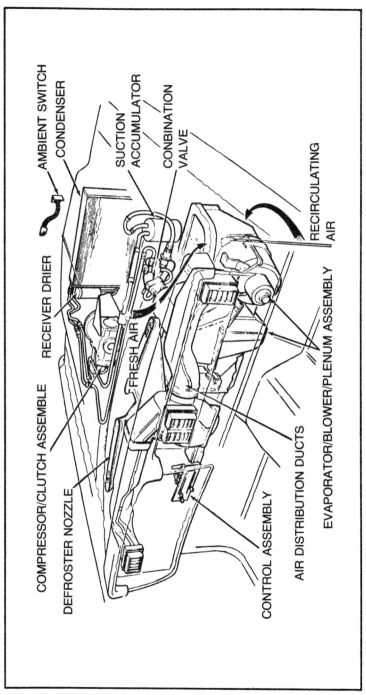

AMBIENT SWITCH

CONDENSER

SUCTION ACCUMULATOR

CONBINATION VALVE

RECIRCULATING AIR

RECEIVER DRIER

FRESH AIR

COMPRESSOR/CLUTCH ASSEMBLE

DEFROSTER NOZZLE

CONTROL ASSEMBLY

AIR DISTRIBUTION DUCTS

EVAPORATOR/BLOWER/PLENUM ASSEMBLY

Fig. 14-6. Evaporator and other air conditioning components as they are positioned in a typical automobile.

215

The refrigerant is extremely cold when it is allowed to escape into the air and will instantly freeze anything it touches. This freezing effect can damage skin tissue and is extremely hazardous when it comes in contact with the eyes. Blindness can be the end result of such exposure. The escaping refrigerant can also cause suffocation if the situation occurs in a closed space, because it displaces all of the air in a room in a short period of time. Explosion is also a hazard and the refrigerant should never be exposed to open flames or high temperatures at any time. Refrigerant which is exposed to open flames in a *non-pressurized* compartment will not explode but will burn and give off a very toxic gas which is fatal to human beings. One other caution when repairing or testing an air conditioning system: prolonged idling of the engine when the temperature is above 85 degrees can create dangerously high pressures within the compressor. An explosion could occur which would fling small parts and components away from the explosion point at dangerously high speeds and possibly spray a fatal dose of refrigerant into the face of the mechanic. *Be careful*.

Problem A: Inoperation Due to
Failure of Compressor to Rotate Properly

1. Check the compressor drive belt for any signs of breakage or wear. This belt may be slipping on the pulley causing erratic rotation of the shaft or no rotation at all. The compressor mounting bracket may need to be adjusted for a tighter pull on the belt, or the belt may have to be replaced completely.
2. The clutch may be slipping. Check this mechanism for signs of dirt or grease on its surface. Clean these areas with carbon tetrachloride.
3. The clutch may not be engaging properly which could be due to low voltage on this component, caused by corroded wiring or loose contacts. Replacement may be necessary if all voltage readings appear to be at the normal value of 13.8 volts. The field coil in the actuator movement may have opened up or the brushes may be worn to the point of inoperation.

Problem B: Intermittent Cooling Temperatures

1. Check the expansion valve which may be jammed. The valve should be tested and replaced if found to be defective or questionable.

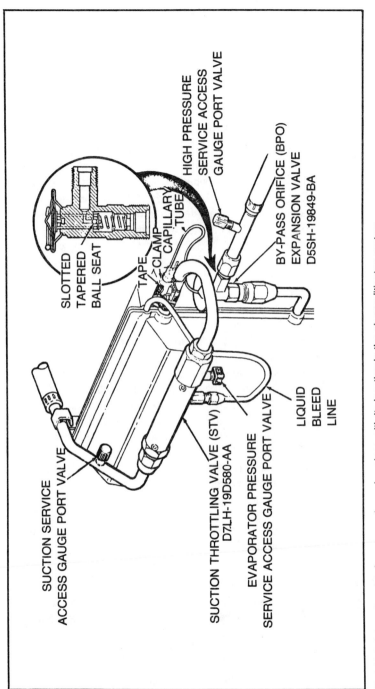

SLOTTED TAPERED BALL SEAT

TAPE

CLAMP

CAPILLARY TUBE

HIGH PRESSURE SERVICE ACCESS GAUGE PORT VALVE

BY-PASS ORIFICE (BPO) EXPANSION VALVE D5SH-19849-BA

SUCTION SERVICE ACCESS GAUGE PORT VALVE

SUCTION THROTTLING VALVE (STV) D7LH-19D580-AA

EVAPORATOR PRESSURE SERVICE ACCESS GAUGE PORT VALVE

LIQUID BLEED LINE

Fig. 14-7. Internal parts of an expansion valve along with its location in the air conditioning system.

2. Check the compressor to make certain that the shaft is rotating properly. A problem here can be analyzed using the steps for the previous problem.

3. Test the suction control valve which may be operating intermittently. Replace this part if questionable or defective.

Problem C: Evaporator Fan Fails to Activate

1. This is more than likely an electrical problem caused by current not being properly transferred to the motor. With a voltmeter, determine whether the proper voltage is being applied to the motor power leads. Adequate voltage measured here points to a defective motor which may have to be replaced or rewound by a motor technician.

2. Lack of voltage on these leads points to a blown fuse, broken wire, or inoperative power switch. Check the proper slot marked "air conditioner" on the fuse block and test the fuse for continuity with an ohmmeter. Replace the fuse if defective.

3. If replacement fuses continue to blow, a short circuit exists and may point back to a bad motor or shorted leads going to the air conditioning switch. A visual inspection may determine whether the latter problem is causing the trouble.

4. A fuse that checks out as all right should lead the technician to suspect a broken wire or defective switch. Visually inspect the wiring around the switch and check out the switch's operation with an ohmmeter. Replace a defective switch.

5. If all else fails, trace the voltage from the fuse block to a point where all indication of voltage is lost. This point is where the problem begins to occur and any trouble that has not, before, been analyzed may show up here. Look for signs of burnt wiring or insulation scrapes that may have been burnt away.

Problem D: Low Suction Pressure

1. Check refrigerant level. If low, add more refrigerant.

2. Examine the compressor drive belt for proper operation. Correct if necessary.

3. Visually examine liquid line for signs of a blockage or restriction of flow. These areas will be indicated by a bit of ice or frost over the problem spots.

4. Expansion valve may be defective. Check this component and replace if questionable or defective.

SUMMARY

Air conditioning systems for automobiles, while only a few years ago were considered as luxury items, have fast become almost standard equipment on many American automobiles. Their dependability, considering the many abuses and the many demands made upon them, is almost unbelievable. Generally, preventive maintenance and occasional recharging of the coolant is all that these systems will require throughout the life of the vehicle.

Air conditioners may seem like highly complicated pieces of equipment, but with the proper test and servicing equipment and knowhow they are easy to service. Safe and effective repairs on this system are easily accomplished in the well-equipped shop.

Remember the safety precautions that have been stressed in this chapter. Each year, many people are seriously injured or even killed in accidents that involve refrigerants and high, stored pressures which are always found in automotive air conditioning systems.

Chapter 15

Accessories

One of the largest determining factors regarding the price of a modern automobile is the amount of accessories ordered with the vehicle. In the past, accessories may have included only a heater, AM radio, courtesy lights and not much else. But today, CB radios, AM-FM, eight track quadraphonic systems, air conditioning, tape players, rear window defoggers and many other items are not only available but are standard on many automobiles. In addition, instrumentation is far more complex. Accessories in this area often include a tachometer, clock, ammeter, and even fuel economy gauges in addition to the speedometer and odometer.

Accessories play a big role in the purchase price of an automobile, and they also can be a major factor when it comes to repairs. Many of these accessories are not electrical or mechanical in nature, as are other systems in the automobile. Many of these items are electronic and must be repaired by a shop which specializes in this type of work. However, proper maintenance of the mechanical brackets which hold these pieces of equipment in place and regular checks on the electrical connections to the car's electric system will minimize problems in the area of automobile electronic accessories. Special tools and instruments usually are required for maintenance, but accuracy can be checked in most shops and the associated cables and conductors can be checked and repaired as needed.

ELECTRONIC ACCESSORIES

The electronic accessories that are normally found in automobiles almost always are powered by the automotive electrical system. Equipment which is especially designed for automotive use will usually require an operating potential of at least 13.8 volts DC, which is the nominal voltage rating of the electrical system when the car is operated at normal driving speeds. Most of these units are designed in such a manner as to resist engine whine or noise which can be a problem when audio equipment such as radios and tape players come into use.

Electrical connections for these accessories are often obtained at the fuse block which is normally located against the firewall on the driver's side of the cockpit. The positive or *hot* lead is connected to a clip on an empty or accessory fuse slot and the negative lead is connected to a clip on an empty or accessory fuse slot and the negative lead is connected to the chassis, often by loosening a bolt under the console and connecting a wire lug before re-tightening. This type of installation works well for many types of accessories, but automotive noise may be a problem because a direct connection has not been made to the battery.

Whenever a connection is made to the fuse block, care must be taken to make certain that the circuit being used is rated to deliver the amount of current which will be drawn by the accessory. Many automobiles now provide fuse blocks which contain circuits labeled *CB radio* or *tape player*. Normally, these fuse slots are vacant and are intended to be filled with the correct size fuse after a home or shop installation of the equipment is accomplished.

If an extra circuit is not provided by the fuse block, low powered devices may be connected to a circuit already in use, such as the accessory position. Make certain that the extra accessory does not overload the circuit. Most of these accessory circuits contain a 20 ampere fuse. If a larger fuse is placed in this circuit to handle a larger drain, there is a danger of severe overload and possibly fire. Check the manufacturer's ratings on the circuit in question. Some information should be provided in the owner's manual and the current ratings of any additional accessories should be stamped on the unit or printed in a schematic or instruction sheet.

Where electrical interference is caused by the engine, a connection of electronic audio equipment to the fuse block and the chassis is often unsatisfactory. A direct connection to the storage battery will often eliminate or greatly reduce this type of interference. An in-line fuse will be necessary in the cable running from the equipment to the battery. Most manufacturers of CB radios, tape players and the like provide these fuses and holders with every unit, but if one must be installed, it should be placed at a point very near the battery, about 6 to 8 inches. A small hole is drilled in the fire wall and rubber grommet placed in this hole. The cable is run through the grommet and through the engine compartment in a way as to avoid any excessively hot components. The cable should also be firmly anchored in place every 8 inches. The positive and negative power cable leads are firmly attached to the positive and negative terminals of the battery. This can be done by lifting the main terminals and wrapping the proper wire around the posts and then replacing the terminals securely. Make certain that both the positive and negative leads are connected directly to the battery. If the negative lead is simply grounded to the chassis, interference may still be a severe problem. Do not attempt to accomplish this wiring without using an in-line fuse. The exclusion of this item could cause a fire or, at the least, cause severe damage to the electronic accessory.

Another means of obtaining entrance to the automotive electrical system is through the cigarette lighter accessory if one is provided. This connection is rated to deliver a high amount of current and will power almost any electronic device likely to be used in an automobile. A special electrical plug is necessary and is available at most electronic supply and hobby stores. The heating element is removed from the socket and the accessory plug is inserted for the power connection. Care must be exercised when wiring the plug to the equipment. Proper polarity must be observed; the positive lead from the accessory must be conected to the positive side of the plug and vice-versa. If improper connections are made and the positive and negative leads reversed, severe damage can result to the accessory. Polarity reversal is the most common cause of failure in electronic equipment used in automobiles when installed after manufacture.

When complete replacement of an electronic accessory with another is required, the job is usually very simple. The same electrical connections can be used and the only problem may be a mechanical one of getting the new accessory to fit into the same space as was occupied by the older unit. Most electronic accessories of similar performance and construction will draw approximately the same amount of current. An AM radio of modern manufacture will require about the same amount of current from the electrical system regardless of who the manufacturer is. The same is true of CB radios, tape players and AM-FM stereo systems. When replacing any of these units, no special electrical considerations are usually necessary as long as the unit being replaced is similar to its replacement.

INSTRUMENTATION

Many of the installation problems and considerations which are common to electronic accessories will also apply to certain types of instrumentation. Many modern instruments are electrical or electronic in nature and will derive power from the electrical system of the automobile. Others are mechanically driven and will be attached through cables to various contacts on the engine. Exact replacement components are available for most modern automobiles, and many models already contain inserts or knock outs for the mounting of accessory instrumentation such as tachometers, clocks, digital clocks and accessory odometers. Where these knockouts are provided, installation times are reduced by a high percentage. Wiring and cable access channels are also provided in many instances when provision has been made by the manufacturer for additional instrumentation.

When mounting slots are not provided or where exact replacement components are not used, below-the-console or outboard mounting is often utilized. A relatively clear area is chosen below the console where adequate display to the driver is available and the instrument or instruments are simply bracketed to this point. The associated electrical and mechanical connections are made to the indicator and installation is complete. Sometimes accessory instruments are mounted above the console, against the windshield, but laws in certain states prohibit this type of mounting, so check local regulations before this method is considered.

When instrumentation breaks, special tools and alignment equipment are required to effect proper repairs. Tiny parts are usually inspected through a jeweler's loupe and microsized tools are used to delicately remove and replace the tiny parts involved. Preventive maintenance will keep most instruments working properly for the life of the automobile if proper tolerance and care were used in manufacture. One very large problem with instruments is dust. Instrument cases are sealed to prevent dust and other particles from entering the delicate movement, but should the instrument be dropped or mishandled, breaks in this shield can occur. If the viewing window of the metered instruments becomes lose or cracked, it will only be a short time before erratic operation of the instrument becomes commonplace. Handle instruments very carefully and attempt to remove as much dust and road grime as possible from them and from around them on a regular basis. Good instruments can be very expensive and deserve regularly scheduled preventive maintenance as do the other portions of the automobile.

An ammeter is an electrical device used to measure DC. The impulses to the meter are converted into corresponding current pulses which are read on the meter scale which is calibrated in amps for monitoring the battery charge rate or in revolutions per minute when used as a tachometer.

Many of the most modern indicating instruments have gone to digital readout which is a direct numerical display of the values being measured. Speedometers, tachometers, clocks, ammeters, and other instruments are now available in digital readout, although very few of these items could be considered standard equipment even yet. For individuals who are troubled by eye problems at close ranges, these digitally indicating instruments are far more easily read.

All digital readouts, other than a few obsolete mechanically controlled digital displays, include sophisticated, electronics circuitry to accomplish their functions. These circuits are constructed by using integrated circuits which may contain thousands of transistors and other electronic components on a tiny piece of quartz crystal no larger than a finger tip. Types of close, solid-state packaging maintains a high level of shock, resistance and, thus, dependability. These instruments will rarely fail due to mild misuse, but are highly subject to severe damage from incorrect voltage polarity and even minor overloads. When damaged, a qualified electronics technician should be called on to perform the repair.

ADDITIONAL ACCESSORIES

Other automotive accessories which are found on many or most newly manufactured models include seatbelt warning devices, power-adjustable seats, rear window defogger, fog and driving lamps, cruise control, dashboard adjustable air shocks, towing packages and many more. These types of accessories range from electronic to mechanical to hydraulic in nature and may cover a very wide range of tool and test equipment requirements when repairs are attempted.

Preventive maintenance, again, is necessary to cut down on these repairs by a large percentage. All electrical cables should be inspected and maintained in a manner which is discussed in the electrical system portion of this text. Mechanically-driven devices usually contain cables which transfer the torque from the control point to the device. These cables must be kept relatively clean and free from road grime and mounted in such a manner as to avoid any severe bending. Hydraulic lines should be inspected often to check for signs of pressure loss of fluid leaks.

TROUBLESHOOTING

When many accessories receive only minor damage or abuse, further deterioration sets in immediately and, in a relatively short period if time, complete inoperation or unsatisfactory operation is the end result. Minor damages should be repaired immediately. Any signs of wear or breakdown of parts or components should be dealt with to prevent further breakdown. Let's examine some accessory problems and possible solutions.

Problem A: Accessory Driving Lights Inoperative

Whenever additional driving lights are added to an automobile by the manufacturer or at a later time, the entire system is isolated from the normal assortment of lamps. It is treated as a separate part of the electrical system with the eventual connection to the storage battery serving as the only mutual connection point.

It can be seen that the driving lights system is controlled by a separate relay which switches the high battery current when the actuator switch is thrown. One electrical leg of the circuit is connected directly to the chassis while the other, the positive lead, is switched by the relay.

Complete inoperation of the driving lights can result from defective lamps, but if both are out simultaneously, the problem probably lies elsewhere in the system. The first check should be made on the relay to see if it is activating properly. While flipping the actuator switch back and forth, listen with the hood raised for the sounds of the relay clicking on and off. If no sounds are heard, the relay coil may be defective or the switch may contain a broken wire or be inoperative.

If the relay seems to be operating properly, the problem may be due to carbon on the internal switching contacts. Using a voltmeter, measure the voltage by placing the probes across the relay input terminal and the automobile chassis. If normal voltage is found at this point, the connection from the battery to the relay is good. If no voltage is indicated, the wiring between this point in the battery is defective and should be spliced or replaced. With a normal voltage input measured at the relay input, switch the positive probe to the relay output terminal and check the reading with the actuator switch in the on position. The absence of any voltage here indicates a bad or burnt relay contact. Depending on the type of relay, cleaning of the contacts may be possible with a standard burnishing tool. Other types may require replacement.

If voltage is present at the relay output terminal, the problem must then be one of three things: bad lamps, a broken hot wire from the relay to the lamps, or a loose or defective ground connection from the lamps to the chassis. Visual inspection and ohmmeter readings with the circuit inactivated will determine which of the problems are causing the inoperative condition.

Other problems may develop with the driving lamp circuit such as intermittent operation, blinking, dimness, etc. These problems may be corrected by referring to the electrical system chapter in this text.

Problem B: Speedometer Inoperative or Operates Erratically

If any foreign matter has entered the speedometer housing, the minute gears may be jamming or dragging which causes improper or non-existent operation. Dust particles can enter the meter movement causing the needle indicator to operate in a jerky manner also. The only serviceable problem without special tools and test equipment is in the connection from the transmission to the speedometer, which is sometimes subject to stresses which cause looseness and corrosion of the fittings.

Lifting the hood of the automobile, locate the transmission connection where the cable attaches to the speedometer. This connection is often covered with engine grease and oil mixed with road tar and other materials. If the connection was not tight originally, some of this material may have seeped inside the connection, jamming the rotation of the cable's internal element. Remove this connection and thoroughly clean away any foreign matter. Examine the connection point and the fitting for any signs of wear or breakage, then replace the connection and tighten securely. If operation still is not correct, examine the connection which attaches to the speedometer, looking for the same problems. Further inoperation indicates a defective cable or defective speedometer indicator.

Problem C: Seatbelt Warning Buzzer and
Light Are On When Seat Belts Are Fastened

This problem is usually cured by repairing switches which would seem to be disassociated completely with the seatbelt system but are, in reality, very much a part of the warning system. In cars with automatic transmissions, the problem will probably be determined to be a defective neutral safety switch on the steering column. To check the operation of this switch, place the transmission in neutral. If the ignition won't activate in this position, the switch is probably defective and should be replaced. If the automobile is equipped with a standard transmission, check the parking brake switch by engaging the brake and looking for the indicator light to activate. If the parking brake indicator light does not come on, the switch is defective and can be located through the owner's manual if necessary and replaced.

Should both of the switches in question check out as good, the problem may lie with broken or high resistance wiring between the pressure sensitive switch or the seatbelt retractor switch. The pressure sensitive switch is found under the seats on both sides of the automobile and the retractor switch is found inside of the well into which the unused belt coils. Examine the wiring at these points and the wiring to the column switch or the brake switch. Look for signs of stripped or torn insulation or loose wires with bare ends.

Problem E: Electrical Accessory Fails To Operate

This problem can be caused by many things including a defect within the accessory (radios, tape players, etc.) which must be repaired by a qualified electronic technician. Problems within the automotive electrical system can also cause inoperation of these devices or erratic, noisy operation for motor-driven and audio devices such as tape players.

When operation ceases, attempt to determine whether or not the accessory is receiving power from the battery. Inoperative panel indicator lights usually indicate that power is not getting through if these lights are supplied with the unit improperly functioning. Using a voltmeter, check the power leads at a point very near the accessory if possible, or at the original connection point to the electrical system. Lack of voltage at this point indicates a blown line or block fuse or a loose, broken ground or hot line conductor. First, check all fuses involved to make certain that they have not opened up. Remember that many electronic accessories may be fused at two points, at the fuse block original connection and in the line near the unit. If all fuses are checked as all right, examine the wiring back to a point where voltage can be read. Check any ground or chassis connections for signs of corrosion, breakage or looseness. Some accessories contain power plugs which are inserted into the back or side of their housings, check this connection for a tight fit.

If it is determined that voltage is reaching the unit or that the accessory is blowing fuses when switched on, the problem lies in the unit and may be repaired at a shop equipped to handle such equipment.

Chapter 16

Emission Controls

Since the late 1960's it has become increasingly evident that the internal combustion engine is probably the major contributor to air pollution. In an attempt to lower the amount of air pollution, engines are now being designed with lower emissions in mind—actual changes in engine design, changes in engine adjustments, and the addition of special devices to reduce or eliminate emissions.

These changes and additions are aimed at the three sources of engine pollution: crankcase vapors, fuel evaporation, and exhaust gasses. Each of these areas will be discussed, including a system description and test procedures for troubleshooting and major components.

CRANKCASE CONTROLS

The engine crankcase receives unburned gasoline that blows by the piston rings. This unburned gasoline tends to dilute the engine oil causing an increase in wear. To overcome this problem, the crankcase has to be ventilated. In pre-emission control engines ventilation was accomplished by simply allowing fresh air to enter through the oil filter cup and to exhaust by way of a vent pipe. The problem with this system is that the unburned gasoline vapors ended up in the air. To alleviate this problem, a system was needed to recirculate these gas vapors. The positive crankcase ventilation (PCV) system was created to do this job.

PCV systems can be separated into two groups, open and closed. As the name implies, open PVC systems allow some of the gasses to escape. In particular, the open system allows gasses to escape through the oil filler tube during full throttle operation. Closed systems recirculate the gas vapors from the oil filler tube to the air cleaner where they can be drawn into the engine and burned.

Both the open and closed PVC systems operate off of engine vacuum. Because of this, the system acts as a large vacuum leak. This vacuum leak would normally create severe operating problems if it weren't for a special valve, the PCV valve.

The PCV valve acts to govern the flow of gasses in the PCV system. This valve slows the flow during periods of high engine vacuum and increases the flow during low vacuum operation. Usually the PCV valve consists of a plunger that operates against a spring. There are also valves that consist of a simply controlled volume orifice having no moving parts. However, the plunger type is more common. The plunger type valve operates by spring tension, pushing the plunger against engine vacuum. The higher the vacuum, the lower the flow.

PCV valves are usually held in the rocker cover by a rubber grommet. These valves can be found attached to the end of the hose leading from the intake manifold—near the base of the carburetor—to the rocker cover.

On the original PCV-equipped engines, the flow of air entered the system at the oil filler cup, but the most recent method draws fresh air from the carburetor air cleaner. Once air enters the system, it goes to the crankcase by way of a hose. This hose runs from the air cleaner to the oil filler cup. The air mixes with the gasoline vapors in the crankcase and is then routed to the intake manifold. From the intake manifold the fuel vapor and air mixture is distributed to each of the cylinders where it can be burned.

As an added measure, most systems have a filter of some type located inside of the air cleaner. This filter is found at the exit point for the hose joint to the crankcase. This filter prevents dirt and other foreign matter from accidentally entering the crankcase.

TESTING THE PCV SYSTEM

Since the PCV system operates off the vacuum, the first test should be to look at the crankcase vacuum, which is checked at the oil filler cup. With the cap removed, start the engine and allow it to idle with the transmission in park or neutral. Take a flat piece of paper and move it close to the air filler hold. The crankcase vacuum is adequate if the paper is sucked against the opening.

If the paper test doesn't indicate crankcase vacuum, the problem may be due to one of the following: inoperative PCV valve, plugged hoses or passages, vacuum leaks at rocker cover or oil pan, or excessive blowby past the rings. Inoperative PCV valves have to be replaced unless they are the type that can be disassembled and cleaned. To check the PCV valve, pull it from the rocker cover and plug the end with your finger. A bad PCV will stop the vacuum. If you don't feel any suction, the valve is bad or the hose is plugged.

After testing the PCV and checking the hoses, check to make sure that all of the bolts on the oil pan and rocker cover are tight. Vacuum leaks at these locations can usually be stopped by tightening any loose bolts. If none of these tests solve the problem, and especially if the engine has a lot of miles on it, ring blowby should be suspected. The best test for excessive blowby is a compression test as discussed in Chapter 4.

FUEL EVAPORATION CONTROLS

The evaporation of fuel—primarily from the fuel tank—also contributes to vehicle emissions. These fuel vapors escape from the fuel tank vent on vehicles without evaporation controls. To prevent these vapors from getting into the atmosphere, hoses are used to channel the vapors from the gas tank to the engine where they are burned. Another way that vapors are eliminated is by pumping them into a special cannister containing charcoal. From the cannister the vapors are pulled into the engine by vacuum so they can be burned by the PCV system.

By putting hoses on the gas tank vent, air is restricted from entering the tank as fuel is drawn out. Since the fuel will stop flowing if air can't get in, a method has to be provided whereby air can enter but vapor can't escape. Each of the major auto manufacturers have different ways of dealing with this problem. Chrysler's crankcase system allows air to enter by way of the breather cap on the engine. American Motors' crankcase system allows air in at the fuel tank cap. In both cases the system is designed to pull air in while preventing vapor escape. Ford crankcase systems employ a three-way valve that operates off vacuum created by the fuel as it leaves the tank.

Engines equipped with charcoal cannisters admit air to the fuel system via a filter in the cannister. These engines also are equipped with vacuum pressure fuel tank caps that admit air but prevent vapor escape.

Both the crankcase and cannister type systems have a special device for preventing liquid fuel from entering the vapor system. These controls are called liquid-vapor separators. Separators are simple liquid traps usually located at the top of the gas tank where the vapor control system starts.

CHECKING THE VAPOR CONTROLS

The vapor control system is relatively maintenance free. The only thing that may need to be done is to replace the cannister air filter. Other than this the system hoses should be checked periodically to make sure they are intact. On very rare occasions the system can become plugged near the fuel tank and interfere with the flow of air into the tank. If this happens, the fuel flow may become erratic and affect engine performance. Correcting this problem is a simple matter of unplugging the system.

EXHAUST EMISSION CONTROLS

Since the exhaust is the primary contributor to vehicle emissions, a vast array of devices have been designed aimed at their control. These devices vary from manufacturer to manufacturer and in some cases from model to model. Here we will deal with the most common systems and leave the special cases to the manufacturer's shop manual.

THE AIR CLEANER

Since an engine that is running lean has fewer unburnt hydrocarbons, a method was needed that would allow the engine to run under lean conditions without sacrificing performance. This method involves the control of incoming air temperature. To control the temperature, the air cleaner was designed to incorporate a door in the snorkel (Fig. 16-1). When the engine is started cold, the door is in a position so that incoming air has been passed over the exhaust manifolds. Since the exhaust manifolds heat up faster than any other external part of the engine, they make an excellent quick heat source for warming the incoming air. As the air temperature rises, the door moves to a position that allows more outside air to enter, keeping the incoming air at a relatively constant temperature. The door opening and closing has to be controlled by a thermostat. This thermostat is usually set to maintain the temperature at around 100 degrees Fahrenheit. In vacuum operated air cleaners, this thermostat operates by allowing engine vacuum to bleed off as the temperature increases.

Since temperatures under the hood can get around 200 degrees Fahrenheit, a source of outside air is needed. All late model vehicles have a long tube that runs from the air cleaner snorkel to the grille.

This allows air outside of the engine compartment to be channeled back to the air cleaner.

There are two ways that the air cleaner door can be actuated. First, the door can be operated by a thermostatic spring or expansion bulb. In this case the movement of the thermostat is responsible for opening the door. The second way uses a vacuum motor. In air cleaners equipped with vacuum motors, the thermostat controls vacuum flow which in turn controls the snorkel door opening. Non-vacuum type air cleaners can be found on some Ford and AMC engines. The vacuum controlled type is found on most other makes and models.

TESTING AIR CLEANER OPERATION

On engines equipped with non-vacuum type air cleaners, testing is a fairly simple procedure. The first step is to make sure the door is free to move. Then with the engine cold, start the engine and check to see if the door is in position to allow warm air to flow. Most of the time this position will be such that the door will close off the end of the snorkel. If thermostat problems are suspected, remove the top of the air cleaner and place a thermometer inside. Replace the cleaner top and start the engine. The door should be in the position that allows outside air in, when the thermometer reads around 130–150 degrees Fahrenheit. If there is a *substantial* temperature difference, the thermostat will have to be replaced.

With vacuum operated systems there are more subsystems that need to be checked. The two main checks concern the snorkel door and the modulator valve. Checking the operation of the door is similar to the non-vacuum systems. The engine should be cold. Before starting the engine, check the door to make sure it is free to move. Start the engine. The door should close off outside air. As the engine warms up, the door should slowly open and admit more and more fresh air. One thing to remember, if the outside air temperature is extremely cold, the valve may remain in the warm air position indefinitely. This normal.

If the air temperature is warm, but the door doesn't change position, the temperature sensor may be at fault. The temperature sensor is located inside the air cleaner. These sensors can not be repaired and must be replaced. Before replacing the sensor, though, recheck the door to make sure it can move freely. Also check all of the hoses for any vacuum leaks.

When the engine is cold, vacuum operated air cleaners divert hot air into the engine. When the engine is suddenly accelerated vacuum suddenly decreases, causing the door to open. This sudden

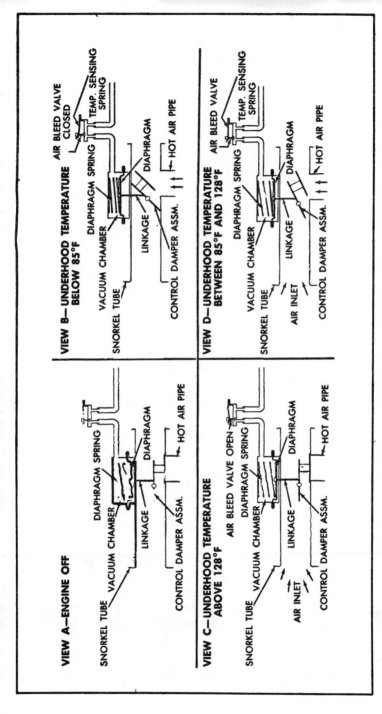

VIEW A—ENGINE OFF

SNORKEL TUBE VACUUM CHAMBER DIAPHRAGM SPRING DIAPHRAGM

LINKAGE

CONTROL DAMPER ASSM. HOT AIR PIPE

VIEW B—UNDERHOOD TEMPERATURE BELOW 85°F

AIR BLEED VALVE CLOSED

TEMP. SENSING SPRING

SNORKEL TUBE DIAPHRAGM SPRING DIAPHRAGM

VACUUM CHAMBER

LINKAGE

CONTROL DAMPER ASSM. HOT AIR PIPE

VIEW C—UNDERHOOD TEMPERATURE ABOVE 128°F

AIR BLEED VALVE OPEN DIAPHRAGM SPRING DIAPHRAGM

SNORKEL TUBE VACUUM CHAMBER

LINKAGE

AIR INLET

CONTROL DAMPER ASSM. HOT AIR PIPE

VIEW D—UNDERHOOD TEMPERATURE BETWEEN 85°F AND 128°F

AIR BLEED VALVE

TEMP. SENSING SPRING

SNORKEL TUBE DIAPHRAGM SPRING DIAPHRAGM

VACUUM CHAMBER

LINKAGE

AIR INLET

CONTROL DAMPER ASSM. HOT AIR PIPE

Fig. 16-1. Various operating modes of thermostatically controlled air cleaner (courtesy Chevrolet Division).

233

surge of cold air will usually make the engine misfire. To prevent this problem, a modulator valve is utilized. This valve operates by blocking the vacuum so that the door doesn't move. Modulator valves can be found on both GM and Ford engines.

Modulator valves are found on the side of the air cleaner. The modulator has two hose connections: one for air temperature and the other for a connection to the vacuum motor.

To test the modulator valve, a vacuum needs to be applied to the hose connection on the edge of the valve. Enough vacuum should be applied to allow the air cleaner door to open to the warm air inlet position. When the door has moved, remove the vacuum. If the valve is functioning, the door should remain in position. If the door does move, the valve should be replaced.

EXHAUST GAS RECIRCULATION (EGR)

Some of the chemical compounds emitted by internal combustion engines are oxides of nitrogen (NOx). These compounds are formed when the combustion chamber temperature reach above 2500 degrees Fahrenheit. At this temperature oxygen and nitrogen react, forming NOx in exceedingly large quantities. To prevent these large amounts of NOx from forming, the combustion chamber temperatures need to be moderated. This is accomplished by recirculating a portion of the exhaust gasses back into the combustion chamber. This process is referred to as exhaust gas recirculation or EGR.

EGR systems operate in two ways; by the floor jet system or by the use of an EGR valve. The floor jet system, which is found in Chrysler engines, allows exhaust gasses to recirculate at all times (Fig. 16-2). As the name implies, special jets are placed in holes between the intake manifold and the exhaust passages. These jets are located below the primary carburetor barrels and meter the flow of exhaust gasses by the size of their orifice. This system allows exhaust gasses to be pulled into the intake manifold continuously. From the intake manifold the gasses are dispersed to the various cylinders where they are burned.

With EGR valve equipped systems, exhaust gasses are only recirculated when the engine vacuum is high. This means that exhaust gasses are only admitted to the intake manifold when the throttle is opened. There are several temperature dependent methods of controlling the vacuum to the EGR valve.

The temperature controls that operate the EGR valve are all designed to close the valve when either or both the engine or air

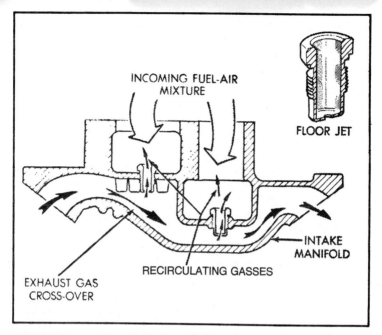

Fig. 16-2. An exhaust gas recirculation (EGR) system employing "floor jets" to bleed exhaust gas into the intake manifold (courtesy Chrysler Corporation).

temperature are cold. On engines that have controls sensing the outside air temperature, the EGR valve stays closed on cold days. Any cars manufactured after March 15, 1973, have EGR controls that sense the engine coolant temperatures or the engine compartment temperature, meaning that the EGR valve is in the open position more often.

CHECKING OUT THE EGR SYSTEM

Engines equipped with an EGR valve should be checked to make sure that exhaust gasses are actually recirculating and that the valve is closed at idle and open when the engine rpm is above idle. To see if exhaust gas is being recirculated, supply an outside vacuum to the EGR valve. This outside vacuum can be supplied by mouth suction or by a hand vacuum pump. In either case disconnect and plug the vacuum line from the valve. Substitute the outside vacuum source and start the engine. Apply vacuum to the valve and listen to see if the engine runs roughly. If the engine runs rough or dies, exhaust gasses are being recirculated. If gasses are not being recirculated, either the valve is stuck or some of the passageways are clogged. Clogged passageways can usually be cleaned by scraping;

this usually solves the problem. However, before disassembling the system, be sure the valve is tested.

To check out the EGR valve, the engine needs to be running. With the engine speed above idle, use your finger to see if the diaphragm stem moves. If the stem doesn't move the valve should be removed and cleaned. Since most valves cannot be disassembled, you will have to try to scrape any fouling material away. If the valve cannot be repaired in this manner, it should be replaced.

Some of the EGR valves used in 1977 have a pressure operated sensor that deactivates the EGR when there is no exhaust pressure. Since the sensor opens a vacuum bleed, mouth suction and hand pumps cannot be used for testing. This set up can only be tested by removing the EGR valve and plugging the parts into the manifold. With the EGR valve out of the system, a comparison should be made of performance with and without the valve. If the engine idles better without the valve, a new EGR valve is needed.

THE CATALYTIC CONVERTER

The idea behind a catalytic converter is to provide a surface on which any excess hydrocarbons in the exhaust can be burned. By providing this surface, oxygen is allowed to combine with the unburnt hydrocarbons, leaving only carbon dioxide and water to be released. There are two basic types of converters, pellet and honeycomb. The pellet type converter, used by GM and AMC, use replaceable catalyst pellets. Ford and Chrysler catalysts have a non-renewable honeycomb catalyst. The only check that can be performed on a catalyst is to look for physical damage.

Since gasoline containing lead ruins the converters, cars equipped with them must use unleaded gasoline. Using fuel containing lead fouls the converter and can plug it to the point that the engine will not run. A single tankful of leaded fuel will not cause any problems, by returning to unleaded fuel further damage will be prevented. Severe damage is caused by repeated use of fuel containing lead.

PROTECTING THE CONVERTER AGAINST OVERHEATING

The catalytic converter can overheat in two ways. First, if the amount of air being pumped to the exhaust is large, excessive heat will be generated. The other way is for the system to become overloaded with hydrocarbons. With Ford products, a device has been incorporated to cut down on the air supply. This system uses a heat sensitive switch to cut off the air pump. The switch actually activates a vacuum solenoid which in turn controls an air pump bypass valve. By shutting off the air supply, burning is stopped and the converter can cool down.

Chrysler Corporation deals with the overheat problem by preventing excessive richness in the exhaust. To prevent this, Chrysler uses a throttle stop solenoid that activates at 2000 rpm. When the solenoid is active it stops the throttle from falling below 1500 rpm setting until the actual engine rpm falls to 2000. By holding the throttle open at this level, fuel doesn't have a chance to build up with respect to the amount of air being allowed through. Since the solenoid quits operating below any engine speed of 2000 rpm, the engine can return to normal idle. Testing this system is simply a matter of watching the solenoid stem. When engine rpm exceeds 2000 rpm the stem should be out; when it is below 2000, the stem should be in the off position.

EXHAUST HEAT RISER VALVES

In an effort to preheat the fuel mixture, the heat riser valve was incorporated in cars a number of years ago. The original valves were spring loaded causing exhaust gas to be diverted under the intake manifold. When the engine warmed up, the spring would lose its tension allowing the exhaust to follow its normal path out the exhaust pipe.

Most new engines are equipped with vacuum operated heat risers. The valve's function is basically the same; the method of operation is just controlled by vacuum. By changing to vacuum, more control over the opening and closing of the valve can be achieved. To control the opening and closing on the valve, heat sensitive vacuum switches are used by Chrysler and Ford. General Motors uses a temperature switch in conjunction with a vacuum solenoid.

TESTING VACUUM HEAT RISER OPERATION

Checking heat risers is a simple matter of disconnecting the vacuum supply. Remove the vacuum line and watch to see if the valve moves to the open position (cold engine). If it does not, the valve is stuck and should be cleaned and lubricated.

AIR INJECTION

To burn excessive hydrocarbons, air needs to be pumped into the exhaust system. This is especially important for catalyst-equipped cars to ensure an adequate oxygen supply for burning the hydrocarbons. To accomplish this, most cars are equipped with an air injection system that pumps air into the exhaust line. The pump supplies air to a series of tubes that connects into the exhaust manifold. To prevent gasses from the exhaust system from getting to the pump, a check valve is used in conjunction with a backfire or a diverter valve. The backfire valve prevents air from being pumped during deceleration when hydrocarbons build up in the exhaust line. By doing this, the rich mixture in the exhaust line is prevented from exploding and backfiring.

On some backfire valves, the ability to dump air out of the system is not automatic on deceleration. On engines equipped with this type of valve, a special valve is used to sense the change in vacuum. This valve is called a vacuum differential valve (VDV). During an increase in vacuum caused by decelerating, the VDV shuts off the vacuum. This causes the backfire valve to divert air pump air into the atomosphere instead of into the exhaust line.

Another method developed for 1976 models is to use ported vacuum instead of manifold vacuum to power the backfire valve. This system gets rid of the VDV since ported vacuum originates above the throttle plate, making the valve operate only when the throttle position exceeds the idle setting. On deceleration the backfire valve dumps air since the throttle position drops below the idle setting.

In addition to these devices there are delay valves and temperature sensing controls. The delay valves are used to slow the drop in vacuum pressure when the driver moves his foot off the accelerator. This stops the air pump unless the driver's foot stays off the accelerator long enough. The temperature controls keep the air pump from working until the engine warms up. As mentioned earlier, temperature controls on the air pump can also be used as overheat protection for the catalytic converter.

CHECKING THE AIR PUMP SYSTEM

The first step in checking the air pumping system is to make sure the pump turns freely. The pump drive belt tension also needs to be checked as do the hoses to make sure there are no leaks. After checking these, the backfire valve should be checked.

To test the backfire valve, disconnect the hose between the check valve and the bypass valve. Run the engine up to 2000 rpm and then allow the throttle to snap shut. This should cause a flow of air out of the air outlet port on the valve. If not, the valve is probably defective and should be replaced.

Test the check valve next. This is done by disconnecting the valve and seeing if any exhaust gas leakage can be felt. If leakage is detected the valve must be replaced.

Testing the VDV requires the use of a vacuum gauge to determine if the valve is stopping vacuum in the backfire valve. Remove the vacuum line at the small hose connection and connect the vacuum gauge. The gauge should read full vacuum for the particular engine at idle. Run the engine at 2500 rpm for a few seconds and then release the throttle. The vacuum gauge reading should momentarily drop to zero. If it does not, the valve will need to be replaced.

DISTRIBUTOR AND CARBURETOR CONTROLS

Both the distributor and the carburetor are used to cut down on engine emissions. As far as the distributor is concerned, the objective is to decrease vacuum advance. By doing this the engine can run with a retarded spark, creating a hotter exhaust. A hotter exhaust is desirable since it provides for an adequate temperature to burn the excess hydrocarbons in the exhaust. The carburetor is used for emission control by adjusting it to the leanest possible setting. When the carburetor is run lean in conjunction with a retarded spark, the vast majority of the fuel is burned before it gets into the exhaust system. This cuts down on the amount of work required by the catalytic converter system.

Both the distributor and the carburetor emission controls are very different from one manufacturer to another. This is also true between models of a single manufacturer. The reason for this is engine design. Cars equipped with eight cylinder engines have different tuneup requirements than those equipped with six cylinder engines. Many other reasons exist to explain the resulting diversity in distributor and carburetor emission controls, but they go beyond the scope of this chpater. The manufacturer's shop manual for a particular model car is the best place to get detailed information.

ENGINE DESIGN AND EMISSION CONTROL

Engine emissions can be reduced by several engine design changes. By reducing the compression ratios, oxides of nitrogen can be reduced since the heat of combustion is lower at lower compressions. Reducing the surface area in the combustion chamber helps to reduce emissions by providing less surface area where fuel can cling and not be burned. This decreases the amount of raw fuel that is pumped out with the exhaust. Since many of these measures drastically alter the performance of the engine, new engine calibrations have to be worked out. Engines today are adjusted for fewer emissions—not best performance. Hopefully, with continuous research into the best engine design, someone will discover the perfect specifications that will return some of the performance while keeping emissions low and economy high. However, until that happens, emissions will continue to be controlled at the expense of performance.

Chapter 17

Improving Gas Mileage

Along with performance, gasoline economy is a major concern among many motorists. As fuel prices continue to soar, more and more drivers look for ways to stretch their gas dollar. Efficiency, economy, and performance are all interrelated. But an efficient engine is only the first step towards maximum fuel economy. Much of this depends on factors not directly related to the engine. Let's consider some of these other conditions so essential to good mileage.

FACTORS AFFECTING GAS MILEAGE

Just as we have assumed that the engine is in good order and properly tuned, we will also assume that the drive train and related areas are satisfactory. This includes proper adjustment of wheel bearings, correct wheel alignment, and freedom from brake-shoe drag. From here on, we will concentrate on the three mileage factors over which the driver has a certain amount of control.

Rolling Friction

This pertains to the force necessary to propel the complete vehicle with its normal load; it has more effect on gas economy than is commonly realized. Most of this rolling friction occurs in the tires. Being elastic, they give or flex with the weight of the vehicle. This flexing represents a force that must be overcome by the engine just to keep the vehicle rolling. The more they flex, the greater the rolling friction. If tires were as hard as roller bearings and the roadway perfectly smooth, rolling friction would be at a minimum. However, this is impractical (except in the case of railways) and would result in an intolerably harsh ride. Tires must provide the best compromise between riding qualities, wear characteristics, and gas mileage.

Since tires represent a compromise to begin with, there is room for variation with respect to both tire types and inflation pressures. Radial tires, for instance, being stiffer, offer less flexing and therefore give better gas mileage as well as longer tread life. However, they may also give a slightly harsher ride and, in some cases, different vehicle handling characteristics.

But regardless of tire type, it is inflation pressure that plays the vital role in mileage efficiency. Car manufacturers, in the interest of promoting riding comfort, usually recommend lower than maximum pressures. A significant increase in mileage, perhaps 5 to 10 percent, can be obtained by increasing pressure close to the maximum recommended amount. This is stated on the tire and is typically 32 psi for most passenger-type tires. It is not recommended to go over the limit, because here the law of diminishing returns sets in. Besides, higher-than-normal pressure makes tires more susceptible to damage from chuck holes, rocks, and other road hazards.

Furthermore, on certain cars, particularly rear-engine models, specified inflation pressures may be essential to safe handling. In these cases, the manufacturer's recommendations should be followed regardless of the tire's rating.

Pressure should always be measured when the tires are cold. Pressure builds up as tire temperature increases with driving. For example, tires that measure 32 psi cold may show 38 psi immediately after a sustained 65 mph run. This is normal and does not mean that they should be bled down. They will then be underinflated when cold. Incidentally, a tire inflated to, say, 30 psi will run cooler than if inflated to 24 psi. Also, keep in mind that initial pressure varies with the seasons. A tire carrying 32 psi (cold) in summer may measure only 25 psi (cold) in the middle of winter. Pressure drops about a pound for each 10 degrees of temperature drop. Check and adjust tire pressure accordingly.

Air Resistance

Air resistance is a seldom-considered mileage factor, although it too can have a significant effect. It is caused by both the vehicle's motion and natural wind. Although it is difficult to make specific statements about its effect on mileage, we can pass on some general observations. Streamlining, or body shape, is a major consideration; the aerodynamically shaped cars of today are less affected by air resistance than the boxy models of the past. But speed is the main consideration.

Air resistance does not increase in direct proportion to speed. A 10-percent increase in speed does not cause merely a 10-percent increase in resistance—it's closer to 20 percent. Likewise, a 20-percent increase in speed may mean over 40-percent increase in resistance. Although air resistance tends to vary as the square of the speed, the effect is complicated because of factors of streamlining, frontal area, and turbulence. To this must be added the resistance effects of natural wind. It makes a significant difference, perhaps 2-4 miles per gallon, if you are driving into, say, a 20 mph wind or driving with it.

Driving Speed

The overall effect of air resistance is to reduce gas mileage. Although we can't drive without experiencing this resistance, we can consider the effect it has. The faster you drive, the less gas mileage you get. And, up to a point, the slower you drive the better the mileage. Although it is not possible to give a definite rule, cars tend to give a reasonably level "plateau" of gas mileage between about 25 and 40 miles per hour. At higher speeds, the mileage begins to drop. How fast it drops depends on many things. Lower powered cars tend to show a faster drop than higher powered ones. However, the lower powered vehicles are usually smaller and lighter and give greater mileage to begin with.

A small car may show a 20-percent drop in mileage in going from 50 to 70 miles per hour. A larger, more powerful model may show less than a 10-percent drop.

The dropoff in mileage is not uniform with speed, either. Because of the nonlinear effect of air resistance and other factors, the mileage loss tends to increase faster than the speed increases. Thus, the loss in gas mileage in going from 50 to 60 mph is less than in going from 60 to 70 mph, and this is less than in going from 70 to 80 mph.

The point to all this is that the slower you drive, the better mileage you get. However, this must be tempered with common sense. It stands to reason that if you drive slow enough, it is possible that you might never arrive at your destination, even though you'll have to keep pouring gasoline into the car to keep it running. This, of course, is a ridiculous extreme. Still, if you do drive too slow, you may become a hazard both to yourself and to others—particularly on two-lane highways. Also, excessively slow driving means you'll take longer to reach your destination, which increases your risk of driving fatigue. It takes 30 percent more driving time if you go 50 mph than if you go 65 mph. On a long trip this could mean an extra night on the road, which would probably cost more than any gas saving.

The key to good gas mileage is only partly due to moderate-speed driving. It's also a matter of how you drive at that speed. Although the previously discussed mileage factors are important, and collectively have a significant effect, driving technique is the most important of all. Fortunately, this is the one the driver has the most control over.

Driving Technique

Why is it that two people driving the same car can show a difference of two to three miles per gallon (or more) in gas economy? The difference is simply driving technique. One driver understands what it is that makes an engine burn excessive gas and then takes steps to minimize these conditions. The other either doesn't know or chooses to ignore economy techniques. Surprisingly enough, these techniques do not mean snail-paced, hazardous driving. You won't be leader of the pack, but you won't be bringing up the rear either.

The first step in developing economical driving techniques is remembering what happens in the carburetor when the accelerator pedal is pressed. First, the throttle plate opens and allows more air-fuel mixture to enter the engine. This, in itself, does not necessarily cause a decrease in mileage, since the increased fuel-air intake is matched by a proportionate increase in speed. But as the speed increases, the engine must produce more and more power to overcome the increasing effects of wind resistance and rolling friction. This increased power or fuel demand is usually met in two ways.

One method uses stepped or tapered *metering rods*, linked to the throttle, moving up or down in the carburetor's main metering jets. This is the orifice through which the gas flows before it is mixed with the incoming air. As the throttle opens, the metering rod moves up, thus increasing the effective opening of the main jet. This allows the richer mixture needed for additional power.

Another method of enriching the mixture is through a *power valve*. This is an extra jet that is opened and closed by a vacuum-operated control. This extra jet, sometimes called a *power jet*, adds to the fuel already flowing through the main jet, thus enriching the mixture. Under light loads and moderate speed conditions, manifold vacuum is relatively high and the power valve is closed. But as the load increases, manifold vacuum falls off. When it drops to a certain level, perhaps 7 to 9 inches of mercury, the power valve begins to open.

THE FOUR-BARREL CARBURETOR

Four-barrel carburetors provide not only mixture enrichment, but additional "breathing" capacity during high speed or heavy load operation. The two front barrels, or *primaries*, provide the normal carburetor functions. The throttle plates of the two rear barrels, called *secondaries*, are closed during cruising and moderate load driving. However, when the primary throttle plates approach full throttle position, the secondary plates begin to open. This mode, although providing additional power, puts a considerable dent in gas mileage.

THE ACCELERATOR PUMP SYSTEM

A second carburetor system adds an extra shot of gasoline each time the throttle is opened. This is the accelerator pump system. Its purpose is to provide momentary enrichment during acceleration. Without it, the engine would not develop the necessary power to accelerate the vehicle smoothly. Bucking, stumbling, and misfiring would ensue (as evidenced when the accelerator pump system fails). A few carburetors, used on very small cars, may not have such a pump and some other carburetors provide acceleration enrichment through other means. Most American vehicles, though, use an accelerator pump system. On some of these, the pump stroke is adjustable.

Although you can't drive effectively without an accelerator pump, you can minimize its action by using only moderate acceleration. The amount of gas it delivers is roughly proportional to throttle opening. A full throttle opening may discharge about a thimblefull of gas. Even though the pump will discharge the same amount of gas whether you press the pedal down slowly or quickly, quick acceleration will also open the power valve or raise the metering rods to the power step. It is this combination that materially affects mileage.

Accelerate with the least amount of throttle opening, consistent with traffic conditions. Some drivers believe that the quicker they reach cruising speed, the better will be their overall mileage. This is not true. The greater the acceleration rate, the richer must be the air-fuel mixture to provide the necessary power.

THROTTLE CONTROL

Poor throttle management is the major cause of poor mileage. The driver who maintains his speed by a continuous series of accelerations and decelerations will never get good mileage. Paradoxically, this is the driving style of many inexperienced or hesitant drivers as well as that of experienced but impatient drivers. The driver who attempts to average, say, 32 miles per hour in a 30 miles per hour traffic flow does so only by a series of heavy accelerations followed by heavy braking.

An interesting corollary is this basic but blunt truth: *Every time you apply the brakes, you are wasting gas*! It works this way: When you use the brakes you are dissipating vehicle energy—energy you no longer want but which you had previously imparted to the vehicle from the gasoline. Therefore, the less you need to use your brakes, the better your gas mileage will be.

This brings us to the cardinal rule for getting the best gas mileage a car can give: Use the *fixed throttle* driving method. Some will tell you to drive at a *fixed speed*. This will help. But the best technique, when it can be applied, is to hold the throttle in one position as steadily as possible. Although it sounds simple, it takes a little practice to become accustomed to it. Our driving instinct subconsciously tells us to keep a steady speed. As a result, we instinctively and subconsciously work the accelerator pedal to accomplish this.

Instead, pick an average level road cruising speed. Let's say, for example, that you want to average about 65 miles per hour. Find the throttle position that gives you this speed on level ground and then simply hold the throttle in that position. As you go uphill, your speed will fall off somewhat. But you'll compensate when you go downhill; you'll slightly exceed your level road speed. This mode of driving gives a relatively consistent and high level of gas mileage.

If you want to accelerate, to pass a car for example, try to do so on a downgrade, if possible. Let gravity supply some of the power. Accelerating while going uphill is doubly hard on mileage. Aside from the power required merely to increase car speed, you need additional power because you are actually lifting the car against gravity. Gas consumption may more than double during this period.

The fixed-throttle method is an optimum driving mode best suited to open-road conditions. Because of driving conditions, traffic, and terrain, it cannot always be employed to the fullest. In mountainous country, you may have to use more throttle movement; you may not make it over the hill if you don't. In heavy traffic, pick a speed equal to the average traffic speed. Under these conditions, it's hard to average more than a few miles per hour over the average flow no matter how you drive. Even though you cannot drive at a fixed throttle, keep the throttle movements to a minimum.

What about the air conditioner? Doesn't it reduce gas mileage? Yes, but it depends to a certain extent on the vehicle and the driving conditions. You'll notice greater mileage loss with small engines than with large ones and at lower speeds than at higher speeds. However, an air conditioner is bought and used for comfort. And just as a home-type air conditioner costs money to operate, so does the one in the car. The loss in gas mileage is merely the price for comfort. Sometimes though, an air conditioner is used more out of habit than necessity. Be sure you really need the air conditioner and not just an open window.

DRIVING GAUGE

Of the dozens of add-on accessories available for the car, one of the most practical, economical, and least known is the *driving gauge*. Actually, it's nothing more than a vacuum gauge designed for permanent mounting under the dash panel.

Use it properly and you can add substantially to your gas mileage. The gauge itself doesn't do anything to cut gas consumption; it simply tells you whether you are driving in an economical or uneconomical manner. It does this by measuring manifold vacuum. The higher you can keep the vacuum while driving, the better will be your mileage. You can see the difference in loading effects between light and heavy acceleration or between low and high speeds. In essence, it teaches you economical driving habits.

It also functions as an overall indicator of engine efficiency. Any engine will produce a certain vacuum when driving under controlled conditions. For example, suppose your engine normally produces a vacuum equal to 12 inches of mercury when going up a particular hill at 40 miles per hour. Should that vacuum fall off to, say, 11 or 10 inches, you know immediately that your car is no longer as efficient as it was. Just what is causing the inefficiency will not be indicated. It could be engine trouble, low tire pressure, or simply extra weight in the car. The important thing is that you have an almost instant indication of possible vehicle trouble.

air filter: operates primarily to remove dust and dirt from the air before it is drawn into the carburetor and engine. Air filters also help to reduce engine noise and quench any flame that may be caused by engine backfiring through the carburetor.

air-fuel ratio: mixture of air and fuel (within the range of 8 to 1 and 18½ to 1) for the engine to run at peak power output, minimum emissions and peak fuel economy.

alternating current: current which reverses direction rapidly, flowing back and forth in the system with regularity. This reversal of current is due to reversal of voltage which occurs at the same frequency. In alternating current circuits, any one wire is first positive, then negative, then positive and so on.

alternator: an electric generator designed to supply alternating current. Some types have a revolving armature and other types have a revolving field.

ampere: the unit of measurement for electric current. It represents the rate at which current flows through a resistance of one ohm by a pressure of one volt.

antifreeze: a substance that is used in place of water in the automotive cooling system to prevent freeze-ups and overheating.

automatic transmission: a system that is controlled automatically by hydraulics or similar pressure to adapt the power of an automotive engine to meet varying driving and road conditions.

battery: a lead-acid energizer for converting chemical energy into electrical energy. It is not a storage tank for electricity—as often believed—but instead stores electrical energy in chemical form.

BDC: stands for bottom dead center—the lowest position the piston travels in its downward motion.

breaker points: part of the ignition system that is used to interrupt the primary circuit in the distributor which includes a high-tension current to fire the spark plugs.

bypass: a controlled separate passage which permits a liquid, gas, or electric current to follow a path other than that normally used.

cam angle: often referred to as contact angle or dwell angle. It is the number of degrees of cam rotation during which the distributor contact points remain closed. It is usually measured with a dwell meter.

camshaft: a shaft with lobes or cams used to operate the engine valves as the camshaft is driven by the crankshaft by means of a gear arrangement.

carburetor: a metering device which mixes fuel with air in the correct proportion and delivers them to the engine cylinders as a combustible mixture.

combustion: the process of burning the air-fuel mixture in the combustion chamber of the engine which produces the power necessary to drive the vehicle.

compression: the act of compressing a substance (such as an air-fuel mixture) to a fraction of its original volume.

compression ratio: a comparison of the volume of the cylinder and combustion chamber when the piston is all the way down, to the volume remaining when the piston is all the way up.

condenser: a capacitor consisting of a roll of two layers of thin metal foil separated by a thin sheet of insulating material and then sealed. It acts like a short circuit. Current flows into the capacitor to minimize arcing at the contacts.

cooling system: used to maintain the engine at its most efficient operating temperature. Two methods are normally employed—water-cooling systems and air-cooling systems.

connecting rods: rods that are connected between the crankshaft and piston.

crankcase: the lower part of the engine block which houses the crankshaft.

cylinder: openings in the engine block that house the pistons as they move up and down.

cylinder block: the upper part of the engine block that houses the cylinders, crankshaft, camshaft, pistons and connecting rods.

cylinder head: a part of the engine that houses the combustion chambers, spark plugs and valve train assembly and detaches from the main cylinder block for repairs, etc.

diagnosis: the use of skills and instruments to evaluate the performance of automobiles and their components.

diode: an electrical device in the alternator which lets current flow continuously in one direction only.

direct current: current which flows in one direction only. One wire is always positive, the other negative.

distributor: an ignition system device that opens and closes the low tension circuit between the source of electrical energy and the ignition coil, so that the primary winding is supplied with intermittent surges of current. It further times these surges with regard to the engine requirements and also directs the high voltage surge through the distributor rotor, cap and high tension wiring to the spark plug, which is ready to fire.

drive train: used in setting a vehicle in motion and includes the transmission, propellor shaft and differential.

dwell angle: see cam angle.

electrical system: the system that furnishes power to crank the engine for starting. It furnishes the spark to the cylinders for combustion and provides current to operate the lighting and the various accessories.

emission control system: a system used on late-model vehicles to reduce exhaust emissions. These emissions result from the combustion process and include hydrocarbons, carbon monoxide and oxides of nitrogen.

exhaust system: the system which safely disposes of engine exhaust behind the vehicle. Components include the exhaust manifold, exhaust pipe, muffler, resonator, tailpipe and various accessories.

fan: a part of the cooling system located behind the radiator and in front of the engine block. The fan draws in air which is used to cool the engine coolant as it flows through the radiator.

feeler gauge: a device used to accurately measure thickness or clearance between two parts.

flywheel: a metal wheel attached to the rear of the crankshaft to help balance engine power. It also acts as part of the clutch and engine-cranking system.

fuel filter: a filter located in the fuel line to clean out all dirt and other foreign matter.

fuel pump: a pump driven by the camshaft to transport fuel from the fuel tank to the carburetor.

fuel system: a system consisting of a fuel tank, fuel-vapor separator, fuel lines, fuel pump, fuel filter and an accelerator linkage. The fuel pump draws gas from the tank and forces it through the filter into the carburetor where it is metered and injected into the air stream. This air-fuel mixture is then drawn into the engine by the vacuum created by the pistons.

gasket: a flat strip of sealing substance used between two surfaces to provide a tight seal between them.

gear: mechanical device with teeth that transmits power or turning effort from one shaft to another.

gear ratio: the ratio or revolutions made by a driving gear compared to the revolutions of a driven gear of a different size.

ground: a conducting connection, whether intentional or accidental, between an electrical circuit or piece of equipment—like to the engine or frame—which returns the current to its source.

hydrometer: an instrument used to measure the specific gravity of the electrolyte in each cell of a battery.

ignition system: the system consisting of spark plugs, wires, distributor, coil, ignition switch and battery which is used to supply a spark in the combustion chamber to ignite the air-fuel mixture.

ignition timing: the accurate timing of the spark in the combustion chamber in relation to the position of the piston in the cylinder.

intake manifold: pipes used to distribute the air-fuel mixture to the individual cylinders.

ohm: unit of measurement of electrical resistance which represents the amount of resistance that permits current to flow at the rate of one ampere under a pressure of one volt. Resistance is measured with an ohmmeter.

oil pan: a part beneath the crankcase which houses the oil pump and stores the oil until needed.

oil pump: a pump located in the oil pan to direct oil to the various moving parts in the engine requiring lubrication.

PCV valve: the positive crankcase ventilation valve which draws crankcase vapors back into the intake manifold to be burned with the air-fuel mixture. It is part of the emission control system.

piston: components that move up and down in an engine to produce power. Pistons are connected to the crankshaft with connecting rods.

piston rings: expandable rings around the piston which seal off the upper cylinder and prevent fluid or gasses from getting past the piston.

polarity: refers to the positive or negative terminal of the battery or an electric circuit.

preignition: occurs when the air-fuel mixture ignites too early.

radiator: a cooling system component comprised of tubing and fins to distribute the heat which the coolant has absorbed from the engine.

rotor: a device used to carry electrical current from a central source to individual uses. One type of rotor is found in the distributor of the ignition system.

spark plugs: electrodes inserted in the combustion chamber to produce a spark and ignite the air-fuel mixture.

specific gravity: the ratio of the weight of a substance to the weight of an equal volume of chemically pure water at 39.2 degrees Fahrenheit.

starting system: includes the battery, starter, wiring, switches and controls necessary to start the engine.

stroke: the distance in up or down movement of piston travel in the cylinder of an engine.

tachometer: instrument used to measure the revolutions per minute of the engine.

thermostat: control used in the cooling system to regulate the flow of water between the engine and radiator to control engine temperature.

timing marks: degree marks located on the crankshaft pulley and on the timing gear cover to enable the timing to be set with a timing light.

torque: a twisting or turning effort.

vacuum advance: a part of the distributor used to advance the spark in accordance with vacuum in the intake manifold.

valve train: the components that control the action of the intake and exhaust valves.

vapor lock: a condition in the fuel system that causes fuel blockage. It is caused by gasoline vapors.

V belts: belts used to power accessories such as the fan, alternator, etc.

voltage: the force which causes electric current to flow in an electric circuit. Its unit of measurement is the volt, which represents the amount of electrical pressure that causes current to flow at the rate of one ampere through a resistance of one ohm.

voltage regulator: a device used in conjunction with the alternator to keep voltage constant and to prevent it from exceeding a predetermined maximum.

water jacket: passages that surround the cylinders and combustion chambers allowing water to circulate and cool hot internal parts.

water pump: pump used to circulate the engine coolant throughout the cooling system between the engine and the radiator.

Metric Measures

The metric system is based on the meter, which is equal to 39.370432 inches. The value commonly used is 39.37 in. and is authorized by the U.S. government.

There are three principal units—the meter, the liter (pronounced "lee-ter"), and the gram, the units of length, capacity, and weight, respectively. Multiples of these units are obtained by prefixing to the names of the principal units the Greek words deca (10), hecto (1000), and kilo (1,000); the sub-multiples, or divisions, are obtained by prefixing the Latin words deci (1/10), centi (1/100), and milli (1/1000). These prefixes form the key to the entire system. The abbreviations of the principal units of these submultiples begin with a small letter, while those of the multiplies begin with a capital letter.

LUBRICANT SPECIFICATIONS

Item	Part Name	Ford Part No.	Ford Specification
Hinges, Hinge Checks and Pivots	Polyethylene Grease	C4AZ-19584-B	ESB-M1C106-B
Front Suspension Ball Joints	Long Life Lubricant	C1AZ-19590-B	ESA-M1C75-B
Steering Linkage	Steering Linkage Lube	C6AZ-19590-A	ESA-M1C92-A Type II
Power Steering Control Valve Ball Stud			
Transmission Linkage	Long Life Lubricant	C1AZ-19590-B	ESA-M1C75-B
Steering Arm Stops	Steering Arm Stop Lube	C7AZ-19590-A	ESB-M1C25-A
Hood Latch and Auxiliary Catch	Polyethylene Grease	C4AZ-19584-B	ESB-M1C106-B
Lock Cylinders	Lock Lubricant	B4A-19587-A	ESB-M2C20-A
Rear Axle (Conventional)	Hypoid Gear Lube	D2AZ-19587-A	ESW-M2C105-A
Rear Axle (Traction-Lok)		C9AZ-19580-A	ESW-M2C119-A
Steering Gear Housing (Manual)	Steering Gear Grease	C3AZ-19578-A	ESW-M1C87-A
Steering Gear (Rack and Pinion)	Hypoid Gear Lube	D2AZ-19580-B	ESW-M2C105-B
Steering - Power (Pump Reservoir) (Lincoln Continental, Continental Mark V)	Power Steering Fluid	D5AZ-14582-A	ESW-M2C128-A
Steering-Power (Pump Reservoir) (Except Lincoln Continental and Continental Mark V)	Auto. Trans. Fluid	C1AZ-19582-A	ESW-M2C33-F (Type F)
Transmission (Automatic) C3, C4 & FMX	Auto. Trans. Fluid	C1AZ-19582-A	ESW-M2C33-F (Type F)*
Transmission (Automatic) C6 & JATCO	Auto. Trans. Fluid	D7AZ-19582-A	ESP-M2C138-CJ*
Transmission (Manual)	Manual Trans. Lube	C3AZ-19C547-B	ESP-M2C83-C
Engine Oil Filter	Long Life Oil Filter	C1AZ-6731-A	ES-C8AF-6714-A/-C
Engine Oil	Long Life Engine Oil	(1)	ESE-M2C144-A
Speedometer Cable	Speedometer Cable Lube	D2AZ-19581-A	ESF-M1C160-A
Engine Coolant	Cooling System Fluid	8A-19549-A or -B	ESE-M97B18-C
Front Wheel Bearings and Hubs	Long Life Lubricant	C1AZ-19590-B	ESA-M1C75-B
Front Wheel Bearing Seals			
Brake Master Cylinder	H.D. Brake Fluid	C6AZ-19542-A	ESA-M6C25-A
Brake Master Cylinder Push Rod and Bushing	SAE 10W-30 Engine Oil	(1)	ESE-M2C144-A
Drum Brake Shoe Ledges	High Temp. Grease		ESR-M13P4-A
Disc Brake Caliper and Anchor Plate Slides	Disc Brake Caliper and Anchor Plate Lubricant	C0AZ-19553 A	ESA-M1C167-A
Rear Disc Brake Caliper (Internal)	Silicone Grease		ESA-M1C169-A
Parking Brake Cable	White Waterproof Grease		ESB-M1C31-A
Brake Pedal Pivot Bushing	SAE 10W-30 Engine Oil	(1)	ESE-M2C144-A
Tire Mounting Bead (of Tire)	Synthetic Rubber Lube		ESA-M99C45-A or ESA-M1BC-A
Clutch Pedal Pivot Bushing	SAE 10W-30 Engine Oil	(1)	ESE-M2C144-A
Clutch Equalizer Bar Assembly Bore & Pivot (Both Ends)			
Clutch Cable Connection (Both Ends)			
Clutch Pedal to Idler Lever Rod (Both Ends)	Long Life Lubricant	C1AZ-19590-B	ESA-M1C75-B
Clutch Release Rod			
Clutch Release Lever-At Fingers (Both Sides and Fulcrum)			
Swivel Clutch Release Idler Lever			
Clutch Release Bearing Retainer			
(1) Part Number depends on viscosity and container size.			

Table A-1. Specifications. *Refer To Vehicle Certification Label on Left Front Door Pillar For Transmission Code To Determine Transmission Type.

Table A-2. Metric and English Weight Measurements.

Metric		English
1 gram	=	15.432 grains
.0648 gram	=	1 grain
28.35 grams	=	1 ounce avoirdupois
1 kilogram	=	2.2046 pounds
4536 kilogram	=	1 pound
1 metric ton	=	.9842 ton of 2240 pounds
1000 kilograms	=	2204.6 pounds

Table A-3. Metric and English Capacity Measurements.

Metric	English
1 liter (= 1 cubic decimeter)	= 61.023 cubuc inches
	.3531 cubic foot
	.2642 gallons (American)
	2.202 pounds of water at 62°F.
28.317 liters..................................	= 1 cubic foot
3.785 liters..................................	= 1 gallon (American)
4.543 liters..................................	= 1 gallon (Imperial)

Table A-4. English conversion Table for Pressure, Power and Water Measurements.

Pressure			
Pounds per square inch	X	2.31	= feet of water (60°Fahrenheit)
Feet of water (60° Fahrenheit)	X	.433	= pounds per square inch
Inches of water (60° Fahrenheit)	X	.0361	= pounds per square inch
Pounds per square inch	X	27.70	= inches of water (60° Fahrenheit)
Pounds per square inch	X	2.041	= inches of Hg. (60° Fahrenheit)
Inches of Hg. (60° Fahrenheit)	X	.490	= pounds per square inch
Power			
Horsepower	X	746746.	= watts
Watts	X	.001341	= horsepower
Horsepower	X	42.4	Btu per minute

Water factors (at point of greatest density—39.2°Fahrenheit)

Miners inch	X	8.976	= U.S. gallons per minute
Cubic inches	X	.57798	= ounces
Cubic inches	X	.036124	= pounds
Cubic inches	X	.004329	= U.S. gallons
Cubic inches	X	.003607	= English gallons
Cubic feet	X	62.425	= pounds
Cubic feet	X	.03121	= tons
Cubic feet	X	7.4805	= U.S. gallons
Cubic feet	X	6.232	= English gallons
Cubic foot of ice	X	57.2	= pounds
Ounces	X	1.73	= cubic inches
Pounds of	X	26.68	= Cubic inches
Pounds	X	.01602	= cubic feet
Pounds	X	.1198	= U.S. gallons
Pounds	X	.0998	= English gallons
Tons	X	32.04	= cubic feet
Tons	X	239.6	= U.S. gallons
Tons	X	199.6	= English gallons
U.S. gallons	X	231.00	= cubic inches
U.S. gallons	X	.13368	= cubic feet
U.S. gallons	X	8.345	= pounds
U.S. gallons	X	.8327	= English gallons
U.S. gallons	X	3.785	= liters
English gallons (Imperial)	X	277.41	= cubic inches
English gallons (Imperial)	X	.1605	= cubic feet
English gallons (Imperial)	X	10.02	= pounds
English gallons (Imperial)	X	1.201	= U.S. gallons
English gallons (Imperial)	X	4.546	= liters

Table A-5. English Conversion Table for Length and Area Measurements.

Inches	X	.0833	= feet
Inches	X	.02778	= yards
Inches	X	.00001578	= miles
Feet	X	.3333	= yards
Feet	X	.00001894	= miles
Yards	X	36.00	= inches
Yards	X	3.00	= feet
Yards	X	.0005681	= miles
Miles	X	63360.00	= inches
Miles	X	5280.00	= feet
Miles	X	1760.00	= Yards
Circumference of circle	X	.3188	= diameter
Diameter of circle	X	3.1416	= circumference
Area			
Square inches	X	.00694	= square feet
Square inches	X	.0007716	= square yards
Square feet	X	144.00	= square inches
Square feet	X	.11111	= square yards
Square yards	X	1296.00	= square inches
Square yards	X	9.00	= square feet
Diameter of circle squared	X	.7854	= area
Diameter sphere squared	X	3.1416	= surface

Table A-6. English Conversion Table for Volume, Weight and Energy Measurements.

Cubic inches	X	.0005787	= cubic feet
Cubic inches	X	.00002143	= cubic yards
Cubic inches	X	.004329	= U.S. gallons
Cubic feet	X	1728.00	= cubic inches
Cubic feet	X	.03704	= cubic yards
Cubic feet	X	7.4805	= U.S. gallons
Cubic yards	X	46656.00	= cubic inches
Cubic yards	X	27.00	= cubic feet
Diameter of sphere cubed	X	.5236	= volume
Weight			
Grains (avoirdupois)	X	.002286	= ounces
Ounces (avoirdupois)	X	.0625	= pounds
Ounces (avoirdupois)	X	.00003125	= tons
Pounds (avoirdupois)	X	16.00	= ounces
Pounds (avoirdupois)	X	.01	= hundredweight
Pounds (avoirdupois)	X	.0005	= tons
Tons (avoirdupois)	X	32000.00	= ounces
Tons (avoirdupois)	X	2000.00	= pounds
Energy			
Horsepower	X	33000.00	
Btu	X	778.00	= ft.-pounds
Ton of refrigeration	X	200.00	= Btu per minute

Table A-7. Metric Conversion Table for Length and Area Measurements.

Length

Millimeters	×	.03937	= inches
Millimeters	÷	25.4	= inches
Centimeters	×	.3937	= inches
Centimeters	×	2.54	= inches
Meters	×	39.37	= inches
Meters	×	3.281	= feet
Meters	×	1.0936	= yards
Kilometers	×	3280.6214	= miles
Kilometers	÷	1.6093	= miles
Kilometers	×	3280.8	= feet

Area

Square Millimeters	×	.00155	= square inch
Square Millimeters	÷	645.2	= square inches
Square Centimeters	×	.155	= square inch
Square Centimeters	÷	6.452	= square inches
Square Meters	÷	10.764	= square inches
Square Kilometers	×	247.1	= acres
Hectares	×	2.471	= acres

Table A-8. Metric Conversion Table for Volume, Weight, Unit Weight and Pressure Measurements.

Volume

Cubic Centimeters	X	16.387	= cubic inches.
Cubic Centimeters	÷	3.69	= fluid dram π USP
Cubic Centimeters	÷	29.57	= fluid ounces # USP
Cubic Meters	X	35.314	= cubic feet
Cubic Meters	X	1.308	= cubic yards
Cubic Meters	X	264.2	= gallons (231 cubic inches)
Liter	X	61.023	= cubic inches
Liters	X	33.82	= fluid ouncesUSP
Liters	X	.2642	= gallons (231 cubic inches)
Liters	÷	3.785	= gallons (231 cubic inches)
Liters	÷	28.317	= cubic feet
Hectoliters	X	3.531	= cubic feet
Hectoliters	X	2.838	= 50.42 cubic inches
Hectoliters	X	26.42	= gallons (231 cubic inches)

Weight

Grams	X	15.432	= grains
Grams	X	981.	= dynes
Grams (water)	X	29.57	= fluid ounces
Grams	X	28.35	= ounce avoirdupois
Kilograms	X	2.2046	= pounds
Kilograms	X	35.27	= ounce avoirdupois
Kilograms	X	.0011023	= tons (2000 pounds)
Tonneau (Metric Ton)	X	1.1023	= tons (2000 pounds)
Tonneau (Metric Ton)	X	2204.6	= pounds

Unit Weight

Grams per cubic centimeter	X	27.68	= pounds, per cubic inch
Kilo per meter	X	.672	= pounds per foot
Kilo per cubic meter	X	.06243	= pounds per cubic foot
Kilo per Cheval	X	2.235	= pounds per horsepower
Grams per liter	X	.06243	= pounds per cubic foot

Pressure

Kilo-grams per sq. cm.	X	14.223	= pounds per square inch
Kilo-grams per sq. cm.	X	32.843	= feet of water (60° Fahrenheit)
Atmospheres	X	14.696	= pounds per square inch

*United States Pharmacopoeia

Table A-9. Metric Conversion Table For Energy and Power Measurements.

Energy

Joule	X	.7376	= foot pounds
Kilogram meters	X	7.233	= foot pounds

Power

Cheval vapeur	X	.9863	= horsepower
Kilo-watts	X	1.341	= horsepower
Watts	÷	746.	= horsepower
Watts	X	.7373	= foot pounds per second

Miscellaneous

Kilogram calorie	X	3.968	= Btu
Standard gravity	÷	980.665	= centimeters per second

Table B-1. Battery state of charge and freezing temperatures.

SPECIFIC GRAVITY	PER CENT OF CHARGE
1.280	100%
1.250	75%
1.220	50%
1.190	25%
1.160	Limited Useful Capacity
1.130	Discharged

BATTERY EFFICIENCY AT VARIOUS TEMPERATURES	
Temperature	Efficiency of a Fully Charged Battery
80° F.	100%
50° F.	82%
30° F.	64%
20° F.	58%
10° F.	50%
0° F.	40%
− 10° F.	33%

FOR ENGINE TESTING

Basic
Compression gauge
Vacuum gauge
Tachometer

Additional
Cylinder leakage tester
Dynamic compression tester

FOR IGNITION SYSTEMS

Basic
Power timing light
Tachometer
Dwellmeter
Voltmeter

Additional
Plug cable checker (ohmmeter)
Ignition analyzer (meter type)
Oscilloscope
Distributor advance tester (on-the-vehicle type with timing light)

FOR ELECTRICAL SYSTEMS

Basic
Voltmeter
Ammeter (0-80 amperes)
Tachometer
Hydrometer

Additional
On-the-vehicle dynamic diode tester
In-circuit diode tester (for alternator bench work)
Battery load tester
Ohmmeter
Ammeter, high range (sometimes part of above ammeter)

Basic
Fuel pump pressure gauge (usually part of vacuum gauge)
Tachometer

Additional
Combustion analyzer
Fuel pump pressure-volume tester

FOR EMISSION SYSTEMS

Basic
Tachometer
Combustion analyzer (with carbon monoxide scale)

Additional
Carbon monoxide analyzer
Infrared analyzer

FOR COOLING SYSTEMS

Basic
Coolant thermometer (to 225°F)
Coolant hydrometer (antifreeze tester)

Additional
Radiator pressure tester

FOR AIR CONDITIONING SYSTEMS

Basic
Thermometer (0-120°F)

Additional
Pressure gauge manifold

FOR BASIC TUNEUP

Compression gauge
Tachometer
Dwellmeter
Timing light
Voltmeter

Fig. B-1. A list of basic troubleshooting instruments.

Table B-2. Typical emission level requirements.

PRIVATELY OWNED VEHICLES		
YEAR	HYDROCARBONS	CARBON MONOXIDE
PRE '68	1000 ppm	6.0%
'68-'69	600	5.0
'70-'74	500	4.0
'74 & AFTER	250	1.5
FLEET OWNED VEHICLES		
PRE '68	600 ppm	5.0%
'68-'69	400	4.5
'70-'74	300	3.5
'74 & AFTER	150	1.3
PASSENGER CARRIERS FOR HIRE (BUSES, ETC.)		
PRE '68	400 ppm	3.0%
'68-'69	300	2.0
'70-'74	300	1.5
'74 & AFTER	100	0.8

VEHICLE MUST NOT EXCEED LEVELS SHOWN AT IDLE AND 2000 RPM.
PPM = PARTS PER MILLION.

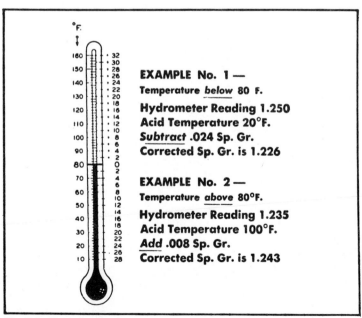

EXAMPLE No. 1 —
Temperature *below* 80 F.
Hydrometer Reading 1.250
Acid Temperature 20°F.
Subtract .024 Sp. Gr.
Corrected Sp. Gr. is 1.226

EXAMPLE No. 2 —
Temperature *above* 80°F.
Hydrometer Reading 1.235
Acid Temperature 100°F.
Add .008 Sp. Gr.
Corrected Sp. Gr. is 1.243

Fig. B-2. Chart showing the proper correction to the specific gravity for various battery temperatures.

Table B-3. Compressor pressures.

AIR TEMP AT CONDENSER (°F)	70	80	90	100	110	120
COMPRESSOR PRESSURE (psi)	130-140	150-160	175-185	205-215	245-255	280-290

Table B-4. Air conditioner outlet temperatures.

AIR TEMP (°F)	70	80	90	100	110
OUTLET TEMP (°F)	38-40	40-43	44-47	46-49	49-52

Index

2285–D3
22–57

5/80